Forging a Better Religious Education
in the Third Millennium

Contributors

NORMA COOK EVERIST

BARBARA J. FLEISCHER

CHARLES R. FOSTER

KENNETH O. GANGEL

JAMES MICHAEL LEE

MARY ELIZABETH MULLINO MOORE

GABRIEL MORAN

RICHARD ROBERT OSMER

ROBERT W. PAZMIÑO

RONNIE PREVOST

ANNE E. STREATY WIMBERLY

Forging a Better Religious Education in the Third Millennium

Edited by
James Michael Lee

Religious Education Press
Birmingham, Alabama

No part of this publication may be reproduced, stored in a retrieval system, or transmitted, in any form or by any means, electronic, photocopying, recording, or otherwise, without the prior permission of the publisher.

The paper in this book meets the guidelines for permanence and durability of the Committee on Production Guidelines of the Council for Library Resources.

Library of Congress Cataloguing-in-Publication Data
Forging a better religious education in the third mllennium /
edited by James Michael Lee.
    p. cm.
  Includes index.
  ISBN 0-89135-113-2 (pbk. : alk. paper)
  1. Christian education. I. Lee, James Michael.

BV1471.2.F66 2000
268—dc21
00-025244

Religious Education Press
5316 Meadow Brook Road
Birmingham, Alabama 35242-3315
10 9 8 7 6 5 4 3 2

Religious Education Press publishes books exclusively in religious education and in areas closely related to religious education. It is committed to enhancing and professionalizing religious education through the publication of serious, significant, and scholarly works.

PUBLISHER TO THE PROFESSION

CONTENTS

INTRODUCTION

*"Come, my friends
'Tis not too late to seek a newer world"*
–Alfred Lord Tennyson

This is a renewal book. Its avowed purpose is to renew the face of religious education

The famous hymn *"Veni Creator Spiritus"* attributed to Rabanus
Maurus (780–856) calls on the Holy Spirit to renew the face of the
earth. In the same general vein as Rabanus Maurus, I have called on
some of the most celebrated and influential American religious educationists to work collaboratively with me in helping to renew the face
of religious education.

As this book is published, it is the dawn of the third millennium.
What are religious persons around the world going to do to bring
themselves closer to God in the third millennium? Specifically, what
are Christian religious educators going to do to bring others closer to
God in the third millennium? This book is an attempt to provide a
broad, composite, and prophetic vision of what a representative sample of the most prominent and most influential Christian religious educationists of the last decade of the second millennium believe are the
most important things that religious educators can do to ransom the
time for Christ over the next hundred years and over the next thousand
years.

In the last five or so years of the second millennium books and articles appeared that purported to provide a broad vision and specific
guideposts to forging a better religious education for the third millennium. To my great chagrin I found almost all of these books and articles to be quite disappointing, to say the least. By and large these

1

books and articles were low level in almost every respect. They lacked genuine vision, they lacked an authentic prophetic spirit, they lacked a solid theoretical base, and they lacked empirical research support. Instead of providing a genuine, broad, and truly eye-opening vision, they more often than not offered an ersatz, generally constricted, and myopically squinted view. Instead of providing a truly bold and groundbreaking prophetic perspective, they typically offered an unoriginal and stale rehash of worn-out ideas and practices that were third-rate to begin with. Instead of providing an outlook that was based on solidly substantiated fruitful theory, they typically offered an essentially unhelpful cocktail of ideology and speculation. Instead of providing a horizon richly supported by empirical research, they typically offered empirically-unsupported musings and dreamy hunches.

As I read these professionally banal books and articles, I thought to myself: "Surely religious education can do better than this. With books and articles like these, no wonder the field of religious education is held in such low repute by church leaders, by theologians, by pastoral psychologists, and by sociologists of religion. No wonder religious educationists and educators are generally not invited by ecclesiastical leaders to major ecclesiastical meetings or task groups whose purpose it is to map out the future directions of the church."

"What is needed," I thought, "is a first-rate book that offers genuinely visionary, authentically prophetic, and truly wide-ranging viewpoints on how religious education can proactively and successfully forge a better religious education for the third millennium." I then began to devise a plan of action to produce a book that would clearly show what religious education must do, and how it should do it, in order to make the enterprise optimally successful in the third millennium at best and more successful than it was in the second millennium at worst.

Thus there are three essential and guiding axes of this book: vision, prophetic stance, and wide-ranging viewpoints.

This book is all about vision. By this I mean that this book provides a broad futuristic landscape of what should be the overall shape of religious education in the third millennium. Vision is essential for successful religious education because vision supplies that sweeping and necessary futuristic perspective that enlarges religious education from where it is now to where it should be in the future. To paraphrase the older English translation of *Proverbs* (29:18), without vision the religious education enterprise will surely perish. It will perish because without vision religious education will be mired in the past and will never grow significantly. But there is a vast difference between vision and dreaming. At every stage of its development vision is anchored to fruitful theory, proven practice, and solid research in the field in which the vision applies. It is this constant anchorage in theory, practice, and research that keeps vision in line and prevents it from degenerating into wild flights of fancy. Vision necessarily grows out of the past and the present. The more that religious education creatively recognizes the endless workable possibilities which lie hidden within past and present theory, practice, and research, the greater and more potentially productive vision is thereby enabled to become. In contrast to vision, dreaming is essentially free-floating speculation and in some cases wishful thinking about what the future can become. Dreaming is free-floating because it is not consciously and constantly anchored in fruitful theory, proven practice, and solid research. One of the most effective ways of killing or at least stifling vision is to replace it with dreaming. Conversely, dreaming can be transformed into something productive by essentially restructuring it into vision.

This book is also all about prophecy, or, more specifically, the prophetic role of religious education. This book unabashedly attempts to change the future. If vision consists in a heuristic perspective for future sweeping possibilities, prophecy organically links vision with action. To be prophetic is not so much to see the future as to make the future—or to hasten the future, as I like to say. In its prophetic dimension, religious education visions a broad sweeping future and then makes that future happen earlier than it would have happened if religious education were not there: this is what hastening the future means. Unlike vision considered in itself, the prophetic role brings with it considerable sacrifice and suffering. Vision in itself is threatening to other persons and to the status quo only conceptually. The prophetic role, in marked contrast, is threatening to other persons and to the status quo all along the line, conceptually, affectively, and, most tellingly, in actual concrete practice. The prophetic role upsets the old order to which persons and institutions have become accustomed and to which they have become satisfied and comfortable. The prophetic role of religious education is therefore a dangerous one to both persons and institutions who enjoy the status quo (though often they do not like to admit that the enjoy the status quo). Thus the forces of the status quo tend to try by every means, including dirty tricks at times, to derail the prophetic role of religious education at every turn.

Finally, this book is all about wide-ranging viewpoints. It presents a panoply of visions and prophecies, some of which are complementary, some of which are diametrically opposed. Unlike some religious educationists, I have always believed strongly that it is absolutely essential to the growth and vitality of any field, including that of religious education, to bring out into the open the whole array of diverse viewpoints on the nature, structure, content, and direction of the field so that in the crucible of critique and evidence, the most viable perspective will prevail.

To ensure as complete a representation of complementary and opposing perspectives, as possible, I endeavored to secure as chapter authors persons from all three major groups within Christianity: Catholics, Mainline Protestants, and Evangelical Protestants. To secure even broader representation, I endeavored to secure chapter authors who spanned the spectrum within their own group and in some cases within the whole array of Christian religious educationists ranging from very conservative theologically and religiously to very liberal. I also attempted to enlist a good representation of younger, middle, and older scholars in the field, though this was not always possible to the extent to which I would have liked because the most important and most influential religious educationists tend to be those who have had long careers in religious education.

I am delighted by the uniformly high caliber of all the chapters in this book. And I am equally delighted that, as far as I am aware, no other religious education book ever published in North America has had under one cover such an outstanding assemblage of the then leading representative authorities in the field of religious education.

I underscore the theme that the major and inviolable criterion governing my invitation to religious educationists to contribute chapters was competence. It was from this criterion that I made my representative selection. I deliberately eschewed any and all political criteria because such criteria are necessarily external to competence, and, indeed, frequently inimical to competence. Such political criteria include a set number of males and females, a set number of persons from all geographical parts of the country, a set number of persons from different ethnic groups, a set number of clergy and laity, a set number of politically correct and politically incorrect persons, and the like. Readers who are primarily interested in political considerations rather than considerations of competence should look elsewhere than this book. Indeed such individuals should go elsewhere than Religious Education Press, where competence has always been the supreme criterion and political considerations have consistently counted for naught.

An interesting sidenote almost necessarily intrudes itself at this juncture. I selected contributors solely on the basis of competence and not because of political considerations, which have always been anathema to me. Yet I noticed after making my selection solely on the basis of competence that every Evangelical Protestant contributor to this volume is a member of the clergy. All of the Mainline Protestant contributors with but two exceptions are clergymembers (and of these two, one is an ordained deacon). None of the Catholic contributors is a cleric. This is somewhat amazing in view of the twin facts that on the one hand Catholicism is allegedly clergy-ridden and on the other hand a cardinal principle of the Protestant Reformation was the declericalization of the church and the concomitant assertion of parity of laity with the clergy in the mission of the church. In his fine chapter, Kenneth Gangel, possibly the most widely known and most respected Evangelical Protestant religious educationist of his era, asserts that in the new millennium laypersons rather than ecclesiastics will have to assume the mantle of leadership in religious education. Speaking for myself, I heartily applaud Gangel's view in this regard. But surely we have a long way to go.

Because the religious educationists whom I invited to contribute chapters are among the most celebrated and influential in the field, it was with some hesitancy that I asked them to contribute because persons of this stature usually have many writing and speaking projects going all at once at any given time. It is a tribute to the importance of the topic that all but three accepted my invitation. One of these, a woman in her middle years for whom I have considerable respect as a circumspect scholar, sent her regrets at being unable to contribute a chapter because she said she was feverishly working night and day to finish writing an important book on which she was then writing. Her contribution will be sorely missed. A second religious educationist who declined to accept my invitation was a well-published woman who pointed to her highly advanced age as the cause for being unable to contribute. Unfortunately the only other two persons in her denom-

ination who had that kind of deservedly high reputation, which is a
precondition for being included in this book, are either close to her in
age or even more ancient than she. Unfortunately, both this woman's
own special mellow perspective and the perspective of the important
Protestant denomination she represents are not included in this book,
surely a loss. The third person who declined my invitation claimed
that the press of work precluded his contributing a chapter, though I
strongly suspect that it was political considerations rather than work
that constituted the basic ground of his refusal. I regret that this chapter will not appear because its inclusion would have further strength-
ened and rounded out the book.

Essentially, what I asked all the chapter contributors to do is to indicate what they believe are the most important things that religious
education must do in the third millennium in order to achieve its enormous and as yet unfulfilled potential. This book provides under one
cover, then, a rich intellectual banquet in which a splendid assemblage
of some of the most celebrated and influential religious educationists
in the last decade of the twentieth century present what they believe
are the singularly most important tasks for religious education to accomplish in the third millennium.

In my letter of invitation to the chapter contributors, I requested
that each chapter embody five major characteristics. I made this request to help ensure a common focus for each chapter and to induce
the distinguished chapter contributors to compress their decades of influential religious education leadership into the highly distilled
essence of what they believe to be some central imperatives for optimum religious education in the third millennium. These five requisite
characteristics are as follows. First, each chapter will be one of solid
substance, quite unlike the lightweight books and articles on the topic
that were published in the waning years of the twentieth century. Second, each chapter will be visionary in that it gives the contributor's
broad perspective of what that contributor believes to constitute the
ideal general and specific contours for religious education in the third
millennium. Third, each chapter will be prophetic in that it is deliberately targeted toward bringing about desirable changes in the theory
and most especially in the practice of religious education. Each chapter should serve as a change agent. Each chapter will forthrightly state
some or many of the most important things that religious education
must do in order to attain its full potential, as the chapter author con-

strues this full potential. Fourth, each chapter will not deal exclusively or even primarily on the present and future of religious education in the chapter author's own faith group but rather will look broadly at the present and future of Christian religious education all across the board. The reason for this request is that the book as a whole should be a broadly based Christian book rather than a denominationally particularistic volume. Of course there will be times when the chapter author naturally and understandably does focus on the present or future of religious education in that contributor's own faith group. But this focus will always be ancillary to the main theme of the chapter and should always be done in a way that advances the general state of all Christian religious education. Fifth and finally, each chapter will be tightly written but in a way that brims with excitement.

I assured the chapter contributors that even though I am the editor of this volume, nonetheless I will not do any substantive editing whatever of any chapter unless that chapter strays significantly from the overall purpose and general requirements of the book. My purpose in refraining from even the least bit of subtantive editing is to enable all the chapter contributors to present their thoughts in as pristine and unalloyed a manner as possible. The only editing that will be done on any of the chapters, including the one that I wrote, is that done for style by REP's outside copyeditor in Wisconsin.

In order to assure a certain evenness and parallelism among the chapters, I asked the chapter contributors to make the length of their chapters from between about twenty five to approximately thirty manuscript pages. I also requested that there be no footnotes, bibliography, or any other kind of scholarly apparatus. I indicated to the contributors that if they believe that they absolutely must mention the name of an author or a book, they should do so in the body of the text (without city, publisher, or page). The reason underlying my request is that there is so much to get compressed into such a short a space that it would not be wise to spend space on scholarly apparatus. Because the scholarly attainments of all the distinguished chapter contributors are so widely known, every reader with even minimal knowledge of the field will recognize that what the contributors write in their chapters is backed by years of long hard reflection and solid research.

This book is intentionally religiously pluralistic in that it brings together in one volume authors from all three major Christian faith groupings: Catholic, Mainline Protestant, and Evangelical Protestant.

In my view, one of the greatest scandals in twentieth century religious education has been the lack of genuine and fructifying pluralism among the leaders of the three major Christian faith groups. I am consistently shocked by how little religious educationists and educators of one faith group seem to know about the religious education theory, patterns, and practices of religious educationists and educators from another faith group. Religious educationists from different faith groups meet each other at conventions to socialize, read scholarly (and not-so-scholarly) papers, and genially participate in interfaith forums, all the while only very seldom digging deep into the religious education theories and especially the practices of the members of the other faith groups with whom they interact. Indeed, Catholic and the Mainline Protestant religious educationists have a separate organization and convention from the Evangelical Protestants, and rarely does the twain meet. Religious educators in the parish and congregation generally know even less than religious educationists about the religious education theory and practices of other faith groups. Genuine cooperation among religious educators at the local level with religious educators of differing faith groups is minimal at best, and rarely goes to a deep level of mutual sharing. To me, all of this is scandalous. Deep knowledge and actual cooperation among members and organizations of different faiths is extraordinarily helpful in ridding Christian religious education of constricting provincialism, particularism, and ignorance—and sometimes, alas, noxious prejudice. Such a sad condition prevents Christian religious education to be fructified by the insights, practices, graces of differing faith groupings. I myself endeavor as best I can to go contrary to growth-asphyxiating insularism of every sort. I still regard as one of my most important professional accomplishments that the initial volume in my foundational trilogy on religious instruction, *The Shape of Religious Instruction* (1970), was, as far as I am aware, the first major religious education book that treated equally and together the theories and practices of all members of differing faith groups. Up to that time virtually all Catholic, Mainline Protestant, and Evangelical Protestant religious education books dealt almost exclusively with the writings and practices of members and institutions within that overall faith grouping. In the relatively rare exceptions to that practice, a very few authors did deal with religious education writings and practices from outside that larger faith grouping, but made sure to treat them separately by faith grouping. As far as

I am aware, I was the first (and still the only) Catholic ever to be a member both of the Association of Professors and Researchers of Religious Education (the Catholic / Mainline Protestant professional association of religious educationists) and the North American Professors of Christian Education (the Evangelical Protestant professional association of religious educationists), and one of only a few non-Evangelical Protestants to be a member of the North American Professors of Christian Education. In my role as the founder and publisher of Religious Education Press (established in 1974), I have always insisted that REP authors utilize and cite insights gained from the writings and practices of religious educationists and educators from outside their own major faith grouping, and that editors of REP volumes include chapters from writers from outside their own major faith group. I mention these facts about myself not to boast in any way but rather to show that if religious educationists and educators truly wish to be religiously pluralistic and in this manner to significantly fecundate their own ministry, they can do so if they really want. In short, I passionately believe that if religious education is to fulfill its as yet unfulfilled promise, then it must be religiously pluralistic.

Before proceeding to a brief summary of each of the chapters in this volume, I wish to return to a theme I mentioned earlier in this Introduction. I have studiously endeavored to include authors who represent very different and sometimes conflicting points of view because only in this way can truth genuinely emerge and significant improvements in theory and practice occur. (En passant, some of the authors whom I invited hold views that are diametrically opposed to the basic positions that I myself embrace about the foundations, contours, and thrust of religious education.) There are distinguished liberal and conservative authors represented in this book. For example, Kenneth Gangel is probably the most conservative of all major current Christian religious educationists (some have even called him a fundamentalist) whereas Gabriel Moran is in all probability one of the most liberal of the contributors. Gangel has written one of the strongest chapters in this volume, and Moran's chapter is a sample of the finest vintage Moran. Within the Evangelical Protestant contingent, there is one highly conservative writer (Gangel), one whose writings and life are infused with a lovely warm Pentecostalism (Pazmiño), and one who can probably be described as a moderate Evangelical Protestant (Prevost). Among the Mainline Protestants, each writer represents a different denomination and a different place on the conservative/liberal continuum: the only exception to this is that there are three Methodists (Moore, Foster, and Wimberly) in recognition both of the sheer number of the Methodists and of Methodism's special religious education dynamism within the Mainline wing of Protestantism. (I hasten to add, however, that I asked Wimberly to contribute a chapter not as a representative of Methodism, but as a representative of the black American churches of which she is quite possibly the most important writer in the final decade of the twentieth century. In this respect, it is only accidental that she is a Methodist). Among the Catholics, there is Gabriel Moran, who appears to be decidedly liberal, myself (a moderate), and Barbara Fleischer, a younger scholar who possibly falls somewhere between Moran and myself on the liberal/conservative continuum. I should not in any way be praised for this broadly based inclusivity of chapter contributors. Such inclusion ought to be a matter of course in the religious education world. I regard it as highly unfortunate and markedly retrogressive that denominational religious education conventions for workaday religious educators typically exclude not only speakers from differing faith groups but ensure that the roster of speakers is thoroughly laundered in such a way that only persons in essential agreement with the leaders of the convention are invited. I regard it as highly regrettable when popular religious education magazines whose target audience is the religious educator in the field, so often only publish articles that advocate a particular "party line" and rarely if ever publish challenging articles written by persons from other faith groups or even from within the same faith group. I regard it as a grave violation of the essence of a university when graduate religious education programs have as faculty members persons who all agree with one another essentially. (The latter need not be so. When I was the director of the Graduate Program of Religious Education at the University of Notre Dame, a man wrote a vigorous and well-reasoned letter to me disagreeing vehemently with one of my positions. I discovered that this man was an up-and coming scholar, and I hired him to be a member of the summer faculty at Notre Dame. He turned out to be a highly-regarded member of our faculty. We have been friends ever since.) I regard it as pathetic when religious educationists present a theory, a set of speculations, or some musings stating that a dialectical encounter between basically conflicting positions is essential to religious education, and then become gravely insulted when persons disagree with one or another aspects of their position.

In arranging the order in which the articles in this book appear, I made as the sole criterion what seems to me to be a natural flow, a logical progression that advances the thesis of this volume in a competent manner. It was this natural organic flow, and not any political or other extraneous consideration which formed the basis of my selection of the order of these chapters. Thus, for example, I did not choose to have an article by a woman followed by a man followed by a woman, or an article by a Mainline Protestant followed by a Catholic followed by an Evangelical Protestant, and so on. This kind of political or other type of extraneous and hence scientifically unsupportable basis for selection would illegitimately replace competence with a woefully misbegotten counterfeit and in the fallacious process significantly dull the sharp edge of this volume.

Surely the ideal chapter to open this volume is the one written by Mary Elizabeth Mullino Moore. First of all, it revolves around the main axis of an existentially grounded allegory about the hard and often excruciating journey that religious educators must take if they are to successfully move into the third millennium. Second, its main focus is on teaching, which is, after all, the specific characteristic that basically differentiates religious education from other areas of religion. In her chapter, "Sacramental Teaching: Mediating the Holy," Moore uses her own difficult last-year-of-the-millennium move from the West Coast to the East Coast as an allegory of the move that religious educators necessarily undertake in going from the second into the third millennium. Moore shows how this move summarizes the two major thrusts of her chapter: the often difficult realities of change and the fundamental future of religious education. Though these difficult realities are usually hard and painful both for religious educators and for the field itself, nonetheless these difficult realities and the acute distress that often accompanies them are essential if we are to forge a brighter future for religious education in the third millennium. Moore goes on to offer some helpful guidelines to religious educators, not only for successfully coping with the difficult realities of changing over to the third millennium but also for transforming these very stress-inducing difficulties into positive opportunities for making religious education more productive in the third millennium than it was in the second. These guidelines include discernment and decision making, preparation for the journey, and acceptance of the chaos and the kind of messiness religious educators will almost inevitably find not only on the way but also when they arrive at their destination. For Moore, the clue to moving successfully into the third millennium is what she calls sacramental teaching, namely, teaching that mediates the holy, teaching that mediates the grace, power, and call of God. In the rest of her chapter, Moore sketches what she regards as four major general characteristics of sacramental teaching: expect the unexpected, seek reversals, nourish new life, and finally reconstruct community and repair the world. Thus the two most important things that religious education and religious educators have to accomplish in order to make the enterprise effective in the third millennium are the ability to persevere successfully during the move and to base religious education activity around the axis of sacramental teaching.

The basic spirit and motif of Moore's opening chapter are continued nicely in the second chapter, "Issues and Ironies of the New Millennium," written by Norma Cook Everist. Using the title of this volume as both entree and axis, Everist explores the nature and operation of forging and in so doing demonstrates how this metaphor is a fruitful one for religious educators endeavoring to shape the soul and structure both of their work and of the field in the third millennium. The bulk of Everist's chapter is devoted to six major issues with which she believes religious educators must constructively and fearlessly grapple as they work hard and with considerable difficulty to forge a better religious education in the third millennium. The first major issue is globalization. Everist regards globalization as an interactive force in which religious educators simultaneously influence and are influenced by a whole panoply of multicultural forces in their efforts to forge a better religious education. The second major issue is diversity, which Everist sees first as a prizing and then an incorporation of the various diverse elements in various Christian and non-Christian faith groups in order to make religious education as wide as the all-embracing arms of Christ. The third major issue is violence of all sorts. Everist believes that violence in all its forms is a truly urgent issue, one that calls on religious educationists and educators to bring the healing love of Jesus to bear on all persons and institutions, both lovable and unlovable. The fourth major issue identified by Everist is time, that seemingly elusive dimension of our lives, but nonetheless a dimension that religious educators ought to utilize in their efforts to help persons sow and harvest their days on earth in ways that lead them to attain more fulfilling religious lives. The fifth major issue is place. This issue has to do with assisting persons to be of service to individuals in a wide variety of places and situations. The sixth and final major issue for religious educators, as they continue to forge a better future for religious education in the third millennium, is the pivotal philosophical and psychological reality of change. The problematic of change is an absolutely central issue for successful religious education in the third millennium. In effectively addressing the reality of change, religious educators help themselves and those whom they serve to retain their basic faith and personal identity not in a static nongrowth fashion but rather by fully utilizing the basic phenomenon of change, which is an essential condition in all human life. It is with her emphasis on change, on the difficult move, on the transformational journey, that Everist's contribution to this volume comes full circle and connects with the basic theme of Moore's opening chapter.

Now that Moore has laid out the dynamism of the journey and Everist has pinpointed some of the major issues that crop up throughout the journey, Robert Pazmiño bids us to step back a bit to realistically assess the worthwhileness of religious education's journey into and through the third millennium. In his chapter "Surviving or Thriving in the Third Millennium?," Pazmiño confronts the issue frontally, as befits a native of Brooklyn, and boldly asks; In the third millennium, will religious education just survive, just hang on, just do the things it has always done, *or* will religious education really begin to make the vital molar innovations that are essential for its improvement, for its thriving? Pazmiño answers this question with gusto, with bold assurance, and with open hope: religious education *must* do whatever it has to do in order to thrive and not merely survive. Pushing forward the major thrust of Everist's chapter, Pazmiño proceeds to identify and discuss four molar implicit areas that religious educators must competently and vigorously address if the field is to thrive. These four molar areas are changing educational technologies, global interdependence, patterns of social interaction, and wisdom versus knowledge. Pazmiño suggests that any satisfactory resolution of these four molar areas must necessarily rest on what he calls an educational trinity: substantive content, persons, and situational context. Utilizing this trinity as the foundation for successful religious education in the third millennium, Pazmiño proposes an action-oriented model for religious educators that consists of five basic tasks: proclamation, community formation, service, advocacy, and celebration. The final section of this chapter throws down the gauntlet of challenge to religious educators wishing to make the third millennium a golden age for their ministry. Pazmiño believes that it is through forthrightly and competently addressing this challenge that religious educators will successfully traverse the third millennium. The challenge is simply this: Be open to God's reviving so that religious education will thereby be enabled to move beyond surviving and even beyond thriving. Being truly open to God's reviving means that religious educationists and educators will be open to hearing the voice of God wherever and whenever this voice manifests itself in the world. This radical and fundamental kind of openness means that religious educationists and educators must abandon every last vestige of closedness, whether ideological or programmatic or psychological. To be closed is to be unreceptive to the voice of God and therefore to stand in the way of God's reviving. The basic and freeing openness to God's reviving suggests that religious educationists and educators ought to be relational rather than institutional, be relevant to the world and to people, exhibit strong leadership, have story as its center, be done in partnership, be innovative, and finally have clarity of mission and vision.

Charles Foster's chapter expands on an important motif coursing through the foregoing Pazmiño piece, namely, that of situation, that of environment. In his chapter, "Why Don't They Remember? Reflections on the Future of Congregational Education," Foster contends that any efforts to improve religious education in the third millennium that focus solely on the religious educator's understanding of substantive content and on pedagogical skills, while absolutely necessary, nonetheless are not sufficient. For Foster, the improvement of religious education in the third millennium must also involve the environment. The teaching act always takes place someplace. This immediate environment is physical—it involves a specific place and the persons and objects in that place. But the environment in which teaching/learning takes place is also contextually sociocultural. This is the overall environment. In religious education, the overall contextual socioemotional environment is the broader congregation or parish. The teaching act always occurs with the religious educator and learner in an immediate concrete situation of one kind or another, a concrete situation that subtly yet inextricably is connected to an overall contextual sociocultural environment. It is in the interactive set of environments, immediate and overall, that the dynamic interplay among the religious educator, the learner, and the subject-matter content occur. The admixture of the immediate environment and the overall environment is a powerful and everpresent variable in shaping the structure and flow of the teaching event, and ought never to be neglected or minimized. Consequently, an imperative task for religious educators in the third millennium is to develop their skills in creating, expanding, and enriching all those kinds of immediate and overall environments in which teaching/learning take place in the congregation. An interactive cluster of nonimmediate environments that go to make up the overall teaching/learning environment, together with the broader congregational environment, include cultural environments, gender environments, intergenerational environments, and religious environments, to name just a few. The second half of Foster's chapter is devoted to presenting general instructional guidelines to help third-millennium religious educators successfully achieve the objectives laid out in the first part of the chapter. Notable among these general guidelines are three. First, third-millennium religious educators should embrace diversity by structuring learning environments in such a way as to be more hospitable and playful. They can accomplish this task by devices as effectively utilizing ritual in an open welcoming manner and by according requisite attention to the differential learning styles of those whom religious educators teach. Second, religious educators in the third millennium should work toward celebrating events in different settings. Different situational contexts bring out different kinds of learning outcomes. Finally, third-millennium religious educators should strive to develop and implement a curriculum that is characterized by polylogic, empathic consciousness, and collaborative critique.

The next chapter written by Kenneth Gangel in a way ties together the various strands developed in the preceding chapters and places these strands in a global framework. It is thus an ideal chapter to conclude the first part of this volume. The title of Gangel's chapter, "Candles in the Darkness," is not only beautiful but also highly instructive. It is a title that implies both hope and struggle. The title implies hope that the third millennium will be lit up by the candles of religious education activity. But on the downside, the title also implies a tough protracted struggle in which both individual religious educators and institutional church structures will have to work long and hard to light up the new millennium out of the darkness bequeathed to it by the twentieth century's myriad unresolved individual and societal problems. Such a struggle is waged in the recognition that our activities are not a bank of searchlights but only candles which always run the danger of being snuffed out by the winds of evil. Gangel sees a major role for religious educators in the new millennium as lighting the candles of hope and making sure that these candles not only continue to burn but in fact burn with ever increasing brightness. The opening section of this illuminating chapter focuses on the necessity of religious education in the third millennium to develop and nourish a deep religious climate. The essential core of this all-pervasive climate is that of living in a thoroughgoing biblical manner. Gangel is not satisfied with simply identifying what he regards as the core of effective religious education activity in the third millennium. He properly goes on to show specifically how religious education can be improved in the third millennium, thus making his chapter an especially helpful one. Gangel identifies eight major candles that religious educators should both light and nourish in the third millennium in order to make their work effective: biblical authority, theological foundation, adequate worldview, spiritually grounded values, communal relationships, excellence in all things including application and procedure, comprehensive scope, and competent leadership. There can be no religious education that is religious, Christian, or authentic without being uncompromisingly rooted in biblical authority. To root religious education in the Bible, asserts Gangel, means that religious education is essentially a theological enterprise assisted by the social sciences as well as other sciences and disciplines. (This point is taken up again by Barbara Fleischer in her chapter in this volume.) It is theology, or more precisely biblically based theology, which informs religious educators what is the correct nature of truth and what is the correct nature of the human person—two of the four molar variables involved in every religious instruction act (subject-matter content and the learner). Gangel then goes on to address the issue of worldview, a seminal though often neglected wellspring of religious education, a wellspring that grounds and deeply influences so much of what religious educators do. Gangel explores the purposes, principles, and consequences of worldview in the religious education enterprise, and how important it is for religious educators in the third millennium to be aware of worldview and to ensure that their worldview is congruent with the biblical worldview. The chapter then goes on to emphasize that the development and teaching of values that are deeply spiritual is an urgent task to which religious educators in the third millennium must perforce attend. Effective religious education in the third millennium, education that is biblical to the core and spiritual in thrust, requires religious educators to eschew any kind of imperial mentality. Religious educators must avoid any tendency to yield to imperialist temptation, and instead adopt a communal model in which religious educators, administrators, learners, and the whole local church work together as an interactive community. Gangel takes pains to emphasize that pervading the entire religious education endeavor must be excellence. The motivation and end result of excellence in all dimensions of religious education can be found in the conviction that every religious education activity, large and small, ought to be done for the glory of God. Excellence in religious education requires the program to be comprehensive in scope and milieu. Finally, Gangel sees effective religious education in the third millennium as depending on lay rather than clergy leadership. Lay leadership is a biblical and a Reformation legacy, a legacy that places high premium on servant leadership.

Gabriel Moran's contribution, "Building on the Past", is a fine bridge chapter between the first part of this book and the second part. The chapters preceding Moran's examine major problems facing third-millennium religious education as viewed from a molar perspective, while the chapters that follow Moran's explore major problems facing third millennium religious education as viewed through the lens of more particular concerns. All chapters look at major problems facing religious education: it is the lens that differentiates the chapters in the first part of this book from those in the second part.

Moran's essay constitutes a serviceable bridge chapter because it overtly links religious education's past and its future. It is a truism in both psychology and history that the past is the best available predictor of the future in general and of future behavior in particular. Thus Moran's chapter is helpful in that it shines the light of the past upon the third millennium and in the process illuminates important past emphases that can be fruitfully continued, major past emphases that are better left on the rubbish heap of history, and selected past emphases that either directly point to or indirectly suggest the way to new and fresh and untried directions for successful third-millennium religious education. Taking seriously the history of religious education, Moran begins his chapter by examining the recent past of religious education. In his examination of the past, Moran seeks to locate clues that in one way or another might point to an improved religious education in the third millennium. Moran takes pains to caution that while religious education for the third millennium must look to the past for some helpful clues on what to do, nonetheless religious education in the third millennium must necessarily improve on what was done in the past; we cannot allow the past to repeat itself. To be useful, the past must be a springboard to leap into the future, to fly higher. Moran then proceeds to examine various Christian and non-Christian faith groups in order to discover some clues on what these faith groups have to offer religious educators during the process of forging a better religious education in the third millennium. In the next section of his chapter, Moran explores the second part of the term "religious education," especially with respect to the intertwined relationship of education and schooling, and to the place of religion in this admixture. In the fourth and final section, Moran adds some new insights to the ones he has already developed in this chapter and places these insights within the famous four-dimensional matrix that he advanced in expanded form in his book *Religious Education as a Second Language* (1989). In such a four-dimensional matrix, religious education in the third millennium should be international, interreligious, interinstitutional, and intergenerational—the "four inter's." All four elements composing this matrix dynamically and continually interact with each other in such a way as to enable the religious education enterprise to break out of its pre third millennium mold and enable it to become a vital and relevant force in the third millennium.

The next three chapters concentrate on one major vantage point or on one cluster of vantage points as an especially potent energizer to forge a better future for religious education in the third millennium.

For Anne Streaty Wimberly, an especially potent and fruitful energizer for the entire gamut of religious education is that of the black experience in America—the black Christian experience in general and the black religious education experience in particular. She looks at the future of religious education in the third millennium through the lens of the black Christian experience in America and demonstrates how this experience holds great transformational promise for forging a bright future for religious education in the third millennium. Wimberly skillfully reveals how the black Christian experience, especially when encapsulated in the black religious education experience, constitutes a privileged gift to all of religious education in the third millennium. The theme of Wimberly's gorgeous essay is concisely yet fully expressed in the title of her chapter: "A Black Christian Pedagogy of Hope: Religious Education in a Black Perspective." She does not center her chapter just on the theme of hope itself but rather on hope as powerfully transformatonal, on hope as transmuting both cognition and action in religious education. Such a sorely needed upward transformation is surely an antidote to the deadening rationalistic emphasis that was so pervasive throughout so much of religious education in the last half of the twentieth century. Running through the centuries-long American black experience as a gyroscope and a stabilizer, as an unfailing source of energy, and as a sure promise of the future, has been the theme, the reality, of hope. Tracing the history of formal legalized slavery in pre Civil War days through the later era of informal, nonlegalized slavery that lasted from the end of the Civil War to the end of the black freedom movement, Wimberly shows that even in those very difficult and parched times Christian hope was kept alive in black religious education and in other areas of black church life. It was this dynamic hope that sustained body and soul for so many black persons in America. It prevented blacks from falling into the pit of despair, into the tomb of hopelessness. There was a future, a bright future, no matter how bleak the circumstances. Herein, states Wimberly, lies a rich lesson for all of religious education in the third millennium: Keep hope burning and alive and prophetic in all of third-millennium religious education, especially when the times are difficult and trying and even anguishing, as surely they will be. Black religious education can bestow on non black religious education in the third millennium both the spirit and the existence of hope, no matter what the circumstance, no matter what the pain, no matter how hopeless the situation seems to be. For Wimberly, one important religious education key to the pedagogy of hope is the griot. This is a person whose role in fostering hope through religious education activity centers around knowing and recalling past stories of hope, and from these stories fashions new forms of hope in genuine dialogue with learners. The hope-filled religious educator of the third millennium must be a guide to the congregation as it walks the path of the pedagogy of hope. The religious educator must also serve as a cross-cultural advocate; here again black religious education has so very much to offer the whole panoply of religious education endeavor. Wimberly identifies eight major values that black religious education has tended to accentuate because of its historical experience. These values can be of signal importance to all of religious education as it seeks to forge a finer future in the third millennium: vigilance, courage, tenacity, faith, love, integrity, community, and respect. One important feature of this chapter is its presentation of various black-inspired models that can serve as helpful contexts for a religious education pedagogy of hope. These models are the exodus model, the exile model, and some alternative models including a homocentric model, and a model that combines the exodus model with the exile model.

If Anne Streaty Wimberly sees the past and present black religious education experience as providing an especially fecund source for enriching religious education all across the board, Richard Robert Osmer regards cross-disciplinary thinking, notably but not solely in the form of the process of evolution, as providing an important path to making religious education achieve optimum vitality and effectiveness in the third millennium. The title of Osmer's chapter concisely encapsulates the axis of his chapter: "A New Clue for Religious Education: Cross-Disciplinary Thinking at the Turn of the Millennium." In a famous 1950 book entitled *The Clue to Christian Education,* Randolph Crump Miller maintained that the clue to all effective religious education lies in theology. Now exactly a half century later, at the dawn of the third millennium, Osmer's chapter sets forth a new major clue, a clue that he contends is uniquely suited to religious education the third millennium. For Osmer, this new, all-encompassing clue is evolutionary thinking, especially when done in a cross-disciplinary mode. He gladly admits that there are other paradigms, other important clues which are significant and highly useful in providing a very helpful direction for a vitalized religious education in the third millennium. But Osmer also maintains that evolutionary thinking represents one necessary core aspect for achieving religious education effectiveness in the third millennium and thus is eminently worthwhile pursuing as we attempt to chart the course of religious education in the third millennium. Surveying the history of the teaching ministry in the church, Osmer finds that this ministry has functioned somewhere between the two poles of integrity and intelligibility. Utilizing the necessary and productive dynamic tension between these two poles as one key way in which evolutionary thinking in religious education has taken place, Osmer uses American Mainline Protestantism in general and the celebrated Coe-Smith debate in particular as especially helpful examples of what happens when evolutionary thinking frontally encounters religious education—and by inference what can happen when cross-disciplinary evolutionary thinking encounters the third millennium. This chapter demonstrates how George Albert Coe's quest for intelligibility on the one hand and Shelton Smith's search for integrity on the other hand represented two opposite poles of the spectrum. Both poles, Osmer maintains, are too extreme, since each excludes valuable aspects contained in the other. Neither pole by itself was successful in religious education in the first half of the twentieth century, and neither is likely to be effective in the third millennium. What is really needed is not a blending or homogenization of the two poles but rather the active, ongoing maintenance of a healthy and necessary dynamic tension between the two poles each of which remains intact. For Osmer, one major imperative of religious education in the third millennium is to provide a balanced, inclusive embrace of all poles of evolutionary thinking done in a cross-disciplinary fashion. Cross-disciplinary thinking above all enables the advancement of creative evolutionary theory and practice in religious education. The remainder of Osmer's chapter is devoted to procedural considerations that are aimed at enhancing educational practice through the use of crossdisciplinary processes. Osmer sees the work of Howard Gardner and his theory of multiple intelligences as representing cross-disciplinary evolutionary theory in practice and therefore representative of an ideal modus operandi for effective religious education thought and action in the third millennium.

Wimberly's chapter looks at the vitalization of all of religious education in the third millennium through the lens of a black pedagogy of hope. Using the lens of some important twentieth century Mainline Protestant religious educational thought, Osmer's chapter sees evolutionary thinking done in a cross-disciplinary mode as the major factor that can bring about the basic improvement of all of religious education in the new millennium. For her part, Barbara Fleischer's lens for forging a better future for religious education in the third millennium is that of practical theology. Fleischer forcefully and unequivocally contends that the basic and absolutely essential overarching key to the maximum success for religious education in the third millennium is practical theology as it is thrusted toward transformative learning. She makes this point repeatedly and with skill in her chapter, "Practical Theology and Transformative Learning: Partnership for Christian Religious Education". Fleischer believes that in dynamically dialectical partnership, practical theology and transformative learning can heal the rift between the religious and the educational in religious education. She stoutly asserts that it is practical theology that provides the necessary overall approach and ecology wherein successful religious education in the third millennium can truly flower. Fleischer boldly maintains that practical theology is not a subspeciality of theology. On the contrary, practical theology constitutes a wholly new mode of envisioning theology and of entering into the religious enterprise. Practical theology accomplishes this dynamic task by the use of praxis, a concept adopted by some influential neo-Marxian thinkers and subsequently appropriated by some theologians, philosophers, and religious educators in an attempt to provide a construct with which to unify in one activity the two poles of theory and practice. Fleischer holds that practical theology constitutes the grounding of religious education work in all of its phases, especially in historical, hermeneutical, and sociocultural analysis. Through this kind of analysis and reflection, practical theology can directly lead to personal and communal spiritual living. Fleischer believes that the most fruitful focus of religious-education-as-practical-theology is the transformation of society in order to help satisfactorily address in a theological mode the issues of social justice. She goes on to make a sharp distinction between transformative learning and instrumental learning, indicating that in her view transformative learning represents a basic paradigm shift for both general education and religious education. Fleischer then briefly deals with the nature and uses of transformative learning, concluding her essay with an illuminative treatment of the interplay between practical theology and transformative learning.

The final two chapters of this book regard the exercise of the prophetic role of religious education as providing the major impetus and metier in bringing about a brighter future for religious education in the third millennium. These two chapters are an ideal conclusion to this book because each in its own way, they both explicitly and directly center on hurtling religious education into the third millennium. For both Ronnie Prevost and James Michael Lee, the ongoing enactment of their prophetic office by religious educationists and educators will enable them to examine critically and without compromise the ongoing state of religious education, and on the basis of this examination forthrightly and courageously propose general and specific prescriptions for the progressive renewal of religious education throughout the third millennium. The Prevost chapter and the Lee chapter have a sense of urgency to them. But the tone of their urgency is different. Prevost's tone is a relatively mellow one as prophetic writings go. It stresses prophecy through proaction, gently. Though it is on the gentle side, nonetheless, it does sound a clarion call to change, and basic change at that. Lee's tone and spirit is more like that of an Old Testament prophet: forthright, direct, no-holds-barred, and going right to the roots. There is no mistaking the grave sense of urgency and grand prophetic renewal for which his chapter cries out.

The prophetic cast of Prevost's chapter is readily discernable in the title of his chapter: "Creating the Undiscovered Country: Religious Education as an Agent of Forging the Third Millennium." He begins his chapter by noting that the last part of the second millennium was characterized by a tremendous amount of significant change in society in general and religious education in particular. He believes that if religious education is to attain its full potential in the third millennium, it must not be reactive to change, as it so often was in the second millennium. Rather, religious education in the third millennium must adapt in such a way as to manage change and skillfully utilize change for its own purposes. Prevost regards change as a problem—or better yet, as a challenge—which religious education must confront boldly if it is to fulfill its great promise. In such productive confrontation with change, religious education should use problem solving processes in its effort to successfully use change for its own purposes. Such problem solving will first concentrate on a careful, nondefensive, widespread examination of the current situation as it faces religious educators in the third millennium. On the basis of this diagnosis, the successful religious educator in the third millennium will offer prognoses for an effective future and then will take prescriptive action that will not just remedy the problems facing the field but more importantly will turn the problems into successful opportunities for religious growth. Prevost goes on to unpack the diagnosis-prescription scenario as the central axis for proaction in religious education. In the diagnosis section of his chapter, he limns the perennial challenge for religious education as beautifully illustrated in religious history from Abraham to the present day. He then goes to the heart of the issue by asserting that the basic nature of the third millennium challenge to religious education is found in the unfortunate fact that institutional religion throughout much of the second millennium was lamentably bound by culture, that is heavily reactive rather than proactive. The chapter goes on to explore expressions of the current challenge to the philosophy of religious education, centering its attention on metaphysics, epistemology, and axiology. Prevost then proceeds to the prescription section of his chapter, but not before noting that there can be no genuinely successful prescription without previous diagnosis and, by inference, no successful prophetic action in the absence of prior analysis. The general prescription that Prevost offers to religious education in the third millennium is twofold: forge a religious education that is simultaneously proactive and prophetic. Such twin prongs— which in the ultimate analysis are essentially the same thing in different expressions—will exert a needed beneficial impact on religious education curriculum, substantive content, and pedagogy. Prevost concludes his chapter with a short prognosis that *if* religious education will become proactive and prophetic throughout the third millennium, there can emerge what he terms "cautious optimism" that the field in all its dimensionalities will improve significantly.

The prophetic thrust of Prevost's chapter is continued and sharpened in James Michael Lee's chapter "Vision, Prophecy, and Forging the Future." Lee begins his chapter by asserting that the spirit of his chapter stands squarely and unabashedly within the venerable prophetic tradition. He defines prophecy as hastening the future, foredoing as well as fore-telling. Thus the goal of the prophetic role in any field, including that of religious instruction, is basic transformation. Borrowing Jean Piaget's terminology, Lee asserts that basic transformation means fostering accommodative learning rather than assimilative learning. Accommodative learning is the process of either radically changing the existing framework or establishing a fundamentally new framework. For its part, assimilative learning is the process of placing new learnings into an already existing framework. Drawing on the witness of history, Lee have reminds us that almost all true prophets in the world, in the church, and in religious instruction all too often have been initially spurned, rejected, or even persecuted because their emphasis on accommodative learning takes persons and institutions out of their comfortable mind-sets and ways, and hurtles them into new and unfamiliar zones. Lee goes on to say that authentic prophecy must always be organically linked to vision. Productive vision, for its part, is anchored in solid theory and appropriate research, and thus differs essentially from daydreaming. In the next section of his chapter, Lee explores the lamentable fact that though religious instruction in all the Christian churches is supposed to be of supreme importance, nonetheless it is not accorded the attention it deserves by ecclesiastical officials. He then goes on to offer some concrete solutions to this problem, solutions which are necessary if religious instruction is to move forward in the third millennium. The next area with which Lee's chapter deals is the frequent lack of requisite emphasis on top-flight scholarship in the field religious instruction. After returning to the theme of the prophetic imperative in religious instruction, Lee spends the rest of his chapter treating the substantive content and the structural content of religious instruction. He repeatedly stresses that the proper substantive content of religious instruction is "red hot religion," a way of being and doing that is fundamentally different from cognitive subtantive content such as theology. Lee then turns his attention to structural content, the way in which religion is taught. Repeatedly he stresses that the here-and-now religious instruction act is central in every phase of the religious instruction enterprise. He forthrightly rejects practical theology as the cornerstone for productive religious instruction, showing how practical theology does not and cannot of itself bring forth educational outcomes and demonstrating that only social science has the potency to accomplish the task that religious instruction is called upon to do. He ends his chapter on a decidedly upbeat note, stating that if religious educators and educationists place the religious instruction act at the dynamically radiating center of their thoughts and feelings and activities, then the field will surely see the dawn of a new era in the third millennium.

With the Lee chapter this volume comes full circle. In the opening pages of the first chapter Mary Elizabeth Mullino Moore showed the great difficulty inherent in the transformative journey of life in general and of religious education in particular. In the closing chapter, James Michael Lee repeatedly returns to the difficulty of the transformative journey and emphasizes that every religious educator and educationist must necessarily endure the heavy burden of their obligatory prophetic role as a prerequisite for ransoming the third millennium unto optimal religious education.

Prefaces and Introductions to books are typically written last when all the other work is completed. So it is with this book. It is Columbus

Day as I key into my computer the concluding words of this Introduction. It is fitting that this book is finished on Columbus Day.

Columbus saw himself as a man with a mission. This book is devoted to a mission—the mission of making religious education in all its forms as effective as possible throughout the third millennium.

Columbus participated in a great adventure. He was the protagonist in a great undertaking. This book hopefully will help all religious educationists and educators to jump aboard the great adventure of teaching learners to know God, love God, and serve God in the best manner possible throughout the third millennium. If Columbus's journey was not a great one, I do not know what was. And if the journey of religious educationists and educators in the third millennium is not a great one, I do not know what is.

Before he set sail, Columbus told the Sovereigns that he would not take any money for his journey but would instead contribute all the proceeds from his great adventure to help reconquer the holy city of Jerusalem and restore to Christian hands the Church of the Holy Sepulcher, which then and now houses both the place where Jesus was crucified and the tomb in which he was laid to rest, which became the site of the Resurrection. All contributors to this volume, including the editor, agreed never to take any royalty whatever for this book.

Columbus was a deeply religious man who prayed often throughout the day. When he first set foot on the New World, he firmly planted on the beach a special banner of Ferdinand and Isabella, one portraying a huge cross in its center. Immediately after that, he and those who waded ashore with him knelt down on the sand and offered prayers of thanksgiving and consecration to God. He called the land he discovered San Salvador, Holy Savior. As far as I know, all the contributors to this volume are deeply religious. And I suspect that all the contributors regard their chapters as firmly planting the banner of the Lord on the beach of the new millennium and have consecrated their chapters to God and his holy work of religion education.

Columbus, who was called The Discoverer, ushered in a whole new world. The modern era really began with Columbus. With his discovery, the Western world was radically transformed and would never be the same again. What all of us authors in the present book have tried to do, each in our own way, is not just to greet the new millennium with a religious education handshake but to help usher a whole new world in a manner that will transform it accomodatively and assimilatively in a religious education manner.

While Columbus did indeed sail into previously uncharted waters, he did not do it unaided or untested. He was an expert in both the science and art of sailing. He had thoroughly immersed himself in the best scientific theories and research of the day, all of which indicated that the earth was indeed round and that he could thus sail west to arrive in the East. Columbus was a highly accomplished mariner, the best of his era, a man highly proficient in the art of sailing. If we religious educationists and educators are to truly usher in a new world, if we are to successfully navigate the uncharted waters of the third millennium and to accomodatively transform religious education in this millennium, then I firmly believe that it is absolutely necessary for us to successfully master the science and art of religious instruction just as Columbus successfully mastered the science and art of sailing.

Forging a Better Religious Education in the Third Millennium will be the very first book which Religious Education Press will publish in the new millennium. That this will come to pass is eminently fitting because here in one volume is beautifully encapsulated the basic philosophy, goals, and modus operandi of REP. Central to the basic philosophy, goals, and modus operandi of Religious Education Press is that religious educationists and educators representing the entire spectrum of Christian faith traditions, and representing quite different (and sometimes highly conflicting) positions on a wide range of substantive and structural issues in the field, come together as colleagues under one umbrella and offer their points of view openly and nonpolitically in the full acceptance that only when the field warmly and nonpunitively welcomes all serious scholarly-grounded positions in brotherly and sisterly fashion will the field grow and prosper. Religious Education Press not only thoroughly embraces the Gamaliel Principle (Acts 5:33–39), but indeed pushes this principle forward in the sense that REP not only accepts various divergent positions on religious education but indeed assiduously works to ensure that these contrasting and often highly conflicting positions are brought to light in books of the highest caliber.

This volume is deliberately scheduled to be published sometime around the very first Feast of the Resurrection of the third millennium. I feel confident that all my distinguished colleagues who contributed chapters to this book enthusiastically join me in hope and prayer that as Jesus rose two millennia ago, so too religious education will rise gloriously and successfully in the third millennium

I began this Introduction with a quotation from one of my favorite poems, "Ulysses", by Alfred Lord Tennyson. I deliberately used this quotation because it deals with reflections on a long journey filled with a great many problems and difficulties which weakened Ulysses and his companions. The action of the poem takes place many years after he finished the journey. Rather than being enervated or discouraged by the tribulations of the journey, the old Ulysses boldly cried out with the hope and the challenge of a new life, a new beginning, in the words I quoted at the beginning of this Introduction.

The long and difficult journey which the religious education enterprise took throughout the last century of the second millennium is not unlike that of Ulysses. The field underwent many obstacles, travails, and setbacks—as well as some triumphs too. Like Ulysses and his companions, religious educationists and educators have been weakened by enervating struggles over the years. In our case, these struggles were with an often inattentive and ungrateful ecclesiasticum, with the proliferation of bankrupt ideologies, with the steadily eroding onrush of sterile rationalism, with a debilitating scarcity of grand vision and all-consuming prophetic fire, with the doom-filled siren songs of fads and gimmicks, and most sadly with the all-too frequent unwillingness to sacrifice everything for the religious education apostolate. But in the concluding lines of Tennyson's inspiring poem, Ulysses gives us who now walk through the open door of the third millennim a clarion call of hope, a vital key to help religious educationists and educators turn the apostolate into a rousing success all across the board. It is with this quotation, one which holds the promise of a better future for religious education in the third millennium, that I close this Introduction.

> *"One equal temper of heroic hearts,*
> *Made weak by time and fate, but strong in will*
> *To strive, to seek, to find, and not to yield."*

Birmingham, Alabama   JAMES MICHAEL LEE
October 12, 1999

Sacramental Teaching:

Mediating the Holy

MARY ELIZABETH MULLINO MOORE

In recent years, much talk in the church has focused on biblical literacy and on teaching moral values. In a world of massive transitions, enormous risks, and horrendous tragedies, this concern for passing on a solid, unchanging faith is understandable. Unfortunately, the very concerns that lead people to cling to a simple and definable faith often lead people to question and even abandon that faith. What are the challenges to religious educators in such a world?

As I prepare this chapter on religious education for the third millenium, I am also preparing to move across the country after living twenty-four years in Claremont, California, and teaching twenty years there. The preparation process is, in some ways, parallel to the preparation process for a third millenium. When people ask me what I am looking forward to in Atlanta, I have difficulty answering. I am confident that the decision to move is a good decision, but the future has many unknowns. As one of my friends said to me, "You do not know who you will be in the new place." I can describe some of the contours of the community, institution, and work to which I go, but I cannot describe the details. I only know that this journey is a calling—a vocation—and I will understand it better in the future.

The purpose of this chapter is to explore realities of change and project the future of religious education. In particular, we ask what kind of religious education can empower Christian people to move into the future, despite cataclysmic changes in their lives and in the world around them. The specific purposes are to uncover insights into the astonishing and messy world in which we live and to point toward possibilities in sacramental teaching—teaching that mediates the Holy in our world. To those ends, we begin with an allegory of moving, followed by analysis of our astonishing and messy world, culminating in sacramental proposals for religious education.

MOVING—AN ALLEGORY

The story of my family's move across country to a new life can be understood as an allegory for the human family's move into a new millenium. Although the whole human family is moving, each religious community makes the move in its own distinctive way. Consider some of the movements involved in such a change.

Preparing to move across the United States has involved many phases of transition for our family. First was the work of discernment—discerning God's call for the future; then came the decision to follow the call that our family discerned. This was a traumatic time— filled with awareness of the life we loved in the Claremont community and of possibilities that beckoned for the future. Finally, in the midst of trauma, we found the courage to make a decision, which involved a major move away from our familiar home and across the country to a new home. Having made this decision, we had next to communicate it to people near and far, people whose lives would also be affected by our move. In a sense, all of us would be traveling together into a new kind of life, with new forms of relationship.

The next months involved much preparation work. I found myself giving everything within me to my Claremont community, realizing that I had only a few months to give my best and bring vital work to a close. Our family also spent much time with dear friends and family, making the most of our time as we valued every fleeting moment. Further, we had much preparation. I had a double load at my school, trying to do the normal work plus the work of making conclusions and transitions. Our family also had much preparation to do. We gave away many books and possessions that we no longer needed, and we recycled hundreds of pounds of paper, glass, and plastic that could now be used to make new items for the future. Then we packed a huge number of boxes that would travel with us, knowing that we were still taking more than we needed; because of time and attachments, we were unable to let go of more. Throughout this preparation time, we discovered the joy of letting go and simplifying our lives. We felt the confidence of a decision well made and the fear of an unknown future.

Having made preparations for months, the days for moving finally came. We spent the last two weeks packing from early to late, saying tearful farewells to family and friends, and loading our car with the items that would travel with us to our new home. Exhausted and unsure of what lay ahead, we loaded ourselves into the car and began the five-day journey. As we traveled, we had moments of sadness for what we had left behind, and moments of delight as we crossed a beautiful countryside. The future was still uncertain, but we were as prepared as we could be, and we were filled with anticipation.

When we finally arrived in Atlanta, we found our house torn apart with building and repair projects. The house was not ready for us to move in but, of course, the movers were coming anyway. We would have to move into the chaos and live in it for some weeks before we settled into a new life. Fortunately, some friends in our new home city had invited us to a meal on the first day of our new life. The joy of being at table with friends would help us survive the chaos, and perhaps even find creativity in it. We were not entering a ready-made life, either in housing or in work. We would have to create our life from the possibilities that lay before us.

The journey of religious education into the third millenium has many of these same features. First is a time of *discernment and decision making*. Unlike my decision to move to a new institution, the third millenium came no matter what we did. On the other hand, the awesome reality of a turning century and a turning millenium awakened people to discern what God is doing in the world and what God is calling them to do. Since the early 1980s, religious communities and many other institutions have been planning ahead for the new millenium. They have anticipated, planned, and launched new initiatives. This planning has been accompanied by excitement and trauma. We have been aware of the many things we love in our present lives, as well as new possibilities that beckon. We ask ourselves what is most important in our traditional beliefs and practices to take with us into the future and what newness we need to receive. This kind of discernment and decision making is important for religious education as people prepare to leave their home in the second millenium and enter the third. This kind of discernment and decision making requires courage if we are to move from the familiar into the unknown. What kind of education do we need for traveling and for settling into our new home? What kind of communication do we need with one another? How do we need to reshape our relationships?

The discernment and decision-making processes finally yield to *preparations for the new millenium*. The preparations may include completing work that is already begun, as well as giving our best to present relationships and present work. This is a time of appreciation for all that has been and making space for what will be. Preparations include giving away those possessions we no longer need (old wineskins) and recycling artifacts of the past that can be made into something new. Preparations also include packing those enduring values and traditions that we need for the future. In short, some traditions need to given away or recycled, and some need to be handled with care so they can travel with us into the next millenium. Discernment, thus, continues as we seek what God wants and needs for us in this journey. Throughout this preparation time, we may be blessed to discover the joy of letting go and simplifying our lives. We will likely have moments of confidence that God is leading us into the future, as well as moments of fear as we glimpse the abyss of the unknown.

Having made preparations for years, *the journey toward the new millenium finally begins*. The final weeks involve a flurry of excitement and final preparations, saying tearful farewells to the memories and attachments of a passing century and millenium, and loading our religious communities with traditions and values for our new home. Exhausted and unsure of what lies ahead, we begin this new journey. As we travel through a transitional year (or years), we will surely have moments of sadness for what we have left behind, as well as moments of delight in traveling through a new era. The future will still be uncertain, but we have prepared as much as possible, and we are filled with anticipation.

After we finally arrive in the new millenium (however one calculates the beginning), *we will likely find chaos*. Our new house may be torn apart with building and repair projects; however, the third millenium arrives, ready or not. We will simply have to move into the chaos of this new era; we may live in it for some time before we settle into a new life. Fortunately, within our religious communities, we have the opportunity to gather at table again and again. For Jews, gathering at table is a holy celebration of *shabbat*. For Christians, table gathering takes its most significant form in the Eucharist. For both, the joy of being at table with other Jews or Christians can help us survive the chaos of a new millenium, and perhaps find seeds of creativity within it. We will not enter a ready-made life; we will have to create our lives from possibilities that lie before us.

This allegorical story follows anthropologists' descriptions of social change and rites of passage. Victor Turner, and others before him, describe social change as crossing a threshold, moving from preliminal to liminal to postliminal existence. Preliminal existence is a time of anticipation and preparation, analogous to the discernment, decision making and preparation times described above. Liminal existence is a time of change—crossing a threshold—analogous to the traveling and chaotic times of moving described in the story. Postliminal existence is the time of adjusting to a new life, a time that is only beginning as my family creates a new life in Atlanta, and as religious communities create a new life in the early months and years of a new millenium. In the postliminal times, we will discover that some of our earlier preparations were helpful, and others were unnecessary or even counterproductive. Our preparations will have awakened us, however, to the reality of change. At the very least, we have girded ourselves with sacred traditions, and we have leaned toward God's new creation, the future that only God can fully understand.

As we live in the liminal transition at the dawning of a new millenium, consider the choices before us. We can engage in religious education that holds tightly to the past; we can let everything go and enter the future without roots. On the other hand, we can engage in the delightful and messy journey of discernment and preparation, traveling through chaos, and making home in a new era. When we engage faith in this way, we open ourselves to face the abyss of future. In those courageous moments, we may not know what lies ahead, but God is with us in each moment and moves ahead of us into the unknown. Such engagement with mystery transforms people from within and without. It opens people to see our astonishing and messy world with full sight, and to respond to God's call with full courage.

AN ASTONISHING WORLD

With that sense of anticipation, we turn now to the astonishing world through which we view the third millenium. This astonishing world provides a lens for understanding and creating religious education for the next thousand years. In fact, the very way Christian communities have marked time in thousand-year increments since Jesus' life on earth reveals something of the wonder that the passage of time holds for people. Whether they focus on the Jewish, Chinese, or Roman calendar, people observe passing time as a wondrous reality—one to be celebrated and held in awe. By marking time, people note the sacramentality of life and the passing of days in God's creation. We thus turn to two stories of ordinary days, which reveal extraordinary wonder.

In his autobiography, Howard Thurman tells stories of his grandmother, an ex-slave, who welcomed him home every day after school (*With Head and Heart*). His father had died, and his mother did domestic work to support the family; his grandmother was always at home. One day, Howard dressed up to go to his Baptist church and be interviewed by the board of deacons for the final step before his baptism. He had prepared carefully for this moment. The deacons asked Howard many questions, especially about the Bible; he gave thoughtful and well-informed answers. At last, the deacons asked young Howard why he wanted to be baptized; he replied that he wanted to be a Christian. The deacons were not pleased with the answer, so they told Howard to take more time. They suggested that, when he knew himself to be a Christian, he could come talk with them again. Howard returned home, dejected. When he told Grandmother his story, she puffed up with anger, took his hand, and marched with him back to the church. They arrived before the meeting had dispersed. Grandmother marched into the room and shamed the deacons; she insisted that they should be able to read the heart of this boy, who had been Christian for a long time. She assured them that Howard was ready to be baptized. The deacons were astonished! And Howard Thurman was baptized the next Sunday.

John Hull, a British scholar in religious education, tells the story of his adulthood journey into blindness (*Touching the Rock*; *On Sight and Insight*). He struggled with depression for more than three years, having been a brilliant and productive scholar whose professional life centered around reading and writing books; his family life had revolved around the care of small children, teaching them how to read and traveling with them to interesting places. Suddenly his world was changing. He could not read books, play in familiar ways with his children, or write the essays for which he was so much appreciated.

Fortunately, John discovered reading machines and books on tape, and he read the Bible every day as well as his class preparations. He made new discoveries about God. One day, many months after he had lost his sight, he was standing at the street corner waiting for the signals that would tell him that he could safely cross to his home. He had a sudden realization that the people driving by were noticing this blind man waiting to cross the street, and they were probably wondering how he was going to manage, especially without a dog. Then he thought to himself about how he would simply step off the curb, cross to the other side, and make his way home. That was a rather common moment, but he wrote about it later as the first time he felt confidence in being a blind person. John was astonished by his own confidence!

What do these stories have in common, and what in the world do they have to do with religious education? I suggest that they are both sacramental moments—ordinary moments when God was revealed in unexpected ways! Both have *an element of surprise*, but not the kind of surprise that you control as when you plan a surprise party. Both of these stories reveal an unexpected turn of events or a reversal in the way people have always thought. In both, the people are astonished! But also, in both, the *people are living with some degree of conflict or discouragement*, whether with communicating one's readiness to be baptized or living with blindness.

In these stories, also, the *people are not always pleased with God*, and they are asking difficult questions about what God is doing in the midst of all this conflict and discouragement. Maybe the people are even wishing that they could control God's actions—get the results or the healing that they want. But in both stories, *a response from God does come*. The answers are not always the expected or hoped-for answers, but they represent a response from God all the same. And the people are astonished!

Biblical stories astonish us further. In fact, the words "astonished" and "amazed" appear frequently in the first and second Testaments. Consider, for example, the story from Matthew (22:15–22) when the Pharisees tried to trap Jesus. They were trying to get him to say that taxes were either wrong to pay (in which case he would anger the Romans) or were important to pay (in which case he would anger the people who hated to pay taxes to the Romans). Jesus knew that the

Pharisees actually produced coins in the precincts of the Temple, so he asked for a coin and gave an indirect answer that turned the whole thing back to them. He said, "Give to the emperor what is the emperor's, and to God the things that are God's" (v. 21). The Pharisees were amazed. Their trap had not worked! They were not able to stir up the conflict they were seeking. They were not able to control Jesus. And so they went away, astonished!

The unexpected turn for the Pharisees was to discover not only that Jesus was clever but also that the people had more than two options in regard to taxes. The people were already aware of two options—to judge taxes as good or to judge them as bad. In a world that wanted predictable and neat categories of good and bad, right and wrong, Jesus was saying, "You can find another way—a way in which taxes do have a place, but their place is limited: Give to the emperor what is the emperor's and to God the things that are God's." The unexpected came from Jesus' teaching. The predictable world of two choices—either/or—was not so predictable after all.

Consider another story from the Hebrew Bible (Exodus 33:12–23). An amazing event took place shortly after Moses became angry with the Hebrew people in the wilderness and threw down the tablets of stone that he had received from God. Moses was certainly not predictable in this story. The commandments were broken to bits, and the people were shattered and condemned because they had been worshiping a golden calf. Moses, however, led the people to a place where God instructed, and he implored God, "Now if I have found favor in your sight, show me your ways, so that I may know you and find favor in your sight. Consider too that this nation is your people" (Exodus 33:13). Moses was asking God to be predictable and take care of everything, especially to show God's ways and God's glory.

God's response to Moses was dramatic:

> "I will make all my goodness pass before you, and will proclaim before you the name, 'The Lord,' and I will be gracious to whom I will be gracious, and will show mercy on whom I will show mercy." God added a caveat, however, saying to Moses, "But you cannot see my face; for no one shall see me and live" (33:19–20).

Then God explained that Moses was to go up on a rock, and God would put him in the cleft of the rock while God's glory passed by;

God's hand would cover Moses. Only after God's glory passed would the hand be removed, and then Moses could see God's back. Yes! Moses was to see the glory of God but not to see God's face. In short, Moses would see God's works but would not stand face-to-face with the Lord.

Do you think that Moses was going to be satisfied with seeing God's glory from behind God's back? Perhaps not, but in the next scene, we see God giving Moses instructions to cut two more tablets of stone and climb Mount Sinai—no predictability here, just more work. Moses did it. Then God actually came and stood with Moses, proclaimed the name, "The Lord," and made a covenant with Moses and the people. Moses quickly bowed his head and worshiped (34:1–8). Moses was astonished!

The promise in the Moses story is simply this—that God *does* come and God *does* act and God *does* make covenant, but we can neither know nor control what God does and how. Does this mean that we are helpless—that God controls every event that happens? Apparently not, at least not if we take the Moses story seriously, because the people chose on their own to make the golden calf. The people of the Moses story made decisions on their own, just as we all-too-human-beings make decisions on our own. We should not be surprised that the world is unpredictable! But Moses was convinced that he also had power to *address* God—to plead with God for himself and for his people. And in the story, God not only came and acted and made covenant but God also listened! And so indeed, we *can* be astonished because God listens even to us and responds. The unexpected does happen: In a world that wants to see God face-to-face—that wants sureness and predictability—we are shown another option—to address God, to plead with God, to trust that God will listen, even if we are only to see the back of God.

As we begin the unpredictability of a third millenium, we live with a God of surprises, who always comes—who comes in sacramental moments every day but not always as we imagine. Let us hope that we never lose our capacity to be astonished! This is the God of mystery who comes to us even as we wonder what lies ahead.

A MESSY WORLD

With a sense of astonishment in God's movements, we turn now to a world that is also very messy. Consider, for example, the wars that rage around our world, the peace processes that flare and fail, the tragic poverty that besets every continent, and the destruction of children in the wake of political and economic conflicts. Consider, also, diversity: the diverse points of view and experiences of the world that make our efforts to live in healthy human community very complex. In this world we often hold our own views so tightly that we cannot appreciate people whose views are different from ours. Not only do we not appreciate the beauty of diversity, we often do not even see the dramatic differences among ourselves, whether due to race, gender, class, abilities, sexual orientation, or other influences. Such messiness is a vivid part of contemporary reality, but it is also part of our past as a Christian people.

Imagine yourself as a member of the first-century church of Rome. Your church was established by a less known missionary sometime before Paul arrived; however, Paul, the thirteenth apostle, is coming to pay a visit. For some reason, Paul seems eager—even overeager—to communicate with your church, so he writes a long letter and sends it ahead. He writes, "Do not be conformed to this world, but be transformed by the renewing of your minds, so that you may discern what is the will of God—what is good and acceptable and perfect" (Romans 12:2). Paul seems quite concerned for people in Rome to hear this message; he sends his carefully composed letter well in advance of his visit. But why does he do this?

Imagine yourself for a moment in a divided Roman Christian community. Some of the people are Jewish Christians and some are Gentile Christians. They do not get along well, and disagreements break out frequently. One fiery dispute focuses on whether the Ten Commandments are binding on Christians; another regards what foods are lawful and appropriate to eat. The community is alive with groups opposing one another. One particular group seems to be a worry for Paul—the militant Jewish Christians who insist that people must obey all of the Jewish law in order to be Christian. Paul becomes intense and repetitive in chapter 3 of his Romans letter; his primary point is that Jews and Greeks alike are "under the power of sin" (Romans 3:9), and they are also alike as recipients of God's care. He says:

> Do you suppose God is the God of the Jews alone? Is [God] not the God of Gentiles also? Certainly, of Gentiles also, if it be true that God is one. And God will therefore justify both the circumcised in virtue of

their faith, and the uncircumcised through their faith. (Romans 3:29–30)

In the same chapter Paul emphasizes his central point to the community in Rome; in verses 21–26 alone, he testifies four times that salvation to the whole community is through Jesus Christ—that Jesus saves! Imagine this fractured Roman community and Paul with his strong message for them.

Paul's clear message regarding God in his letter to the Romans is that God loves and responds faithfully to the whole community; God is the source of salvation. At the same time, God expects goodness and oneness from the whole body—not uniformity but a spirit of community. In this Romans letter, Paul is also concerned with the human condition; thus, he addresses at least three themes regarding human life. As contemporary readers focus attention on transitions to a third millenium, we are aware of our own messy world; Paul's picture of human life can be illuminating.

The first human-life theme is that *the Roman community was living with conflict and pain.* Consider the church community that received Paul's letter to the Romans—a community in which we can see abundant conflict; we can only guess how much of that conflict was above and below the surface. Paul seemed eager for the Romans to hear his message. He wrote with fiery passion at many points. Hear the words from the last chapter of the letter:

> I implore you, my friends, keep your eye on those who stir up quarrels and lead others astray, contrary to the teaching you received. Avoid them, for such people are servants not of Christ our Lord but of their own appetites, and they seduce the minds of innocent people with smooth and specious words. (Romans 16:17–18)

These are strong words indeed! The contemporary tendency is to read Paul's letter as a general theological statement and to miss his intent to respond to concrete issues in the Roman community. I argue that many distortions and abuses have been created by the tendency to abstract Romans into theological dogma. One distortion is that we tend to read the letter for a message of individual salvation and to miss Paul's concern for the broken community. Another distortion, which has become a serious abuse over the centuries, is the tendency to read the letter as a message to the Jews rather than a message to a group of militant Jewish Christians in Rome. Thus texts in Romans have been used for centuries to reinforce anti-Semitism and anti-Judaism, even to justify the annihilation of six million Jews in the Holocaust. What if we were to reread Romans, however, and discover in the particularity of the church at Rome the particularity of our own churches with their squabbles and conflicts? In those conflicts and pains of community life, we might see signals of broken community.

In addition to a community in conflict and pain, *the Romans text also signals a world in turmoil*. The first-century church of Rome calls up the memory of many religious communities in the same region—Jewish, Christian, Hellenistic, Roman, and other—that were divided among themselves and within themselves as they sought to live faithfully in a world of religious conflict and Roman imperialism. The diversity of peoples, the existence of major economic and political inequities, and recurring conflicts over religious truth created a world in which stress was high and the quest for identity was intense. Such questing for identity only added fuel to debates within the Roman church over Christian beliefs and practices. The people of the church lived in a world of turmoil, and their Christian faith did not exempt them from feeling it.

But *this is also a community seeking new life*. We see a church in which people were willing to put their commitments forward, to struggle with difficult questions, to seek understanding of the gospel, and to follow Jesus Christ. On the other hand, we see a church touched by mean-spiritedness, and we see Paul, a missionary, who perhaps wanted more than anything else for Roman Christians to be transformed into a community befitting the gospel that they proclaimed.

In the Roman church we see a messy world, not unlike the one we face as we journey into a new century. We can also see the challenge in Paul's words to live holy lives, both as a community and as individuals. In such a messy world, people need more than biblical literacy and moral teachings; they need sacramental teaching—teaching that mediates the Holy in our daily lives. This is what Paul sought to do for the Roman community. This is also the challenge to religious education in the third millenium.

SACRAMENTAL TEACHING

We cannot presume that the communities represented by readers of this volume are the same as the Roman Christian community, nor that the journey to a new century is the same as Paul's journey to chasten and strengthen the young Roman church. We *can* presume, however, that most communities face conflict and pain—sometimes visible and sometimes hidden. We can also presume that most communities (then and now) live in a world of turmoil, and most hunger and search for new life. In a church of broken community and a world of turmoil, what is the calling of Christian religious educators? I propose that our calling is to *sacramental teaching—teaching that mediates the Holy, teaching that mediates the grace, power and call of God.*

A word is needed first about sacrament, and then I will sketch some acts of sacramental teaching. The definitions of sacrament are many, but the most common and enduring is "an outward and visible sign of an inward and spiritual grace." Some recent work on the sacraments moves toward recognizing that all creation is sacred; thus, the formal sacraments of the church awaken us to the sacredness of God's whole creation. The sacraments mediate God's grace and enable us to participate more fully in the grace of God that is everywhere revealed. The actual definitions and identification of sacraments have varied widely through Christian history; at one time thirty sacraments were listed. Even with such change, however, the basic definitional elements have remained constant: sacraments represent a flow of the free grace of God through the concrete stuff of creation (water in the baptism and bread and wine in the Eucharist) for the sanctification of human beings. The Orthodox Church and many contemporary churches add, also, the care of creation. Thus, to propose that Christian teaching is a sacramental activity is to say that *the heart of Christian teaching is mediating the free grace of God through the concrete stuff of creation for the sanctification of human communities and for the well-being of all God's creation.*

My purpose here is not to multiply the number of formal sacraments in the church by adding a sacrament of teaching alongside others; my purpose is rather to cast a bright light on the sacramental nature of religious education. With that in mind, we turn to four acts of sacramental teaching.

Expect the Unexpected

The first act of sacramental teaching is to expect the unexpected; that is, expect that God *is* present and *will* act. One mark of the sacraments is that they convey mystery and point to mystery even beyond what they directly convey. Baptism and Eucharist have usually been associated with the paschal mystery (the death and resurrection of Jesus Christ), but the mystery of Christ includes all aspects of Jesus' remarkable life—his birth, baptism, teaching, healing, and transfiguration, as well as his death and resurrection. Jesus Christ, with all of the mystery surrounding his being, has been considered God's primary sacrament by Protestant, Roman Catholic, and Orthodox Christians, for Christ reveals and mediates God's grace to us. At the same time, the mysterious workings of God are everywhere and always around us. The mysterious Spirit of God was present from the beginning in the creating days and it is with us now, even in these days—hearing, seeing, and responding to the moans and laughter of our churches and our world.

With that in mind, consider the sacrament of teaching, which invites people to give reverence to the holy and mysterious God, whose works transcend our imagination and yet whose presence in the ordinary moments of life can be taken for granted. With such a large vocation in mind, sacramental teaching naturally begins with the practice of expecting the unexpected. We might, for example, expect that peace *will* come to the Middle East and hurting countries of Central Europe; that reunification *will* come to Korea and other divided countries; that indigenous peoples in every land *will* be allowed to flourish; and that wounded victims of child abuse *will* be healed. We can even expect that wounded teachers will be healers. These are not statements of optimism but statements of hope that God can perform miracles in the most difficult situations. Thus we expect that God suffers with human communities in their misery and God will finally keep the promise to repair the world (what Jews call *tikkun olam*).

The sacramental practice of expecting the unexpected shapes the way we live with one another. We are called to live with hope and also to nurture hope by giving ourselves to prayer and good works in the world. Expecting the unexpected also shapes the way we study and teach sacred texts. It calls forth a *hermeneutic of wonder*, or what Walter Brueggemann calls abiding astonishment. We approach texts with a spirit of anticipation that mysteries and visions will be unfolded, that the words will help us to see God's work, feel God's presence, and be transformed by God's power.

Expecting the unexpected also turns us to texts that evoke mystery. These may be narratives that reveal the astonishing and messy world in which God lives and moves. They may also be texts that are difficult to understand or texts that are troublesome for contemporary readers or texts that are frequently misunderstood or used for destructive purposes. The unexpected often comes from texts of poetry as well. One of the major functions of the Psalms, for example, is to touch mystery and open persons to a deeper relation with God and creation. Such an experience of mystery is expressed vividly in writings of contemplatives, such as Thomas Merton. The Psalms invite people to seek the spiritual depths of poetry, thus penetrating the actual words and literal sense. Merton recognizes that the Psalms, with all of their depth and hiddenness, have a primary role in Christian life (*Bread in the Wilderness*). Biblical scholars often sound a similar note, exemplified by Patrick Miller in *Interpreting the Psalms*. The Psalms simultaneously reveal God and the experience of the people who wrote them, revealing truths born of the God-human encounter.

The Psalms, like biblical narratives and other religious texts, evoke imagination; they inspire people to expect the unexpected. These are, therefore, important texts for sacramental teaching. At the same time, the approach to texts (through a hermeneutic of wonder) is also critical. In fact, our approach to the whole array of human experiences is critical to our being awake to the astonishing world in which we live. We are not only to be teachers of evocative texts but also interpreters of the astonishing world revealed in our sacred texts and ordinary lives. This is our challenge as religious educators—to be sacramental teachers and to inspire others in sacramental living.

Seek Reversals

A second act of sacramental teaching is to seek reversals. Our Jewish-Christian tradition is filled with reversals. Consider the "reversal thinking" in our biblical tradition. Think of the reversals when Moses saw a burning bush while tending sheep (Exodus 3:1–6). First, the bush was not consumed. Second, God was speaking out of the burning bush—the same God of Moses's ancestors—but God was not appearing this time in normal ways. Further, God was mourning the pain of the people and sending Moses to Pharoah to deliver the people (the same Moses who had fled the former Pharoah because he had murdered an Egyptian).

Now consider the New Testament tradition, which reveals Jesus—the teller of parables—as the one who proclaims reversals at every turning and whose very life is a reversal. As Luke tells the story, Jesus' birth is announced to Mary by an angel—a reversal—and Mary responds by sharing the news with her cousin Elizabeth in the Magnificat—a song of reversals:

> My soul magnifies the Lord, . . . for [God] has looked with favor on the lowliness of [God's] servant. . . . [God] has brought down the powerful from their thrones, and lifted up the lowly; [God] has filled the hungry with good things and sent the rich away empty. (Luke 1:47–48, 52–53, NRSV)

In Luke, as in the other gospels, we see Jesus' life as a parable—a life that subverted expectations, "brought down the powerful from their thrones and lifted up the lowly." Jesus' entire life represented reversals. To follow this man Jesus, and to live in the biblical tradition that we inherit, is to seek reversals and to participate in reversal living.

So how do we engage in sacramental teaching in such a tradition? I will draw a few clues from this hasty journey through the reversal tradition of Jews and Christians. These clues suggest that a *hermeneutic of suspicion* needs to be added to the hermeneutic of wonder. First, Christians can expect the tradition to offer as many questions as answers and to upset comfortable beliefs and values and social structures. Second, teaching can be an opportunity to follow Jesus in telling parables and to follow the Gospels in telling the parable of Jesus. Third, teaching can open questions without completing the answers, as Jesus did with his parables and Luke did with his Jesus stories. Fourth, teaching can invite a community to return to its traditions when people are confused or rudderless. And finally, teaching may also need to offer people support and encouragement when their traditions do not bring comfort; at such times, traditions may upset the status quo and give rise to something new (new insight, new action, new life). People need encouragement to face the challenges and demands of such a subversive gospel.

Nourish New Life

This leads to the third act of teaching as sacrament—nourishing new life. We earlier reflected on the church in first-century Rome, a church that, despite conflict and turmoil, was actively seeking new life. How does one nourish new life in such a church? Paul did it by urging the early Roman Christians to understand God in a larger, more gracious and challenging way, and to build community with one another. Consider another story from recent times.

I know a woman in a small town of Louisiana who gives leadership to a five-member Presbyterian church. This church cares for people who are ill in their town and maintains the beauty of their sacred place so that people can come to the church for prayer and for weddings and funerals. Together the five people clean and polish their sacred space, maintain the grounds, and keep the sanctuary alive with growing plants. The congregation rents their manse for income so they can bring ministers from all over Louisiana to preach and administer the sacraments. They always pay these ministers and give them a nice meal after the service; the ministers often return the money, however, because they enjoy being with the community.

The life of this congregation, when viewed from the outside, is minimal; but when viewed from the inside, they are a community that nourishes life in one another and in their larger community. They are a Christian presence in their small town, and they often join with other churches in the area to witness to their faith in a unified way. When you talk to the leader of this congregation, you will not hear her talk about the woes of her church, although she might laugh when the congregation dwindles to two on a Sunday morning and the music does not sound very melodious. You can always expect to hear this woman's excitement about what happened last Sunday or about what their little church will be doing with the Methodists next month.

Reflecting on this story as a metaphor of sacramental teaching, we can employ a *hermeneutic of nurture*, seeking seeds of life in the ordinary days of an ordinary community. To do this is to follow the pattern of Paul, who sought seeds of life in the early Roman Christian community. From the small-town Louisiana story I discover several insights. First, small communities can be powerful witnesses in their teaching; and they witness just by *being* a community. Second, sacramental teaching involves caring for the space and daily routine of church life—tending church land as sacred space and tending Sundays as Sabbath time. Third, one loving, committed leader can engage in sacramental teaching and, by so doing, inspire others to join her. Finally, sacramental teaching is an act of joy that mediates the joy of God's Spirit to others. To say that teaching is sacramental is to say that it nourishes new life, even when life is hardly visible—only a seed or a remnant.

Reconstruct Community and Repair the World

This leads to one final act of sacramental living—to reconstruct community and repair the world. Sacramental teaching has to do with more than expecting, seeking, and nourishing; it has also to do with mediating God's prophetic call in the church and world. Paul called the Roman community to be more than they were. Mary, in the Magnificat, recognized the hand of God at work in creating reversals in the world. Even the Psalms, known to evoke wonder, contribute to constructing and reconstructing the world. Walter Brueggemann explains that the Psalms can be used to make and unmake a world. They invoke what he calls a "counter-world," which is intergenerational, covenantal, morally serious, dialogical, and politically demanding; thus they stand over against a narrow and indifferent world (*Abiding Astonishment*, 21–28). This is the work of reconstructing community and repairing the world.

We in the Christian tradition have often thought of prophecy as the ministry of a few daring and charismatic leaders—Jeremiah, Amos, Martin Luther King Jr. But prophecy is an action of God to be received and enacted by all God's people; the role of the Jeremiahs, Amoses, and Kings is to mediate the call of God to the whole people—to call the people into prophetic action. As James Lawson once said to our Claremont community, Martin Luther King Jr. would have accomplished nothing had it not been for "the tramping of feet." In fact, the decisions to involve people in marching and campaigning for the vote were some of the most critical decisions that King made, and a secret to the civil rights movement. King could be called a sacramental teacher, for he mediated the prophetic call he heard from God. He was clearly concerned with reconstructing Christian community, for the quality of Christian action was important to him; he was also concerned with repairing the world, for the quality of human justice in the world was his passion. As far as he was concerned, the quality of

Christian community and the quality of justice in the world were completely intertwined.

If we take seriously the communal spirit of Judaism and early Christianity, we can begin to think of prophetic teaching as a work, not only of prophetic leaders but also of prophetic communities. What would happen if we looked toward prophetic communities for inspiration and guidance instead of simply looking toward individual prophetic leaders? We would encourage sacramental communities to discern God's call and to respond by reconstructing their community life and repairing the world. Sacramental teaching would have to do with some primary tasks: upbuilding the community; praying and listening as a community to the call of God and the cries of the world; analyzing the brokenness of the church and world; seeking guidance; engaging in action to protest the destruction of life; and reconstructing communities and social structures to protect and nourish life.

One vision of such communal prophecy comes from a story shared at a graduation ceremony of the University of Judaism in Los Angeles. A rabbinic student was graduating with a master of arts in Hebrew literature before proceeding to the next step in her education to become a rabbi. She told a story about her first day at the University of Judaism. All of the students gathered to meet one another and learn about the University of Judaism. A person was present who had just conducted a vast demographic study of Judaism in the United States, discovering, for example, that the rate of Jewish intermarriage with persons in other religions is more than 50 percent. He presented some of his findings on that day and concluded by saying, "I have good news and bad news." His good news was that, in two generations, Jews will still exist in the United States; the bad news was that they probably will not exist in recognizable forms. In short, Judaism will diverge from the traditions that present and past generations have known.

Lisa Bonnay went on to tell of the first-century Jewish people in the years before the Temple was destroyed. The Romans were closing in, and the Jews experienced much fear. The worship they cherished was going to the Temple to make sacrifices three times a day. Further, they lived in a Mediterranean world where most people thought that destroying a temple was the same as destroying a people's God.

Into that world came a rabbi who gained favor somehow with the rulers of Rome. They told him that they would grant him one request;

his request was for a safe place where he could gather Jews together to study and pray. The request was granted, and a few people gathered regularly to read Torah together. Meanwhile, most of the Jews stayed in Jerusalem to defend the Temple and, with it, their God and their faith. They fought for their Temple but, finally, they lost and the Temple was destroyed.

This rabbi, in the meantime, had been gathering people together to reconstruct Judaism—building a new form of Judaism in which faith was not centered in the Temple but in small groups of people gathering together to study Torah. Further, these groups did not worship God through sacrifices but through prayer three times a day—a practice that continues to this day.

Bonnay made the connection with modern Judaism, which finds itself in a very similar situation—on the verge of destruction in all recognizable forms. Modern Jews are posed with a choice of trying to preserve the tradition exactly as it is or to reconstruct the tradition and carry it on. She concluded, "We are the people faced with that choice."

This small group of first-century Jews, as Bonnay described them, engaged in a *hermeneutic of social construction*. They received and valued their traditions, and they reflected deeply on what was happening in their world. Recognizing that they faced a new era, they followed the guidance of God to begin gathering in new ways—to construct a new way of being a religious community. The new way was not altogether different from the old, and it was certainly not a new experiment purely for the sake of innovation; it was revolutionary, all the same. The people sought to understand, to discern where God was leading, and to respond, drawing upon the sources of their tradition and the guiding Spirit of God.

In a similar way, Martin Luther King Jr. and those who worked with him engaged in a hermeneutic of social construction. They studied the situation of the United States, particularly as regards racism, and they studied their Christian traditions. All the while, they sought to discern God's hand leading them into ever new ways of responding. In so doing, they discerned the responses that God was calling them to make, both for reconstructing their own communities and repairing the world. They thus constructed ways of nonviolent protest and resistance from their Christian traditions, drawing also from Mahatma Gandhi and others. Most radically, they sought guidance from God. Their nonviolent ways represented a radical shift from conventional forms of dealing with human conflict. They rejected the conventions of meeting violence with violence, and they introduced a new way of being in the world.

Readers of this book are also religious people—people whose hearts burn with love for God and a sense of calling to serve God in the world. But we are also faced with changes that threaten to destroy Christian faith, the church, the well-being of the human family, and the earth as we know it. How will we respond? How will we teach in the new millenium? Will we defend the Temple or will we seek to reconstruct our communities and repair the world? Will we meet violence with violence or will we find another way? How can our teaching empower prophetic communities in such a church and such a world?

Sacramental teaching is teaching in which the conflicts in the church and the turmoil of the world are not cause to defend what has always been and to escape into some other world but to gather together with others for study and prayer. Sacramental teaching takes place when we respond to the drama in our particular place and time in history, just as the civil rights leaders and marchers were called to respond. Our actions will usually have as much uncertainty as the story of moving with which I began this chapter. Rarely do we know the outcomes of our actions in advance; we are simply called to follow the leading of God.

Sacramental teaching thus requires courage—courage to seek new life, even in the midst of conflict and turmoil. The sacraments of Baptism and Eucharist, after all, are a promise of what is to come—a foretaste of God's new creation. Sacramental teaching represents a movement of hoping for God's future by seeking to reconstruct the community and repair the world.

CONCLUSION

I have named four acts of sacramental teaching—expect the unexpected, seek reversals, nourish new life, and reconstruct community and repair the world. All of these are acts that mediate the Holy. The unexpected is God in our midst; the reversals are God's parables; the new life is God's creation; and the reconstruction and repair are God's redemptive works, which empower us to be transformed and to participate in the transformation of a broken world.

When we come to see teaching as sacramental, we recognize the sacredness of our task and the transformative power of God. This power is real in any teaching event, and it will likely transform our teaching beyond what we now imagine. As we live the first years of a new millenium, we travel on an awesome and fearsome journey, filled with chaos and the promises of God. On such a journey, we are called to be sacramental teachers—to mediate God's mysteries, even when we do not fully comprehend them. We are called to gather courage and travel with God into the unknown!

2

Issues and Ironies of the New Millennium

ELCA

NORMA COOK EVERIST

As religious educators who lead faith communities in the new millennium, we need to read the contexts in which we serve. In this chapter I shall describe six societal issues that face religious educators, note intriguing ironies, and then give implications, including a brief image, for theory and practice.

Readers may identify more issues or altogether different issues. No matter. We cannot be fortune—tellers, but we can be leaders who genuinely listen to the culture, reflect theologically, and lead boldly into God's promised future. We are called daily to radical change—radical meaning going to the root of the issue and discerning a courageous stance and creative practice.

To forge a better religious education for the third millennium is to shape strong practice. "Forge" as a noun is the place—a workshop— with a furnace in which metals are heated and wrought. "Forge" also is a verb—the act of shaping by heating and beating by hammer. It can mean to advance slowly but surely or to advance quickly and abruptly. Another meaning of "forge" is to make or reproduce for deceptive or fraudulent purposes.

The image of metals being "wrought" belongs more to the nineteenth century than the twenty-first. And the hammer metaphor may seem violent when applied to religious education. But one could play with that metaphor, alluding to the fire of the Spirit, calling for a

51

radical reshaping of our task, hoping our work will not be a lukewarm endeavor. One even could say we need to "strike while the iron is hot," a phrase that originated in the "forge."

These various meanings of the verb form leave much room for diverse, even divergent, strategies. Do we forge ahead rapidly or advance slowly but surely? What if we make abrupt changes when we ought to conserve and exercise patience? Or what if we move too slowly when quick action is required?

Forging ahead shall be wrought with problems. How can we know our own motives lest we "make or reproduce for deceptive purposes"? When we shape new contours for religious education out of desperation or fear for our own institutional survival, we shape fraudulently. When we produce a program for our own self-aggrandizement—or refrain from bold action in self-deprecation—we produce a fake.

We cannot know or predict or control how religious educators will forge ahead in the new millennium. Predictions are inadequate if not erroneous. In 1949, 85 percent of Americans believed there would be a cure for cancer by the end of the century, and only 15 percent thought human beings would reach the moon by that time.

If it is impossible to say where we are going, it may be as difficult to describe where we have been. Suffice it to note two ironies. A century-ending air victory was not a rocket but a balloon race, nonstop around the world. And as we travel the information highway into a new age, a calligrapher from Great Britain is spending six years at St. John's University in Collegeville, Minnesota, copying the entire Bible by hand. Where is change?

As we peer into the twenty-first century we are tempted, if not to retreat, at least to retrieve the past. To write and speak and act prophetically may simply mean to look hard at the world from our present reality, to listen to the context, and to identify the issues, as best we can. (In this chapter I speak from my own context, the United States, not because it is primary or definitive but because each of us lives in a particular context; I invite readers to discern their own contexts and issues.) Here are six issues to ponder. They may seem to have little to do with religious education, but that is only if our definition of religious education is too small. We begin globally.

GLOBALIZATION

Issues and Ironies

The growing process of globalization—economic, cultural, missiological, though incomplete, is a reality from which there is no return. "Cross-cultural" religious education must be assumed and transcended. We are not so much learning from cultures foreign to us as being infused by a multiplicity of global cultural influences. Religious education utilizes music from Nigeria and Brazil and Japan as easily as from Sweden, Germany, and Italy. Religious education classes in the mid-twentieth century learned about the world through stories of missionaries; children today directly access classes around the world on the Internet. Young people understand and accept globalization.

Adults in the local congregation also connect with the world—and not just through their heritage. The insurance representative checks global markets daily. The college teacher attends annual conferences in Dar Es-Salaam, Montreal, or Bangalore. Although parishioners travel broadly for business or leisure, they may separate these activities from their faith life. The church is a global reality. Religious educators will need to invite people to bring their entire world, with all the inherent economic and political problems, into the religious education arena.

In this global community we are inextricably dependent upon each other economically, but old debts keep underdeveloped nations from carrying out their own educational and health goals. The gap between North and South is widening. Citizens of overdeveloped nations live off the labors of the poor. While people have more direct access to one another globally, fear of the foreign has not subsided. Many of the globalization issues have religious overtones, even religious foundations.

Ironically, people in the United States (the world's superpower with instantaneous access to "remote" villages around the world) may be the most isolated and therefore the most ignorant. Our daily news carries almost exclusively stories only about the United States or its "self—interest"—a telling fact theologically. Meanwhile, for their survival, people who live in those stereotypically remote villages must (and do) know about global economics and particularly about the one nation whose power affects most aspects of their daily lives. In short, people around the world know much more about the United States than people living in the United States know about the rest of the world.

Implications

Religious education needs to be global. The Christian church is a Pentecost church and therefore a global community. On Pentecost, people of faith began speaking in other languages as the Spirit enabled them. Almost immediately these teachers of the faith were in trouble, and in order to keep the gospel from spreading, they were warned not to speak, not to teach. A few weeks earlier, after the Resurrection, religious leaders tried to bribe the soldiers to say the resurrection was a hoax. In fact, the guards took the bribe, but the disciples responded to Christ's command to go and teach—everywhere. Religious educators entering the third millennium also must refuse to keep silent. Now we are called also to listen and learn from those around the world who, having heard, have much to teach.

- Use the gifts of young people to teach and lead the church in global access.
- Set learning environments that invite parishioners to connect their global realities with their growth in faith and empowerment for faith action in daily life.
- Forge an outreach ecclesiology for religious education, shaped by the Great Commission.
- Develop global religious education learning partners, becoming missionaries to one another across the continents, congregation by congregation, church to church.
- Dig deeper into the Scriptures and continue Jubilee economic justice efforts, engaged by many faith communities at the millennium mark, as an integral part of religious education.

Image

I sat at a back table at a regional church meeting next to two other clergy delegates, a husband and wife and their four-month-old son. On the table was a small Bread for the World box. Each of the four sides displayed a picture of a child from a different country. The business meeting necessitated keeping the baby as quiet as possible, yet occupied. After all, the child was merely present because he had to be, surely not because he could actually participate in the assembly.

The box was beyond the child's grasp physically. Its full meaning was beyond this infant's grasp intellectually. It contained two ounces of rice, symbolizing all the food millions of people have to eat each day. The child noticed one of the pictures and connected with the face of the other child. As he stared at that image, his own face lit up. His mother, noticing her son's eye contact, slowly turned the box, about every thirty seconds, giving opportunity to see yet another and another child from around the world. This went on for ten or fifteen minutes, the baby displaying an attention span well beyond developmental expectations.

When is a child old enough to learn about world hunger? When does a child become aware of similarities and differences? When does a child begin to learn he is part of the global community and part of a global church? When do children begin not only to attend church meetings but to *be* church? This religious education experience was an auspicious beginning, in silence, in the back of the room.

DIVERSITY

Issues and Ironies

We entered a new millennium living closer to one another than ever before. The world is crowded and it is urbanized. At the dawn of the twentieth century, when one grew angry with one's neighbors, one could still push out to a new frontier—but no more. People still grow angry with their neighbors; today thousands are made homeless, the refugees of wars, political upheaval, famine and an inability to share resources. Perhaps the century turned politically about ten or twelve years before 2000, when the cold war and apartheid officially ended. Power shifted and has not sifted out neatly. The world is caught in a myriad of tribal wars and ethnic cleansing. Reconciliation is incomplete. We have not learned to deal with our differences.

We live closer to each other religiously as well. We no longer can teach about "other religions" at a distance. World religions is a local subject. My neighbor of a different color or religion lives next door or in my own home. Religious education encompasses learning about the diversity within my own belief system, and perhaps within my own heart. How do we teach commitment to a specific faith so that we can live among people of many faiths?

Images of our inability to live together abound. Churches are frequently the places of most excruciating conflict. Ecclesial structures are changing but often not rapidly enough. Patriarchy and other oppressive systems of power die slowly. We are only beginning to move beyond fear to shape an entirely new way of being partners as men and women in church and society. We acknowledge racism, but eleven o'clock on Sunday morning is still the most segregated hour of the week; the preceding religious education hour is no less so. We know we are to learn from the oppressed, but classist attitudes still support inappropriate hierarchy. Every community in America—urban, suburban, rural—must face the issues of racism, sexism and classism. Religious education which teaches reconciliation must embrace in structure and method reconciliation of human community

Implications

One of the first questions the early church faced was how to deal with difference. The very entrance rite into the Jewish religious community was shattered. Gentiles were to be welcomed into full membership in the church. The content and rituals of religious instruction were new, and inclusive. These teachers of the faith could not consider anything unclean that God had declared clean.

Religious education in the third millennium will include doctrines and ethics and rituals, but these must not become stumbling blocks to the faith. In a time of changing structures we are tempted to cling to the familiar, but the best way to preserve the teachings of the past is to use them in constructive dialog with new partnerships for the future. This calls for not just comparative religion, nor even necessarily consensus, but trust to speak in different voices for the well-being of all humankind. In the process we will discover new ways for distinct faiths and cultures to interact.

• Religious education must cross race, class, and gender boundaries, and empower people to work for justice to remove barriers that oppress.
• Religious education curricula need to continue, and to strengthen, study of creedal foundations so that people, firmly grounded, with be able to deal with diversity within and among cultures.

- In order to step outside carefully structured ecclesiastical boxes, religious educators need to discover or create arenas in which people can meet on new and common ground.
- Religious educators need to help students not only tolerate but celebrate differences, teaching for competence, service, and community.
- Religious educators need to include study about religion in history and contemporary society, developing effective methods for interfaith and cross-cultural experiential learning.

Image

The newest addition to the bright, modern school building in Wha'Ti in the Northwest Territories is a set of nine green computers, all connected to the Internet. Above them, on the knotty pine wall, hang pairs of beaded moosehide gloves and a half dozen pairs of moccasins made from caribou. Beside them, handmade wooden snowshoes provide living symbols of the welcome of the season when this village becomes accessible to the outside world by winter roads across lake ice.

On this spring day, a team from On Eagle's Wings has flown in. This ecumenical ministry serves the church and individuals in remote and isolated areas of northern Canada, crossing barriers of roadless land and water, and bridging diverse cultures and time. On Eagle's Wings comes only when invited. They are there to support the local community, not to change it into their image of the church. Among other things, they bring resources to local religious educators and equip the saints by walking with them in a time of great transition.

In a land of extremes—nearly total night or endless daylight, depressing poverty and a high cost of living—the villagers know that for vocational purposes, some will need to leave and they will need the skills of the outside world. The Internet provides global connectedness but not at the expense of losing their identity. The people love who they are and will pass this on to their children.

VIOLENCE

Issues and Ironies

Just as the issue of globalization leads to the issue of diversity, so our inability to deal with difference leads to the issue of violence. Not only can we not afford to "teach war anymore," we need to creatively teach alternatives to violence. Religious educators recognize the basic human predicament of sin, the broken relationship with God that manifests itself in every human relationship. Even if we were to eradicate war and manage to feign pleasantries, human beings still would find ways to kill each other "nicely." The mere avoidance of profanity in polite conversation, "dressing up" for church, bespeaks a fraudulent religious education. Violence is an insidious evil, in whatever form.

As we entered the third millennium, surprisingly, one did not hear the church but public commentators asking, "Whatever happened to civility?" A leading criminologist advises not more sophisticated technological means to detect crime nor building more prisons, but society concentrating on avoiding savagery and cruelty. He says that the large issues are not as important as manners. "Are people polite? Do they recognize the rights of other people? Do they take turns? Those things matter." Perpetrators of violent acts frequently say, "I simply wanted respect."

We are barraged by combative language daily; win/lose alternatives substitute for thoughtful deliberation. News media report even conciliatory decisions saying, "The two came out swinging." Even the weather is reported: "Clayton county is still under the gun for storms until 11 P.M. tonight." Of "peacekeeping" endeavors, however, military strategists say, "We have to meet the objective, finish the job." The fact that the only place we do not use combat imagery is in war presents an intriguing, frightening irony.

The late 1990's epidemic of school shootings and bombings has led society and its leaders to look harder at the issue of gun control. But will communal commitment last once the news cameras leave? And will the solutions proposed—such as giving guns to teachers—address the underlying problems? One of the saddest testimonies concerning the erection of modern wailing walls at the site of the violence may be the woman who said, "People now know what to bring: pictures, candles, letters, teddy bears." A man said "I'm not a churchgoing person, but this is almost a sacred space."

When our sacred places and rituals are public memorials of violent acts, we build community only in response to tragedy. The challenge for religious educators is to become leaders and teachers for sustainable change. Faith communities must not tolerate an "acceptable" level of violence in someone else's neighborhood. Forty teenagers a week are murdered in this country, nearly 90 percent by guns. While fewer than a hundred people are killed by firearms each year in Great Britain, Canada, and Japan, over 38,000 people in the United States each year die from firearm-related homicides, suicides, and accidents. The risk of suicide is five times greater for people living in homes with guns.

Psychological, mental, spiritual, and sexual abuse abounds, sometimes hidden within faith communities; the results of such violation have lifelong consequences. One out of four youth in this society have considered suicide, and by age eighteen one in ten has either attempted or developed a plan for suicide, the rate being highest for those who have been violated. Abuse, disrespect, fear, and hatred weave devastating webs of violence.

Implications

The core of Christianity is love for the neighbor; resurrection is for life. But ironically, Christian history is full of acts of violence under the guise of "conquering for Christ." Religious educators need to help people recognize the depths of hatred, fear and violence in the human heart and to teach reverence for life in the Creator's image, reconciliation as the work of Christ, and peacemaking ways of building Spirit-led community. This will not be easy because even though people may complain about societal rudeness, many believe that pushiness is necessary in order to get anywhere in this competitive culture. Religious educators need to be not only leaders in rituals of grief but also teachers of peace in the third millennium.

- Religious educators need to help communities move beyond avoidance and judgment to discern the basic roots of violence and practices that perpetuate it.
- Religious educators need to shape curricular content and methods forged on and congruent with the biblical concept of reconciliation.
- Faith communities can sponsor and lead workshops on mutual respect, moral deliberation, and conflict resolution.
- Through ecumenical and interfaith endeavors, religious educators need to network with agencies in the community to discern youth assets and provide mentoring relationships.
- Religious communities need to look at their own histories of abusive, sometimes violent behavior and develop mission strategies of respect.

Image

A small group of people from the three churches in a town of 2,000 invited youth and community leaders from the public school, police department, chamber of commerce, and service agencies to a meeting to talk about assets and needs of youth. Conversation started slowly, but people listened to one another. The group gathered a second time and three young teenage girls wrote a story about the meeting for the weekly town newspaper. The coalition will continue to meet, together building a network of care and concern, affirming the gifts of their young people, and developing a safe haven for youth to meet with each other and with caring adults.

TIME

Issues and Ironies

If they were asked, "What is most difficult for you as you move into the new century?" many people in this society would answer, "Feeling stressed out due to time pressures." In an era of unprecedented time-saving devices, people feel overwhelmed and irritable in the midst of crowded schedules and hectic days. Religious educators often see volunteers simply stepping out of their Sunday school teaching responsibilities because they are too busy.

With cellular phones and microwave ovens, how did time become so scarce? We seldom realize that modern conveniences, such as garage-door openers, multiple bathrooms and stereo systems, themselves take time in terms of maintenance. And the immediacy of technological community disallows delays. The "pause" has evaporated; we need our fast food and fax machine replies now! We are not a patient people.

Never before in history have a people had to work fewer hours and exert less physical labor to put food on the table. But we collectively suffer from sleep deprivation, a serious problem on the job and on the road. In the new millennium, people may be more conscious of centuries past and unlimited time ahead. But even at this historic moment, we are not a history-conscious people. We do not have a sense that we are a part of time.

Parents and religious educators have settled for quality time, since quantity is unavailable. Will the days in the next millennium spin by even quicker? Troubled by such prospects, some people have recently turned from time-management seminars to spirituality retreats. But while the public is asking the deeper questions about the meaning of life, churches schedule more committee meetings, more classes, more elaborate ways to compete with entertainment for people's "free" time.

People desire a vast array of choices in regard to things like restaurants, CDs, and vacation opportunities, but there is little time to do it all. Freedom of choice has become a bondage of choice. So, ironically, people are going fewer places, spending more time at home, drawing in rather than joining up. People build larger master bedrooms, plan a home office, purchase houseplants. Kitchens are once again designed for the whole family to gather to cook together, but nobody has time to actually cook. Attendance in most organized activities—not just at church—is down.

Implications

Religious educators know that the hunger which fast food cannot fill is a deep spiritual hunger. Building home altars to worship one's collectibles will not long suffice. People long for a simpler life but are unable to extricate themselves from the complexities and demands of consumer society. The God of the Sabbath calls Christians to holy work and Sabbath rest. The new millennium spiritual challenge may be less, rather than more, individual acquisition and consumption. The early Christian community sold their property and distributed the money to all as had need. They gathered not to claim each other's time but as gifts to one another.

Developmental psychologists now say that although quality time is important, it is stressful at the culmination of full days. We don't have all the time in the world, but we do need time with no structure, no purpose, and no agenda just to be with one another. Religious educators will be tempted to compete because the church receives little enough of people's precious time—only one hour a week, every three or four weeks. But the most important responsibility may be to center people in Baptism, which makes all things new.

People who have no time to eat together are purchasing religious books and videos in record numbers to use at home. Although they are turning away from organized religion with its nightly committee meetings, they need mentors on how to be really present to each other and to God. Religious educators are needed to heal time-urgency obsessions to help people hallow time.

- Since religious education will never have enough class time, design approaches that help people connect each hour of the week with basic religious questions of fear and faith, values and commitments, obsessions and forgiveness.
- Specifically address the issues of time urgency, frenzy, and fatigue, and study together the meaning of Sabbath, teaching spiritual disciplines that promote growth in faith.
- Involve the faith community in creatively designing times and places, including the home, which provide a variety of learning opportunities, such as "time-out" devotional study minutes at work and retreats that really refresh. (This may include eliminating some time-consuming church activities.)
- Even though securing teachers is more difficult today, dare to plan together for which no one has time: teacher education. Dare to assume religious education needs to be central.
- Utilize each stage of the life cycle, helping people connect their lives with a timeless God, the historic church, and an intergenerational caring community.

Image

The Mason City High School concert choir, invited to sing at an official State Department luncheon hosted by the vice president of the United States for the prime minister of Japan, waited in the John Quincy Adams reception room. Security was heavy. The seventy-eight young people, who ordinarily would have been focused on each other, chattering away, were instructed to not talk. They quietly moved about the room and began to notice chairs in which presidents had sat through the years. There was the writing desk of Thomas Jefferson and the Rembrandt Peale portrait of George Washington. Later, after they had sung for the dignitaries (and could again talk) one said, "It was amazing to know this wasn't an exhibit, but real, especially when I noticed the half-empty glasses from which the vice president and prime minister had toasted just minutes before." Turned to look beyond themselves, they too had become participants in history.

PLACE

Issues and Ironies

Some would contend that a core problem today is that people are simply too self-centered. Others would argue that people are not self-centered enough. Each individual in this society lives as though he or she has a right to a huge share of the world's resources. Personal goals and problems dominate people's waking hours. And yet they suffer from identity confusion, loss of grounding, lack of a sense of their place in the universe—or even in the corporate world. Every time an astronomer makes another discovery we have to admit that we're not at the center of the universe but at the periphery, off to the edge of a very minor galaxy. What is our place? Do we make a difference? Can we change things?

The result is that people can suffer from being self-centered and "lost in space" at the same time. We suffer from "just me'ism" and feeling obscure among millions of people." In a world of limited resources, one might think, "I'm told I matter, but how can I? I know I should turn off the light and walk rather than drive, but I'm just one person and look at the waste around me, so it doesn't matter."

Churches struggle with the issue of identity as well. In a time of ever increasing marginalization, an individual congregation is tempted to turn inward for survival. Mission dollars are spent at home. The large institutional church is seen as remote, if not a threat to the church's survival at the local level. Likewise religious education may seem a small, insignificant part, not only of the larger society but even of the church. Parents say outright that there are more important activities for their time-stressed youngsters, such as learning to compete through sports or getting an after-school job so they can learn work skills. Church council members worry that the roof leaks: "Those repair dollars will have to come from somewhere and surely the Sunday school can get by on last year's budget."

The issue of place refers also to relationships. In a society that reveres independence, people hunger to belong. Young adults want to make it on their own but frequently return home when relationships or career opportunities do not work out. Citizens complain about politicians and the media; voting numbers are at an apathetic low. People yearn to know they have an important role to play in this life but immerse themselves as mere audience to talk shows about other people's lives.

Implications

In a society of Internet stock trading and Superbowl spectator sports, religious education would seem to have a very small place that is getting smaller. The challenge may not be to compete for time or space in a crowded world but to teach through helping people gain perspective. The small band of disciples at Jesus' Ascension were asked, "Why are you standing there looking up at the sky?" They were given a task, told to go and to gather. They would matter, every single one of them, sons and daughters, young and old, servants, women and men. And together they would change the world. They were sent forth to teach and preach, and to heal.

In a society stuffed with commodities yet hungering for meaning, the challenge for religious educators may be to touch people's lack of self-worth, which is clothed in self-centeredness. From this marginalized place, religious education may be in the best position to teach perspectives on power and significance without control. In a strange time and uncertain places, the gospel, which has always been out of place in the world, is needed.

- Religious educators need to let the entire universe into the classroom, to teach awareness of the Creator God's immense realm and the significance of each individual.
- Religious education needs to fully claim its place in the life of the church, and the church's importance in the community.
- People are finding virtual community via the Internet; but while technology can facilitate communication it cannot substitute for real human community.
- In a spectator world grown cynical, religious education needs to offer fully participatory learning and serving opportunities.
- Religious education, living as the body of Christ, needs to emphasize both the particular gifts of each individual and the importance of the faith community as a whole.

Image

How do people learn to be of service? How do they learn that they have gifts to help a community in impending disaster? When forces of nature sent rivers out of their banks, local residents felt powerless to save their homes. Two youth in wheel chairs joined other members of their community to try to protect their town from the rising waters. While crews filled sand bags, the two helped transport them to the dikes, one bag at a time, on the back of their wheelchairs. Each one's efforts seemed so small. But together they could do something. Would they succeed? There are no guarantees. But every one in the community learned to serve together that day. Everyone was disabled. And yet there were no specifically disabled people, only differently-abled, definitely-abled members of the community.

CHANGE

Issues and Ironies

Time is asymmetrical. We can know about the past but cannot influence it; we can influence the future but cannot actually know what is going to happen. Probabilities can be statistically computed; the number of things that may occur that are completely improbable is much greater. And since it is the improbable that will probably occur, all that is certain is that we will be deeply surprised. We will need to deal with change and with a more rapid rate of change than we have known in the amazing twentieth century; at least we probably will.

Although people say they enjoy surprises, few do in matters that threaten identity or unsettle security. One hundred years ago people could be quite certain the technology of their parents' generation would be similar to theirs. Some things changed, of course, but not so many that the entire society would be remade. Now that our entire world reconfigures itself every few years, there is little time to think through moral interpretation.

At the beginning of the twentieth century, there was a clash between theology and science. At the start of the next there is a new-found willingness to acknowledge that while science can say how the physical world works, theology is needed to answer, "Why?" This openness to the role of religion in dealing with change goes beyond religion, filling in the gaps in human knowledge to playing a significant role in the decisions necessitated by scientific and technological development. This raises new challenges for religious education. For example, medical research now indicates that people who pray recover better from surgery and illness. Doctors may be open to praying with patients, but is not the challenge of religious education to make clear that God is not the ultimate Band-Aid but the all-powerful one in whose hands all life resides? Some corporations now hire chaplains to meet with workers, but is that simply another part of one's personal benefit package? How does a religious educator challenge the concept that a little religion may be a nice add-on, and present in its place the radical nature of membership in the body of Christ?

There are at least two ironies here. The first is that while religious educators and institutions may have adjusted to being on the periphery of the worlds of science, business, and politics, some of these decision makers have been rediscovering the importance of the contributions of religious education. A second is that other institutions may depend on the centeredness religion provides to help people deal with change, even while religious institutions continue to be viewed as conservative or even reactionary by society. It would be easy to conclude that religious education—meaning values and morality—can be found outside the church.

Churches have problems with change. Institutional religion by definition seeks to preserve itself. Religion builds on tradition, which gives meaning to the essence of life. When things all around are changing, people fear the shaking of religious foundations. Any current generation of committed religious educators, intent on teaching new approaches, new ideas, and new stances on ethical issues, must contend with what faithful parishioners may have learned from equally committed religious educators a few years before. Religious education both builds on the past and introduces patterns of growth.

Implications

In an era of unprecedented change, and future change we cannot even imagine, to be teachers in faith traditions is not only a privilege but a societal necessity. Religious educators can with conviction teach of the surprise of God's creation, the open tomb and Pentecost. This both grounds and frees people for life in a world of change beyond their control.

To teach is to purposely plan change. Faith development requires growth for a lifetime. But how do we teach about change and how it affects individuals and communities? The proliferation of technological communication both connects and alienates. Who charts the course? Religious education may choose simply to follow, utilize, and react to technological medical, scientific, economic, and political change. Or religious educators can help ground people securely in the knowledge and love of God in order to proactively make moral and ethical decisions. This will require careful consideration of questions concerning criteria for religious education in each faith community.

- What is the central goal of religious education in this faith community?
- How does a particular technological medium build and sustain or compromise community?
- How is this curricula appropriately grounded in tradition, conserving the essence of the faith, and how is it relating to people in this time and in their context?
- How can Scripture study meet people at the point of their basic fears, both challenging and securing them with God's unconditional love?
- What changes can be made to reach people who are looking elsewhere for their spirituality and values education?

Image

Mary reached the age of ninety-six before dying at the very end of the second millennium. Born in 1903, she had seen change unknown to most people in history. Mary learned how to change with her changing world. Deeply anchored in her faith, she served in her church for decades; the community loved and listened to her. She daily e-mailed members of her five-generation family, never missing a date or a detail of their lives.

Mary continued to play with her senior chimes choir at church and other community events until three months before her death. Every night before bed, she and her daughter had family devotions. Mary's pastor, calling on her shortly before her death, spoke to what he anticipated was her fear of death. "I'm not afraid", she said. "I just don't know whether to expect I will die or live." Neither do we, but Mary knew her changeless God held her securely to the end.

CONCLUSION

How can we conclude what we have not yet begun? None of us knows the specific challenges ahead, nor even if these will be the pressing issues a decade or even a year from now. But we can know the basics of Christian community and the foundations of religious education that we shall use to forge—shape—practices that speak directly to human need: scriptural mandate to go into the world and teach, radical inclusivity of a gracious God, reconciliation that frees for service, a trustworthy God in an anxious yet apathetic age.

We will not know how quickly or patiently to make change. We will be tempted to offer a simplistic, reactionary, and therefore fraudulent product, rather than engage the people in a process of growth in faith. From the infant and the elder we will need to listen and learn and to respond with vigorous engagement, beyond our (or their) expectations. We will need to go places religious education has not dared to venture, into the daily lives of people who, while saying they no longer need religious education and the church, give every sign that they desperately need both. As religious educators, we will need to be people of vision, fully claiming the task with which we are entrusted for the future.

3

Surviving or Thriving in the
Third Millennium?

ROBERT W. PAZMIÑO

The future of religious education in the third millennium can be compared with what was the preoccupation with the year 2000 (Y2K) computer problem. What did the passing into the year 2000 mean for the continued viability of life in faith communities? How could religious believers more than survive the transition? What might enable a faith community to thrive in a computerized world with increased technological dependence and a persistent spiritual hunger not always satisfied by organized religion? Survivalists made extensive preparations for the drastic changes they anticipated occurring on January 1, 2000. How can persons of faith respond to the invitations of the third millennium in ways that are faithful to their religious traditions?

The parental advice I have shared with my son, who has taught wilderness cooking classes and is a chef teaching at a culinary school, is to write his first book, entitled *A Y2K Survival Cookbook*. This work would find a ready market. However, the task before me in this chapter is not to present an easily followed recipe for religious education that assures a digestible response to the changes anticipated in the third millennium. The preoccupation with the future in the current societal climate may fail to discern essential points of continuity with previous millennia. Religious believers are called upon in every time and place to discern both points of continuity and change that serve to guide a faithful response to what they understand to be God's calling

69

in the world. For Christians this calling is to make disciples and teach all that Jesus taught (Matthew 28:18–20). For Christians a faithful response also requires openness to the surprises with which God the Spirit will bless Christians in the third millennium.

Y2K: FOUR IMPLICIT ISSUES

From the perspective of eternity, January 1, 2000, was only another day in God's time or for Christians in the year of the Lord. According to some calendar calculations in the west, the third millennium began back in 1997. Non-Christian calendars, such as Jewish and Chinese dating, do not note a third millennium on the first day of 2000. Nevertheless, as Y2K survivalists reminded us, this day took on its momentous character because of the current reliance upon computer technology in the West and now around the globe. Thus, this reliance becomes an important issue in thinking about religious education in the third millennium. How should religious educators make use of changing technologies to share the content of their faith with the rising computer literate generations?

Changing Educational Technologies

Responses to the innovative presentation of biblical stories in the *Veggie Tales* video series, for example, have posed a challenge for some. Christians who question computer-assisted animation and the extensive use of music to communicate Christian truth as recorded in Scripture raise questions. They indicate that the reliance upon visual and affective approaches may fail to transmit essential Christian beliefs and to pose adequately the intellectual challenges of the faith. It can be further asked: Are *Veggie Tales* filled with sufficient spiritual nutrients to satisfy the needs of faith development? What more may be required to supplement the reliance upon the media for a balanced spiritual diet that fosters the formation of faithful and creative disciples of a religious tradition?

As an educator, I value the place of variety in educational technologies that include the use of computer-generated formats and creative approaches to "hook" a media literate generation. I also value the development of critical cognitive skills that are not directly fostered by such teaching. The development of cognitive skills calls for adequate questioning following a media presentation. The issues raised in response to *Veggie Tales* may not be unlike the responses of some Christians to the introduction of print technologies in the fifteenth century. The shift from an oral to a print culture disrupted previous patterns of religious instruction. When Martin Luther, of all people, set the Christian catechism to music, changes were brought to religious education. These changes were not unlike the nailing up of the ninety-five theses for public consideration. The appreciation of historical developments in religious education can provide perspective on issues that are emerging at the dawn of the third millennium. Persons of faith can be prepared and not paranoid in response to changes similar to those that previous generations have addressed.

Global Interdependence

A second issue posed by the Y2K computer problem is the reality of global interdependence. One news report noted that in mainland China efforts to address the Y2K problem were complicated by the fact that their computer systems made use of components from the United States, Germany, and Japan. This situation greatly complicated efforts to correct the difficulty that might not be easily resolved by December 31, 1999. The very reliance upon international cooperation and the use of resources from a variety of sources added complexity not only to computers but also to other dimensions of everyday life. In relation to the ministries of religious education, religious pluralism and multicultural realities complicate the easy formulas or recipes that were proposed by earlier generations. In addressing both the present and future, religious educators are called upon to exercise sensitivity to a wide range of contextual factors and diverse perspectives not readily embraced by one's immediate and wider audience.

As an educator, I have explored this second issue as a metaphor for teaching. I define teaching as artfully setting an inviting table that welcomes all persons present to participate; joyful celebration can result. This assumes that no one is intentionally placed under the table. Rather, everyone is welcomed as a contributing member at the table. For this to occur today and into the third millennium, religious educators must grapple with increased diversity that breaks out of previous forms and expectations. At the same time when the bonds of inclusion stretch with this diversity, persons express a hunger for a new sense of unity within both the wider human community and the particular faith community. Every religious community struggles with the need for

permeable boundaries that serve to foster a sense of purpose and identity. While fostering a clear sense of identity with what folks hold in
common, the diversity evident in the wider societal context always
confronts the community consensus. This consensus contends with
what to do with the strangers who present themselves at the table and
seek fellowship or at least dialog in sharing a common future. Religious educators need to be millennium ready and not millennium anxious in response to increasing diversity.

Patterns of Social Interaction

A third issue that emerges from the Y2K problem relates to the relationships among individuals at their computer screens and the wider
social computer network of interdependence that is now in danger of
collapse. The potential computer collapse also threatened the accustomed channels of social interchange and life. With the increased cultural preoccupation with individuals and a personalism divorced from
the wider community and society, the computer problem confronted
us anew with the interdependence of the human community. Coming
to terms with this reality and the possible need to renegotiate the terms
of interchange produces anxiety in some but calls for reflection by all.
Some persons and groups, like survivalists in the United States, are
made extensive preparations and hoarding resources in anticipation of
a massive breakdown of services. The call that is implied for me in
this response is a return to a rugged individualism and a survival mentality when the ordinary support structures of life are not reliable.
Such a response reflects the genuine need for preparation but may
suggest the need to return to historically earlier ways of social life un-
encumbered by technological advances and dependencies. Certain religious groups like the Amish communities have long modeled such a
life and had much to teach if the Y2K computer crisis actually materi-
alized, which it never did.

For religious educators, this third issue suggests the need to pose
perennial questions about the nature of personal, communal, and public life in the light of a potential societal breakdown and crisis. On
what can folks rely or trust when the norms for life shift? Is self-suffi-
ciency the answer? How does religious faith and hope operate in the
face of societal crisis? What is the loving response to a loss of basic
services in any setting, not just one that is computer dependent? How
do personal or familial needs interface with communal needs and how

are they negotiated in a societal crisis? What difference does or should one's faith make? How have and do persons of faith respond in the face of conflict when survival is at stake?

The history of Christian millennialism in its various formulations (premillennialism, postmillennialism, and amillennialism) may provide insights to guide present and future responses to the questions posed. This is not to ignore the faith perspective of panmillennialism that everything will pan out in the end. Panmillennialism suggests a reliance upon God and the wider community in the light of any problem or crisis, including Y2K, that has been ignored by many for the last forty years. A *Time* article (January 18, 1999) relates Y2K to "the original sin of technological society" and "the enduring American fascination with ingenuity and self-reliance." This fascination in the United States has been exported globally. Faith perspectives address the realities of and remedies for sin along with the importance of reliance upon God and others that emerge from various understandings of the creation. A crisis like Y2K provides the occasion, the "teachable moment," to reaffirm religious virtues and values when other sources of stability are threatened.

Knowledge versus Wisdom

A fourth issue that emerges for me in relation to Y2K is the extensive growth of information characteristic of a computer age itself. The proliferation of knowledge and its easy computer accessibility in some cases has overwhelmed persons while at the same time liberating others. The greater challenge for religious educators is to foster the discernment of wisdom amid the diverse sources of knowledge and the creation of spaces for critical and creative reflection in which persons can grapple with the meaning they derive for their lives. Religious traditions provide the wellsprings of the search for wisdom, and religious communities have throughout history provided the sacred time and space for inquiry into wisdom. The worthiness and fruits of this search for wisdom, in turn, pass on to others through education.

Beyond the Y2K concern, religious educators need to consider what will assure the long term care and growth of faith communities and continue effective witness and service in the wider community and society. This important larger question can be explored in relation to going "back to the future." In my work *Principles and Practices of Christian Education* I proposed two underlying forms for Christian education that emerge from my reading of the past. Revisiting these forms in relation to current challenges will serve to indicate points of continuity with the past and to consider changes on the horizon in the third millennium. These two forms are the *educational trinity*—content, persons, and context and the *five-task model*—proclamation, community formation, service, advocacy, and worship. These five tasks may have parallels with those in diverse religious traditions in which the faith passes on to rising generations. Looking back serves to provide perspective on the present and suggest contours for the road ahead into the future.

AN EDUCATIONAL TRINITY
FOR THE THIRD MILLENNIUM

Education can be defined as the process of sharing content with persons in the context of their community and society. Engaging in education in the third millennium requires giving careful attention to the *content, persons,* and *context* of religious education. Religious educators need to ask ourselves, Upon what are we relying in the third millennium? Upon whom are we trusting in addressing new challenges? What specific preparations are we making to pass on to future generations a living and vital faith that makes a difference in the world?

Content

One suggestion I propose for religious educators in answering these questions is to return to the sources of faith and to encourage others to do the same. Such a return raises awareness regarding the content of our religious teaching in critical and creative ways. Going back to the future in the third millennium calls for a return to the basics of a faith community. Our computer and technological competencies should not blur our vision about the human condition and the provisions of faith for life. God has created us; as God's creatures in any age, the most significant affirmation we can make in faith is that we are the children of God. Being a child of God involves a host of responsibilities and privileges that require religious believers to wrestle with their diverse callings in life. Because we are the children of God in both our private and public lives, persons of faith must live out their religious beliefs within a market place of diverse beliefs.

The realities of religious pluralism in the third millennium pose the challenge of how a child of God in a particular religious household relates to other households of belief and diverse expressions of secular faiths that jettison supernaturalism. This requires the affirmation of one's own traditions and a willingness to learn from others, balancing the particularity of faith expression and the universal realities of the shared human condition. For Christians, the teaching of the content of their religious faith is to sustain persons in the third millennium. Such a task calls for a return to God's revelation, an appreciation of God's holiness, and the human response to Gods' consuming and revolutionary love in Jesus Christ. Similarly, religious educators are called upon to affirm the living traditions of their faith and to learn from both the lights and shadows of our past efforts to educate within and beyond their tradition. Without gaining historical perspective, educators are limited. In addition, current and future efforts are truncated and fail to provide creative and critical alternatives.

Religious educators must address the biblical, theological and liturgical illiteracy that characterizes faith communities of diverse theological persuasion. The sharing of the core Christian beliefs and their narrative sources provides the occasion for the transformative work of God the Spirit in the lives of persons, churches, local communities, wider society, and the global community. Christians preoccupied with parochial or denominational concerns need a new awareness of world Christianity that will stretch conceptions regarding mission. In fact, the call of the Christian church will need to be transformed in relation to a focus on mission and missions beyond the parameters of institutional survival and the perpetuation of traditional patterns and forms.

Persons

A consideration of the persons of religious education for the third millennium will need to recognize the issues raised by various age cohorts. The emergence of Generation X and its embrace of postmodernity will require careful attention to matters of community and personal relationships. In a high-tech culture, the interest in "high touch" educational contacts or encounters (as John Naisbitt identified in *Megatrends* in 1982) has come to fruition. In addition, the fast pace of society has resulted in a hunger for Sabbath or retreat that various religious traditions have honored.

Among baby boomers, integrity issues loom large, particularly in an "age of disbelief" that has fragmented private and public life. Spiritual hunger leads them to see life as whole and holy with great interest in the recovery of spirituality. Among those identified as Generation Y, who follow Generation X as the next age cohort, the issues most apparent include the impacts of global consumerism and the restoration of a sense of hope for those not functioning on the competitive edge. For both the youngest and oldest generations, their issues cluster around survival with the increased precarious conditions of local communities and the diminished commitments to support a safety net of services to those least able to care for themselves. In response to these realities, religious educators are called upon to be more explicit in their advocacy for persons most at risk and marginalized.

Across the various age divisions and cohorts the issue of age segregation must be raised, with its attendant danger of increased fragmentation of the human community. The task before religious educators is to explore intergenerational interdependence through various local, regional, national, and global programs. The only time during the week when generations interface, besides walking past each other in shopping malls, may be when they gather in their religious communities.

The additional challenge in considering persons is for religious educators to develop, in conversation with other practical theologians, theological anthropologies that serve to guide religious communities. For Christians this calls for considering how the Holy Spirit interfaces with the human spirit and the community spirit, the societal spirit, and the global spirit to reclaim created and human life that is viable for all God's creatures. This is no small task in an age preoccupied with the bottom-line realities of the market and the use of power to gain personal advantage in all areas of human life. This task involves the willingness to confront modern day idolatries that have been embraced by faith communities as well as by individuals.

Context

The advent of the third millennium requires religious educators to study the global context and its shifting contours. Five particulars of this context are worthy of attention, first continuing urbanization. Globally there has been a steady movement, with some exceptions, to urban centers. This trend calls for renewed efforts to address human need in relation to economic, social, and political systems, structures and opportunities that enhance and not destroy human life.

A second factor of increased global concern is the ecological crisis that calls for concerted efforts to cooperate extensively to sustain human and created life on a scale not considered in past centuries. This will require the reevaluation of national security ideologies that fail to embrace universal human values and rights. This is related to the Christian sense of stewardship and the full appreciation of God's creation. God's call to humanity is to care for the earth along with persons who inhabit the earth. The earth itself is a heritage we pass on to successive generations and much can be learned from indigenous communities in this area of global concern. These communities consider the heritage that passes on to the seventh generation in relation to contemporary decisions and public policies.

A third feature of third millennium is the multicultural character of life. Every day, persons encounter and interface with persons of different family and community of origin. Religious educators must continue to address the realities of racism, sexism, and classism that ravage the human community and the intolerance based upon religious beliefs. God reserves the right to speak through and use persons with whom I disagree, and thank God for that reality! Religious educators need to be stretched beyond our narrow parochialism and reductionism, and encounter the fullness of what Christians name as the fullness of what God's Spirit is doing in the world. For Christians a sense of world Christianity will be essential for the Northern Hemisphere to appreciate the nature of God's work in Africa, Latin America, and Asia.

A fourth feature of the next millennium is character of an "age of disbelief" that Stephen Carter identified. Countering this trend calls for religious educators to connect spiritual realities to everyday life. The rise of interest in corporate chaplaincy and the connections between spirituality and business is one example of countering the great of divorce of faith from life that typified modernity. Recognition of the great hunger for spirituality is a first step as religious educators share the resources of their faith traditions. The need is to honor diverse forms of spiritual life, and for Christians, to honor the person and work of God the Spirit beyond human controls and formulations. Religious educators need to help persons see God as active in the world and open to encounter persons where they are and with their diverse needs.

The fifth feature of the context for the consideration of religious educators is what I have initially identified in relation to the Y2K problem, namely, the media dependency of global culture. Religious educators need to gain historical perspective regarding diverse educational methodologies. The reactions to *Veggie Tales* cited above point up the importance of studying the interface of religious education with media developments. The danger of "morphological fundamentalism" exists in every age as the forms of faith themselves take on a quality that resists change. Change and transformation is required of every faith community in sharing religious traditions with persons in a rapidly changing context. That change should not diminish the complementary need for the continuity of faith and the celebration of essentials not subject to the passage of time and custom. Other features may be named, but these five serve to outline some of the contours of the third millennium calling for the attention and faithful response of religious educators. Religious educators should also consider the specific tasks related to their ministries.

A FIVE-TASK MODEL FOR EDUCATORS

The five tasks I identify to guide religious educators apply to the tasks of religious educators from diverse traditions who seek to effectively teach in the third millennium. The five tasks, as noted above, are proclamation, community formation, service, advocacy, and worship.

Proclamation

Proclamation involves the sharing of faith stories or accounts and their connection to both personal and communal stories. Religious educators must address various forms of illiteracy within their communities, which for Christians include biblical, theological, liturgical, moral, behavioral, and emotional illiteracies. The ownership of faith stories or perspectives requires that attention be given to the intricacies of personal, familial, and communal realities. Forging the links of faith to life and beyond life to death, religious educators wrestle with perennial human questions of identity and meaning in life. Religious educators pose essential questions that others may exclude or ignore. The formation of a religious identity in the future will require a connection to the past and the present. The great teacher of the Christian tradition Augustine in his *Confessions* suggested that educators attend to three areas: the present of things past, the present of things present, and the present of things future. In sharing a sense of lived time, educators from Augustine's perspective explore memory, intuition, and expectation respectively. Memory links persons to their past and shares a variety of sources that inform life and common connections with the human race. Intuition links persons to their present and can foster a sense of relationship to others as a basis for identity. Expectation links persons to the invitation of a new day with all of its possibilities. Proclamation in religious education sustains the web of life that links the past, present, and future of religious persons. Related to this proclamation are the virtues of truth and integrity that religious educators seek to incarnate and foster in the lives of others.

Community Formation

In the human family a deep hunger exists for peace—shalom or reconciliation. Postmodernity's impacts upon the rising generations also suggest a hunger for community and relationships. These realities suggest for the third millennium the need for an intentional effort by religious educators to foster community formation. Explicit consideration needs to focus on the nature of human commitments and basic expectations. How can persons have a sense of communion with God and others? How can expressions of care for God, self, others, and the world be encouraged? Small groups provide a sense of connection but cannot succumb to the dangers of parochialism and sectarianism. These dangers fail to embrace the call for welcoming strangers and the mission outside the relationships of care and support in a faith community. Can the small groups of the future be inclusive of various generations and life experiences, both single and married folk, for example? Related to the question of inclusion is the question of boundaries and boundary crossings in religious education programs. For Christians, openness to the realities of world Christianity is a concern. Western Europe and North America can no longer dominate Christianity. Distinct perspectives from Africa, Asia and Latin America need to be heeded in the formation of a global community. The redefinition of the wider community and who serves as its gatekeepers are matters for future consideration. The task of community formation has local and global implications for all religious communities, and the virtues of love and care take on concrete expression in planning for the third millennium.

Service

Service provides an entry point to express faith commitments in action and to be a viable witness in the world. Religious educators in the third millennium will need to prepare persons and the entire faith community for diverse expressions of service, mission, and outreach in the world. The gap between the "haves" and the "have-nots" on the global scale, with increased numbers of refugees and those deprived of basic human services, call for creative and compassionate responses. The extent of need and its scale require international cooperation across religious and national boundaries. The educational task is not to overwhelm persons with a sense of hopelessness or futility in raising awareness but to analyze the causes, develop strategies, and act in concrete ways to make a difference. With diminishing and competing resources, careful study and learning the lessons from past efforts are crucial. In addition, service must be sustained over time and value the mutual ministry that must be explored if the integrity of the effort is to be maintained. Too many efforts have resorted to quick fixes; the persons served have not been empowered to work as partners for the common future. Religious education for such service is a costly effort that calls for the careful counting of the costs.

Advocacy

For religious educators the task of advocacy requires raising the consciousness of persons to the realities of those marginalized and oppressed. This experience is particularly, though not exclusively, visited upon the poor of the world. Another group particularly impacted is the children of many nations. Other groups include women and various racial, ethnic, and cultural minorities. The ministry of advocacy involves giving voice to those who remain voiceless and denouncing the societal arrangements that sustain oppression. Historical patterns will not suddenly revert to just and peaceful arrangements with the coming of the third millennium. Advocacy will require in the future the expression of outrage regarding the continuing conditions that destroy the worth, dignity, and life chances of all persons. Vigilance is also required in all areas of social life to confront the entrenchment of new forms of oppression that will emerge in the future. No easy formulas

can be proposed or passed along to religious educators, but accounts
in which persons have made a difference can foster courage and a
sense of hope. In addition, the demands for justice, peace, and equity
can be shared as perennial ideals that call for reappropriation by each
rising generation. Those who struggle for survival and others who
support them will need to wrestle with the interlocking web of
structures that can support economic, political, social, cultural, and religious justice. The realization of justice may invite the voluntary re-
distribution of resources before other means of correcting the wrongs
are explored. Religious educators can explore and strategize with persons the various alternatives and reflect upon direct efforts of social
ministry and outreach.

Celebration

The task of celebration reserves the place of wonder, awe, reverence,
joy, play, and worship in religious education. Beyond a task, celebration is a place of renewal, refreshment, and recreation on the educational landscape. The ideal is for this task to undergird the four other
tasks of proclamation, community formation, service and advocacy.
This dimension can serve to distinguish religious education from other
forms of educational practice (this should be distinguished from arro-
gance). God can be present in the educational practice of those not explicitly conscious of a religious agenda. This assumes a faith perspective with God as the source of all of life and all good gifts experienced
by humanity, which includes education. The ultimate teacher from a
religious perspective is God, who invites humanity to a banquet. The
response of persons to the invitation and the conscious awareness of
the host vary with the persons who gather at the table. Nevertheless,
the explicit task of religious educators is to make explicit the source of
the invitation and the delight of the host with those who partake of the
meal carefully prepared.

The task of celebration requires religious education in the third millennium to honor creativity and imagination in the teaching and learning process. Reflection is required to discern the illumination over
against the illusion that imagination may bring, but religious educators
can reintroduce the adventure and joy. This adventure and joy comes
in the pilgrimage of mind, heart, and body as persons renew their partnership with God. For Christians this journey of faith includes expecting surprises that God the Spirit will bring into reality as new visions

and dreams take form, recognizing the place of incarnation, embodiment, and sacrament in the Christian tradition. It also celebrates the emergence of new forms and sacraments that will be called forth in the third millennium. One form that I conceive on the horizon emerges from either a sports or dance event in which participants both huddle together and mix in varying combinations.

HUDDLE AND MIX

The question of religious educational ministries thriving and not just surviving in the third millennium may require reviving commitments in a number of settings. The level of commitment to religious education among Christians, varies despite the conclusions of a study like *Effective Christian Education*, which the Search Institute conducted on the national level. This study pointed up the crucial role that educational ministries have in fostering the faith development of persons across the life span. Neglecting such findings and their implications for local Christian parishes and churches reduces the discussion of the future to the question of survival. Perpetuating the faith in the rising generations is the task of each mature generation of believers and calls attention to the need for regular intergenerational contact and interaction. Such contact and interaction fosters the passing on of a living faith and can occasion spiritual formation and mentoring. It includes nonformal and informal educational encounters among persons of varying ages and levels of faith maturity in addition to formal education. A gathered faith community may remain one of the last vehicles for intergenerational contact in a society increasingly fragmented by age segregation.

The educational shorthand I propose to honor both intergenerational mutual ministry and the grouping of persons with common interests or characteristics is "huddle and mix." Educational programs in the third millennium will need to balance the mixing of persons intergenerationally and culturally with the huddling of persons with more focused needs. The huddling that has been effective in small group ministries, traditional classes, and in various parachurch or paraparochial programs can complement the larger or more diverse gatherings that stretch folks beyond the comfort of their immediate affinities. Huddling in smaller groupings can also stretch folks who have avoided the challenges of intimacy and vulnerability. This huddling in turn must avoid the insular and exclusive outlooks that fail to embrace the call for mission, service, and advocacy in the wider community and world. Because easy formulas cannot be proposed to sustain a balance between huddling and mixing, each educational ministry setting must wrestle with the parameters and emphases of its particular calling.

The huddling and mixing metaphor can also apply to addressing the challenge of religious pluralism in the third millennium. Huddling within faith communities serves to establish and sustain a religious identity. However, a mixing with persons from diverse religious backgrounds complements this huddling. This assumes that a genuine openness to the others and even to strangers operates on the boundaries or borders of the faith community. The complexity of life in many communities necessitates weekly or even more frequent huddling to nurture faith and foster interpersonal edification. However, mixing is a characteristic of life in the third millennium and calls for faithful persons to formulate a public theology or vision to complement the private and parochial concerns that are the focus of huddling efforts. Huddling also honors the particular identities and missions of persons, whereas mixing holds the potential of affirming universal human values and what can be gained from interacting with others different from one's religious affiliation and identity.

BEYOND SURVIVING OR THRIVING: OPENNESS TO GOD'S REVIVING

Beyond surviving or thriving in the third millennium, persons of faith are called upon to discern the contours of God's work and time in the world. Beyond prognosticating the future, religious persons honor the place of no-knowledge, mystery, wonder, and awe in human life. For Christians this requires recognition of God's gracious working through the person of the Holy Spirit. God the Spirit is active in the world to bring renewal, reformation, revival, and new life in confronting current and future challenges. Reviving religious education for the future requires a reappropriation of a living tradition that provides continuity and encourages change.

From the storehouse of Christian tradition, three anchors on the ark of the church as it launches into the future are the faith, hope, and love of which the Apostle Paul spoke. Faith in God and God's resources assures religious persons of strength and wisdom beyond our human limitations in response to educational challenges. Hope in new possibilities calls believers to honor the visions and dreams of our youth and children as God prepares them for leadership. Love, centered in the love of God for all time, enables persons of faith to love others who are different and yet share a common future.

In November 1996 I had an opportunity to participate in a denominational educational conference in New England that was called Envisioning the Future of Christian Education at the Turn of the Century. The three-day consultation brought together persons from all levels of educational ministry in New England and national leadership to explore a common future. A jointly crafted one-page document outlined the directions emerging from the consultation that serve to envision possibilities not only for this denominational body but also for religious educators more broadly. The document identified seven mandates for the future that can foster the revival of religious education: be relational versus institutional; be relevant; have strong leadership; have at its center story; be done in partnership; be innovative; and have clarity of mission and vision. Each of these seven mandates is suggestive for educational programming in the third millennium, with noted provisos and my interpretation.

Be Relational versus Institutional

This mandate proposes the need to empower persons through caring and supportive relationships. Given the fragmentation experienced by many in the wider societal context and the sense of distrust of institutions among some age cohorts, religious educators need to attend to the task of community formation identified above. Because of time pressures and the dissociation that reliance upon technology can bring, persons hunger for human face-to-face contacts. Religious education programs can offer such contacts. A danger exists in maintaining an anti-institutional bias with the institutionalized character of corporate life. Nevertheless, the challenge within institutions is to foster a sense of the value and worth of individual persons and of allowing time for social interaction as a complement to a task orientation. The emphasis on persons and on being relational cannot ignore the place of both content and context in an educational trinity. Such a mandate suggests a possible entry point for an educational program in terms of recognizing the persons of participants and fostering a sense of community. The danger in an exclusively "people-centered" approach is the experience of pooled ignorance when educators only serve as facilitators and fail to share the wisdom of their religious traditions.

Be Relevant
Though this mandate is often viewed as a trite expectation for religious education, it denotes the need to contextualize efforts. The emphasis upon connection in this chapter is crucial for religious education. Religious educators need to connect their faith perspectives to the lives and realities of participants and encourage the relevance of the educational content to contemporary concerns. The rapidly changing contours of personal and corporate life call for religious educators to read the culture and to listen to the stories of persons. Life situations for age cohorts vary and what is effective with one audience or setting may not be with different persons in another context. In order to be relevant, religious educators need to be flexible as well as carefully prepared for their teaching. Relevance also implies sensitivity to cultural and multicultural variables. The search for unity in the religious and human communities through education cannot ignore diversity.

Have Strong Leadership
Many religious education programs ignore the important human resources that require care and support. Those who teach need to be personally recruited, equipped, and recognized for their service. This applies to both voluntary and paid staff persons. The level of commitment and faithful service diminishes if the supportive network is unattended in most religious communities. The terms of service and the expectations for leaders ought to be clear and in writing whenever possible. Regular times for evaluation of educational leadership can strengthen the actual practice of education and encourage others to consider service. The functioning of leadership also improves with regular times for Sabbath or re-creation. The high stress in some settings involves leaders in dealing with many hurting persons and regular conflict. The partnership that is noted in a separate mandate can serve to support leaders from the dysfunctional stance of the "lone ranger." One gap identified by colleagues who work with congregations in conflict is the limited

interpersonal skills of some persons who are serving in religious leader-ship. The development of these skills is a priority for the future.

Have Story at its Center

The increased fragmentation of community and family in the experi-ence of persons indicates the need for a narrative approach in a number of settings. Patterns of social interaction reduce the opportu-nity for persons to be known, but sharing personal stories provides an occasion for disclosure and establishing relationships. The impact of film media has provided an alternative to sharing of personal stories in face-to-face encounters, which religious education can foster. The ad-ditional challenge is to help persons discover the connections between their personal stories and the communal and faith stories. Religious education happens where personal, communal, and faith stories inter-face. The proposed emphasis upon story cannot neglect other forms of literature and religious discourse. The exclusive emphasis upon story in the wider culture may require a counter-cultural stance in some set-tings with the need for rigorous analytical and reflective dialogue.

Be Done in Partnership

The wide diversity of persons and perspectives that characterizes so-cial life will require the intentional effort to develop and sustain part-nerships. Learning from those with whom I disagree on religious questions provides the opportunity to explore common concerns and commitments. The development of partnerships will require the hard work of establishing trust where suspicion may have dominated past interactions. Adequate time must be committed to such an effort, as well as a willingness to deal with the shadows as well as the lights of past experiences. The work of reconciliation across human differences requires risk and provides no easy fixes. In coming to a common table for the shared future, persons must come as equal partners with no one positioned under the table. Coming together requires the sharing of differences and the concerted effort to find a common ground. The naming of partnership relates to the earlier mandate of leadership be-cause it serves as one model to promote in the third millennium.

Be Innovative

The openness to change and innovation requires the willingness of re-ligious educators to venture out beyond customary patterns. The risks and costs of innovation are real but are worth the taking. Religious educators must honor the variety of creative gifts that are present in any religious community. However, in advocating change and experimentation, religious educators must communicate with others the rationale for any proposals and address openly any questions or concerns that will be raised. Change for the sake of change alone will not be well received in religious communities that many view as a safe haven in the sea of societal changes. The challenge for religious educators is to balance change with the affirmation of continuity so that growth occurs across the entire community. In some religious settings, any change will be viewed as a threat. Change and its embrace by a religious community can be viewed as an educational process. As such, it requires dealing with affective, cognitive, and behavioral responses.

Have Clarity of Mission and Vision

Religious persons need to gain clarity regarding the "what" and "why" of their ministries. The what and why questions are first-order questions to raise in any educational venture for the present and future. Havoc emerges when persons lack clarity regarding their mission and vision. Religious educators can pose the first-order questions and facilitate the process of religious communities in their dialogue about future commitments, strategies and directions. The landscape of the third millennium, as in previous millennia, will require the emergence of new vision and mission. Celebrating the new and honoring the continuing heritage of the old are the tools of the religious educator's trade.

The seven mandates for the future of religious education interpreted through my experiences are suggestions. Each religious educator must filter them through the demands and requirements of her or his particular tradition. All religious traditions affirm a God who is alive and eager to bring a reviving presence into all of life, which certainly includes religious education. This is the invitation of the third millennium for religious educators and all persons of faith.

CONCLUSION

In this chapter I have explored religious education in the third millennium with the possibilities of surviving or thriving. The Y2K computer problem posed four issues for religious educators to address. In response to these issues, I propose two forms of continuing viability for religious education: an educational trinity that considers the content, persons, and context of education, and a five-task model of proclamation, community formation, service, advocacy, and worship. These forms can provide a rootedness and continuity for religious education. Two additional considerations for the future include the educational formula of "huddle and mix" and the seven mandates that can foster an openness to God's reviving religious education in the years to come.

4

"Why Don't They Remember?"

Reflections on the Future of
Congregational Education

CHARLES R. FOSTER

Why don't people remember much of what they have been taught? That question has haunted me for nearly thirty years. Certainly we remember something associated with a dramatic moment, event, or relationship. We usually do not forget something repeated so often it becomes embedded in our subconscious. And we typically remember something that illumines or makes sense of a question or a problem that dominates our attention or captures our imagination.

As teachers, we take delight in student remembering, but student forgetting bothers us—the missed answers on a test, the difficulty in recalling a discussion from a prior class session, the inability to use information we have provided to analyze a text or issue or to solve a problem, the blank look when we ask a question. We seek an explanation. We know some students forget because they are not interested in the subject. We know some students have the facility to remember some things—for example, the parts of a motor—yet struggle to recall other things—for example, dates and names. We also realize that some students do not remember because they do not practice what they have been taught. This is as true in the study of Scripture as in music or sports.

Few writers in education struggle directly with the question of student forgetting. The concern is present in guidebooks to improve teaching effectiveness, in manuals to increase student accountability (a nice euphemism for student remembering), and in handbooks to enhance the administrative efficiency of an educational program or institution. In other words, the problem of not remembering can be remedied according to these writers—whenever teachers do their work more effectively or educational administrators can improve the efficiency of the learning enterprise. Undoubtedly these conclusions are wise. But they are not adequate. More attention must be given to the contexts that support teaching and reinforce learning. Perhaps a story from my own teaching in a congregation may focus the issue.

NOT-REMEMBERING

While in seminary back in the 1960s, I taught a group of ninth graders in a large congregation in an affluent suburb near New York City. I knew them from our contacts the previous year to be bright, multi-talented leaders in school. Most came from families with a strong commitment to education. We met for our first session on a Sunday in September. The curriculum unit guiding our teaching and learning for the next six months would lead them in an exploration of the life and teaching of Paul. I began the session with a series of exercises to discover what this group of young people had remembered about Paul from prior Sunday school classes, sermons, family discussions, and their own reading of scripture. Although they had a vague recollection that he was a New Testament figure, they could not answer a single question. Repetition of that experience on different topics through the years with other groups of children, youth, and adults has only intensified my curiosity about why our students in faith communities do not remember much of what we teach them.

A closer examination of the education in the congregation where I was teaching this group of ninth graders may provide several contextual clues to their not remembering. Highly trained teachers, sophisticated curriculum resources, strong financial support, and a model organizational structure for the religious education of that congregation were not adequate to the task. Something was missing. In retrospect, I am convinced, much was missing—indeed, little of what I have begun to call the basic infrastructure of a community or congregation which sustains and intensifies learning over time, could be found in that congregation.

Lack of Interinstitutional Support

This congregation's education no longer existed in the interdependence of the ecology of educational agencies that supported the teaching and learning of congregations several decades earlier. Although most families strongly supported the congregation's efforts in teaching their children and many parents took their turn teaching in the Sunday school, few families assumed direct responsibility for formal religious instruction in the home. Few parents engaged in any formal religious education for themselves. Although prayer at certain public school events and religious music for holiday concerts were still common, values of competition, privilege, and individualism dominated the agenda for students in the local schools, undermining congregational efforts to inculcate values of compassion, collaboration, and reconciliation. Little of the education in their families or in the schools, in other words, indicated to these young people that remembering something about Paul and his teachings would be important.

Lack of Intergenerational Support

Most families in this congregation had moved to this community. They had left their hometowns and extended families in the Midwest, South, and Northeast to work in the corporate world of the metropolitan area. The lack of intergenerational connections in the family were intensified by the lack of ties in the church with people of other ages. These ninth graders knew few adults other than their parents who might undergird and reinforce the congregation's teachings. They rarely found themselves in relationships or settings in which they might encounter, in more informal ways, a discussion of what they were being taught. The age-segmented isolation of the congregation's teaching was compounded by the structure of the curriculum resources used in the Sunday school. They were designed to repeat themes in age-appropriate ways through the life cycle. So those young people, who had been in the congregation during most of their school years, had previously encountered curriculum units on Paul in the third and sixth grades. This meant that the congregation's teaching for children divided their learning into discrete, sequential, and separated units—in much the same fashion as the digital watch fragments the flow of time. Little, in other words, reinforced the efforts of teachers or sustained the learning of students across time.

Inattention to Student Diversity

Although training programs for teachers in that congregation sensitized us to the developmental tasks of children and youth in the congregation and thereby to the variation in student readiness for certain learning tasks, at the time, we were simply unaware of the influence of gender, class, and culture on how people learn. We simply assumed that all students could learn in the same way—and that the task of the teacher was to find the methods that would most effectively facilitate the learning of all students. Since our approach to teaching had been informed by the writings of John Dewey, we did not assume that students would learn what we wanted them to know through transmissive methods. But we lacked the knowledge of the complexity in human learning patterns to recognize that the challenge of helping students remember what we taught was more difficult than we knew.

Information Overload

If the range of the differences we are discovering about how the students in any group or class learn did not create enough complexity for our teaching, the challenge of deciding what to teach from all the information we have about the subject matter we are teaching becomes more complex each year. Kenneth Gergen in *The Saturated Self* has observed that we experience all this information as overload. Robert Kegan describes the experience as being *In Over Our Heads*. Both metaphors indicate conditions for teaching and learning alien to remembering. They challenge the confidence of teachers at the very point of their desire to encourage student remembering. For example, if I were to teach another group of ninth graders today something about Paul and his teachings, I would first have to ask what of all that has been written about Paul would I choose to teach. I would also need to ask what I know about the students I am teaching to help them learn what I want them to know. Some students would be more interested in pursuing historical questions, others more theological questions, and others would prefer to explore practices of faith and morality associated with Paul's view of discipleship. The result is that whatever I would choose to emphasize, each student would "hear" my teaching differently, respond to it differently, and incorporate it into their worldviews in a variety of ways—that is, if they happened to remember it. The complexity of the environment for learning, in other words, creates a set of conditions that enhances the possibility for students to forget what we attempt to teach.

A common theme runs through these challenges to the possibility of student remembering in this and many other congregations. A pattern of isolation and disconnectedness runs counter to the intensive institutional efforts of the congregation to maintain an effective educational program. These ninth graders did not participate in an ethos of strong intergenerational relationships or with the cultural reinforcement of their other primary contexts for learning. The curriculum resources guiding their study functioned as topical sound bytes. They may have been developmentally responsible, but insensitive at the same time, to the dynamics of reinforcement integral to sustained learning. As for those of us who were teaching, we simply lacked awareness of what C. A. Bowers in *Responsive Teaching* has called the ecology of learning styles and cultural patterns to be found in any educational setting. Despite the organizational unity of the congregation's education, its most dominant characteristics may well have been the isolation and fragmentation many associate with the conditions of postmodernity. This congregation lacked the integrative processes typically found in relatively homogeneous and stable congregations that link and reinforce their teaching and learning over time. Among the most important of these integrating processes—especially in educational settings dominated by student diversity and attentive to the explosion of information—is the informal conversation usually associated with strong kinship and interinstitutional relationships. It provides, I contend, the curricular infrastructure for the congregation's educational practices.

Congregational Conversation

The importance of a congregation's conversational patterns for their ministries of teaching and learning was highlighted for me during a study of three congregations described in *We Are the Church Together* and in *Embracing Diversity*. A major feature distinguishing these congregations from those surrounding them was the explicit embrace of the racial and cultural diversity of their neighborhoods in their ministries. This meant people had to learn how to talk to each other across the experience of different races, cultures, and in some instances languages. In observing their struggle to become familiar enough with each other's speech patterns and rhythms, idioms and metaphors to communicate informally with each other, I discovered something about the ways in which the communication patterns in a congregation spill over into family discussions, nurture intergenerational relationships, inform and challenge public values and perceptions, and in the process frame, undergird, contextualize, and sustain their teaching and learning.

We may see something of the same dynamic at work when small children learn to speak the language of their families. Parents, older siblings, grandparents take time to instruct young children in the use of certain words, but much of their language learning occurs in overhearing its use in daily conversations, on the radio and on television. We learn the vocabulary of faith in much the same manner. Our teaching functions as a catalyst to student learning. It establishes a framework and channel for their remembering. Our teaching has a chance of taking root in the memories and imaginations of our students if it is reinforced through the informal conversations of congregations.

These observations bring me to my thesis: Attention must be given to nurturing a lively and vital consensual conversational infrastructure for the congregation's educational ministry if students are to remember more of what they are taught. This means that congregations seeking to extend and renew their faith traditions into the future must counter the loss of institutional and intergenerational reinforcements for their teaching. They must be more responsive to the diversity of student learning styles and cultural patterns. And they must find ways to create coherence out of the proliferation of information that could be taught.

INFORMAL CONVERSATION AS CONGREGATIONAL INFRASTRUCTURE

Several years ago Walter Brueggemann challenged religious educators to develop an educational strategy of bilinguality so that faith communities might converse not only among themselves but also engage in public discourse with others—including their enemies. Drawing on the story of the encounter between the Assyrians and Judah in 2 Kings 18:17–27, he underscored the necessity for both a communal conversation "behind the wall," in which the members of a community of faith have the freedom to sort out the issues before them in their own language without being overheard, and the importance of their public conversation at the wall in which they must negotiate their futures with their neighbors—both friends and enemies. Brueggemann did not describe in this essay (in *Educating for Citizenship and Discipleship*), what an education for conversation either "behind the wall" or "at the wall" might look like. In *The Creative Word*, he explored the necessary interdependence of the community's canons of Torah, prophecy, and wisdom in both the content and method for that education. Many contemporary communities of faith however, lack any such coherent structure for education to ensure either the continuity and relevance of their conversations behind the wall among themselves or the efficacy of their conversations at the wall with others. This, I would suggest, is located in the lack of attention to the very structure of the conversations that sustain their organized efforts at teaching and learning. What might such a conversational infrastructure for a congregation's education look like? Some definitions are in order.

Relationships || Gospel

Congregational Conversation is Relational

Conversation involves more than the words we may speak to each other. Conversation is a form of relationship. But it is not just any type of relationship. Its root meanings point to a relationship in which we find ourselves involved in a company of others. These relationships with others involve continuously negotiated exchanges in and through which we may find ourselves moving in a different direction from those with whom we speak. Conversation has the power to influence and to be influenced, to shape and to misshape, to form and to transform, to bind and to free those who participate in it. To engage in conversation is not to enter into a neutral relationship. It creates an interaction of invitation and response. It involves risk and negotiation. It sets the stage for changes in us, in others, and in the relationship between or among us. Hence conversation is always political; it persistently engages us in the dynamics of power at work in those relationships.

Congregational Conversation is Consensual

Congregational or community conversation is consensual in much the same way that any shared language depends on a consensus of meaning in communication. This consensus does not have so much to do with agreement over the meaning of words. Rather it has to do with the confluence of shared values, perspectives, and sensibilities with shared rhythms, metaphors, images, and patterns for speaking and listening that create in a congregation or community a sense of being at-one-with-each-other, of shared identity and vocation, and of common tradition and mission. The consensual nature of a community's conversations may be hard to define, but we certainly know it when we find ourselves in situations in which the words may be familiar but the meanings attached to them escape us, when we miss the humor in the jokes that are told, when we stumble over the patterns and rhythms of the verbal interaction, when we experience ourselves as marginalized and outsiders, and when we find ourselves victimized or oppressed. We may be less aware of its characteristics when we find ourselves experiencing the intimacy of the comraderie or the intensity of the mutuality that occurs when our interaction is most interdependent. Through this consensual give-and-take, however, conversation nurtures the corporate ethos of a community. In this regard it has the potential to nurture in congregations the communality that undergirds both the congregation's identity and mission.

The Infrastructure of Congregational Conversation

One other term in my thesis needs clarifying. By "conversational infrastructure" I have in mind the interactive communication patterns in a group that convey, support and renew a group or community's values, perspectives, and practices. In this regard I draw upon the research of Edward Hall and Edward Trager described in *The Silent Language*. They observed that the cultural patterns that inform our speaking and listening exist on three levels. Hall and Trager simply labeled them the informal, the formal, and the technical. Together they make up the infrastructure integral to the communal conversations that function as the communal contexts for our teaching and learning.

The *informal vocabulary* of conversation is situational and imprecise. It establishes predispositions to mutuality, gives momentum to the rhythms of our communicative interactions, and creates a contextual framework to facilitate the hearing we seek. It gathers people into a common experience—that frames and channels the message to be delivered. It makes use of story, jokes, commentary, and instruction. Its critique tends to be self-referential-drawing on the authority of the experience and traditions of the group. In whatever form, it functions to create the conditions for a common hearing.

Until the 1960s at least, the sources and catalysts to this informal religious vocabulary for most mainline Protestants existed primarily in the interplay of congregational and denominational life that cut across their ideological lines. People were not necessarily aware of the differences in the gospel accounts of the birth of Christ or that Genesis contained two accounts of creation, but their basic encounters with the confluence of stories like these provided a common framework for hearing sermons, participating in Bible study groups, commenting on political events, or making ethical or moral decisions. In the words of the hymn text, this was the faith of the fathers (and mothers) living still. The Baltimore Catechism and the weekly rhythm of the liturgy and other rituals fulfilled a similar function for the more formal teaching and learning sponsored by Roman Catholics. The consensual framework of religious conversations across the nation in other words, included a rather broad spectrum of the population. Today, the sources and catalysts to the informal religious vocabulary in congregations is just as likely to come from the media (video versions of Bible stories and mass market movies that are based on biblical stories or engage religious themes), the marketing of religious artifacts such as WWJD (What Would Jesus Do) bracelets, or the publicizing of religious experience in the testimonials of sports and media heroes and mass rallies (e.g., Promise Keepers) as it is from the liturgical, educational, and missional life of the congregation.

The result of this relatively new situation is that decreasing numbers of congregations have an adequate informal vocabulary to ground any education directed to sustaining and renewing their faith traditions. This loss may be due primarily to a lack of attention to the necessity of nurturing the informal conversation that functions as context and agent for sustained teaching and learning. When people in the congregation do not live in the same neighborhood, when they participate only in structured meetings, or participate only occasionally in the liturgical life of the congregation, their informal conversations are reduced to words of greeting and safe generalities or are limited to the formal and technical vocabularies of the congregation's leadership. People do not have enough to say to negotiate matters of faith and practice with each other. I have called informal vocabulary the curricular infrastructure of congregations. Without its presence the intentional efforts of pastors and teachers to convey doctrines, stories, polity practices, and the like are much more difficult to sustain. Without the testing, reinforcing, and supportive role of a lively and vital informal vocabulary many people simply have difficulty recalling what they have heard in any formal setting.

The *formal vocabulary* of conversation in a community typically forms the content of our deliberate efforts at teaching and learning, most liturgy, and much preaching. It consists of the vocabulary of faith that must be known by anyone seeking to participate in a congregation's communal traditions. It typically provides the basic content to the informal vocabulary of a community—so that Bible narratives, hymns, catechisms, modes of interpretation, and practices of piety and morality establish the basic content distinguishing faith practices from one congregation to another. It functions as the controlling tradition in our communication with each other. It is embodied in the doctrines, articulated in mission statements, ordered in liturgical practices, and formulated in policy and governance documents that establish the boundaries between one community and another—between the private realm of the community and the public realm of the world at large. The formal vocabulary of a community in the old Sunday school vernacular becomes "the lesson,"—which must be learned to become a full participant in the life of the community. This formal vocabulary is what E. D. Hirsch Jr. meant by the phrase "cultural literacy"—that composite of information through which people make sense of their world out of the resources of a particular cultural or, in our case, religious tradition.

Hall and Trager also noted that communities make use of *technical vocabularies* in their conversations. These vocabularies are primarily used by specialists; in religious communities this means biblical scholars, theologians, and ethicists as well as congregational leaders who mediate their specialized language. We find these vocabularies in Bible commentaries, theological works, and the constitutions and polity handbooks of denominations and congregations. People rarely use technical vocabularies in day to day conversation except in formal educational or research settings. Indeed, evidence would indicate that many clergy do not draw on the technical vocabularies of biblical and theological scholars in their teaching and preaching as much as their predecessors did. And yet, I would argue, their lack of attention to the technical vocabulary of a faith community diminishes the depth and stability of the formal conversations that challenge and renew the informal conversations that sustain the faith traditions of a congregation or community.

I rehearse these distinctions because educators and theologians primarily attend to the technical and formal vocabularies of a community in their teaching. Some, like David Tracy, who has written provocatively on the dynamics of scholarly conversation in *The Analogical Imagination*, seem to denigrate the significance of informal conversation in the quest to know and understand. At one point he distinguishes the chatter of everyday talk from the authentic conversation that occurs when the pursuit of a question carries those involved into the rare experience of thinking. This experience, however, is not confined to the use of formal and technical vocabularies. It may occur at any time and among any group of people—including children. The danger for teaching and learning in congregations, however, is that the processes of thinking together typically lack enough continuity of relationship, enough familiarity with the language of the community, to gather folk into the reciprocity of exploring a question, an issue, or a practice. If the teaching and learning of a congregation is to contribute to personal and communal remembering, it must give attention not only to the formal vocabularies of curriculum and formal teaching strategies but also to the nurture of its informal conversations.

PEDAGOGICAL PRACTICES FOR INFORMAL CONGREGATIONAL CONVERSATION

So how do pastors and teachers create conditions for the informal conversations that help undergird and sustain the remembering crucial to the tasks of maintaining, deepening, and renewing both personal and corporate faith? The answer begins by acknowledging that traditional patterns for congregational governance are no longer adequate to the task of holding in community the diversity of groups and experience found in them. In both parish and voluntary forms of congregational life over the past one hundred years, more and more substructures have been instituted to respond to the growing consciousness of folk to the differences of people in the congregation: women's groups, youth groups, and men's groups; classes for persons of different ages and abilities—even to the point of distinguishing among children and youth by the year of their birth; groups for people interested in the

arts, mission, social action, spirituality, a variety of sports and fellowship. More recently, congregations have sought to accommodate the
growing social, racial, cultural, and economic diversity among the
people they serve. This has led to worship services in a variety of languages, self-help and dependency groups, and advocacy programs and
an ever wider array of social services. While responsive to the interests of persons, each new group also separates and often isolates people from each other and in the process, diminishes the conversation
that holds everything together.

Once in a while we hear of congregations in which the diversity becomes unbearable—usually around some political, social, or ethical
issue having theological overtones. Rarely do we hear on those same
news reports stories of people leaving congregations because they no
longer know enough people like them to warrant their continuing loy-
alty. If the consciousness of pluralism is indeed a prevailing characteristic of the contemporary era, the vitality, if not the future, of these
congregations is in doubt. So once again, how do congregational leaders nurture the conversation that supports and sustains their education? In *Educating Congregations* and in *Embracing Diversity*, I have
suggested two practices that may be responsive to the challenge of educating to remember.

Embracing Diversity

Despite biblical injunctions to the effect that strangers bear God's
gifts, through most of Christian history, congregations have generally
been suspicious of strangers. Whenever stability, continuity, and ho-
mogeneity dominate the consciousness of peoples, the gifts of
strangers often require change, lead to transformation, and call for
flexibility and adaptability. We need only think of the impact a new
baby has on a household or of the challenges to our settled ways that
occur when a grandparent moves into the house; and these strangers
are expected or are familiar to us. The changes we face in our view of
ourselves and the world is even more profound when someone from a
different culture, religious tradition, political perspective, or economic
experience moves next door to us. Or joins our congregation.

An encounter with strangers is more subtle. Whether or not it was
true, most middle to older adults in our congregations grew up with a
sense of the interconnectedness of their communities. When someone
was sick, the news spread through the community. When a death

occurred in a family, folks from around the community gathered around. When a child received some special recognition at school, word spread quickly. Such familiarity of expectation rarely happens today in most of our communities—even in many rural areas still marked by relative stability. We are not likely to hear about illness or death in a family until we hear it announced during worship. We may never hear about the accomplishments of the children who live just down the street or sit in a pew with their families in congregational worship.

I make these observations because we, at least, used to assume a continuity of experience in the places where our lives touched each other—especially in the fellowships of our congregations. Now it is my observation that we have so little continuous contact with each other that our meetings are often awkward and the things we might say to each other are typically left unsaid. In reality we meet one another as strangers. We are challenged in biblical tradition to view the strangers we meet as neighbors. Increasingly however, we experience our neighbors as strangers. This means that the embrace of the diversity that is central to the ministries of congregations in neighborhoods with changing populations is also crucial to the ministries of congregations in what appear to be stable and relatively homogeneous neighborhoods. We can no longer assume the continuity of experience that cradles the informal conversations among people who know each other well.

The ecology of learning styles and cultural patterns that distinguish our various ways of experiencing the world in the life of a congregation are complicated even further by the range of our belief systems or worldviews and the varieties of our personal and social experience. When a group of us gathers to teach and learn or to meet to decide on some program or policy or to worship together, some among us may well experience anything said or done as unfamiliar, alien, or even hostile. And yet that which seems threatening may also be a gift. It may bring new possibility or be the bearer of hope. As such, given the new consciousness of the pluralism in the human experience, the very experience of that which is unfamiliar or strange may be a catalyst to the conversations that will bind us into new expressions of community. This new possibility for congregational life in the twenty-first century underscores several characteristics of a pedagogy for the congregation that embraces diversity.

It is hospitable. This insight has long been associated with Martin Buber. We do not become "thous" to each other—that condition essential for mutual and revelatory conversation to take place—unless the space that separates us conveys invitation, openness, and candor. Hospitality is the condition for conversation, as it is for learning. There is much discussion in educational literature about the importance of "safe spaces" for learning to take place. I am not sure that any learning environment can truly be safe; the learning we seek or the learning we do may turn our worlds completely upside down. But those spaces can be hospitable. They can make us feel welcome, at home with each other. They can create the conditions for trusting in the possibility of the unknown—even the unknown that may lead to changes we do not seek or transformations we have not anticipated.

It is contentious. Charles Tilly, in a provocative essay in a *Social Research* journal colloquy on conversation, observes that when conversation takes seriously people's experience and commitments, it embodies both mutual and contradictory claims. The embrace of diversity collapses if people's interactions convey superficiality or are limited to conventional politeness. The candor central to the conversation that nurtures community only begins with the recognition that we can never fully appreciate or understand one another. Some postmodern scholars describe this condition as incommensurability—the recognition that empathy has its limits and that any truth claim is culturally and socially limited. Those limits are rooted in the diverse and often contrary commitments, beliefs, values, and practices we encounter in each other. Typically we seek to accommodate these contrarieties as in the ways husbands and wives often sublimate the differences in beliefs, values, or practices they discover in each other, or in the ways that dominant peoples have always tried to subjugate those they did not understand through acts of oppression. In the embrace of difference, however, that which is not familiar or fully understood may catalyze imaginative activity and may be valued as resources for new learning.

It is playful. As we embrace differences in the human community, our attention shifts from the quest for conformity to an appreciation for the incongruity and lack of complementarity often made visible in the encounter of the limits of our knowledge of the other or of the cultural values and customs that inform their worlds. Conversation that is playful has a spontaneity about it, but in the embrace of difference that spontaneity occurs not at the point of our control of what we know but at the edges of what we do not know. It reflects a willingness to risk, to suspend judgment, to try on that which is unfamiliar. It subverts traditional patterns of order and efforts at control and domination, and it creates places where we might encounter each other more fully. Playfulness is laced with humor as C. A. Bowers, in his study *Responsive Teaching* has observed. It becomes an expression of solidarity—a solidarity rooted not in uniformity but in the embrace of differences. Laughter may indeed be one of the most effective gauges of the hospitality that involves informal conversation.

It is empowered by rituals. Rituals of gathering authorize the participation of all who are present. They declare that all who are present are full participants—neighbors if you will, and not strangers to one another. As such, rituals of gathering energize the engagement of diverse peoples with each other. They give permission to those who are present to enter into the task at hand. They link old timers with newcomers so they might become partners with each other into the journey of the experience before them. Rituals of gathering give way to rituals of intensification—corporate actions that renew, extend, and deepen a sense of identification with one another. Rituals of dispersal or sending forth become reminders that even when people will not see each other from one meeting or class session to the next, a tie does bind them together.

Most liturgies have rituals of gathering (processionals and calls to worship), rituals of intensification (prayers of confession and forgiveness, prayers of recommitment), and rituals of dispersal (benedictions and recessionals). For many people, however, these ritual acts do not empower, renew, or intensify their participation in that community. They have been inherited from the past when the language, actions, and rhythms of the rituals spilled over into the language, actions, and rhythms of the week and have not become embedded in their own views of the world. A call to worship functions differently, in other words, in a setting in which people are called together to focus on the praise of God out of a week of interaction with one another on the economic and social matters of living together, from a setting in which people neither see or talk to one another all week. A ritual of dispersal for people who leave the liturgy to encounter each other during the week extends the unifying activity of worship into and through their interactions with each other. Those ties that bind them in community are simply missing for those who never meet each other anyplace but in the church.

Practices of embracing diversity alone, however, are not adequate to a pedagogy that prompts and sustains the informal conversations of a congregation. A second and intersecting set of practices is also needed. These practices do not originate in the organizational or programmatic structures of the congregation but in the events that give rise to and sustain those structures—including those concerned with education.

Celebrating Events

The dominant organizational model for formal education in most congregations has been the school. In an earlier day in Catholic, Lutheran, and some Presbyterian and Episcopalian congregations it was the catechism. In many congregations the catechetical process became lodged in the school. Both have much to commend them. They work on the notion that learning is progressive and accumulative; that learning can be ordered in sequential segments; that cohorts of learners can move through these sequences in orderly and timely fashion; and that the training of the mind can influence the formation of values, sensibilities, habits, and practices crucial to participation in the life of the larger community.

The embrace of diversity does not diminish the power of the school or the catechism as an educative instrument, but it challenges the adequacy of these assumptions. Learning in individuals has a progressive and an accumulative character, but it also includes forward spurts and backward slides. It is often unpredictable and unmanageable. All people do not learn in the same fashion or at the same speed. The learning of students in any group therefore is typically experienced by teachers as discontinuous, disorderly, and disconnected. Recent research, especially in studies of neurological patterns in the brain that affect learning, further confounds our efforts to view the dynamics of teaching and learning in systematic or controlled patterns. These studies demonstrate that the mind, for example, does influence the formation of values, sensibilities, habits, and practices, but not necessarily in any cause and effect manner. Indeed the emotions may be as important in triggering mental functions as cognitive activity.

Another structure for ordering teaching and learning is required—one that does not diminish the contribution of the school as a set of practices contributing to the teaching and learning of a community or invalidate the usefulness of sequential and accumulative curricular strategies. A structure is needed that will function as a catalyst to the informal conversations that inform and sustain the learning of formal and technical faith vocabularies so that they may in turn, ground, critique and renew congregational life and mission. Any such structure for congregational education must have within it the capacity to create the conditions for the learning of all in the community. I have described this practice elsewhere as the ordering of teaching and learning to prepare people for participation in the primary events in the life of a congregation or community. For congregations this obviously includes occasions of worship and mission and the rhythmic repetition of seasonal events that both mark the movement of the community through the year and intensify the identification of its members with its mission—the season of Lent culminating in Holy Week, a planning process leading to a mission trip, or the preparation for saints' days and revivals.

The pedagogical structure of congregational events is a simple one. It involves the preparation of congregants for participation in the event (in this period of Christian history, congregational leaders cannot assume they will have the knowledge and skill to do so), the act of participation in the event, and the recollection and critique of that experience to discern and respond to the claims of that event in their lives. All of this is discussed in *Educating Congregations*.

I did not discuss in that volume, however, how this pedagogical process nurtures the conversation in the congregation that becomes, in turn, the curricular undercurrent for the teaching and learning that occurs in these three phases of any event in its life. The primary events in the cycles of a congregation's life function both as catalyst and agency to its informal conversation. Like a rock thrown into a pond, an event contributes to congregational identity and mission through the informal conversations that ripple out across the congregation in ways that no one can order or control. These conversations, often originating in planning sessions, spill over into rehearsals and are reinforced in study sessions to ground them in the congregation's faith traditions. Because many congregational events are inherently intergenerational, the stories and practices associated with an event come up in family discussions in the car and at the dinner table. They require phone calls among the people involved in the event to address an issue or a problem associated with the event. They may prompt requests or plans for formal study that become the occasion for formal conversation. In other words, congregational events have the potential to connect, reconnect, and even disconnect people from each other.

Congregational events nurture the informal vocabulary of the congregation. As people rehearse together certain songs and prayers, scripts and texts, missional and caring practices, they begin to develop a common vocabulary through which they interpret their experience of an event or draw upon its resources for some issue or question they find themselves addressing. The event of Christmas provides a good example. Certain hymns are practiced in formal and informal settings repeatedly. *Silent Night, Away in a* Manger, and O *Little Town of Bethlehem* become associated with the celebration of the season through the repetition of the season. Their sounds and rhythms mean Christmas. The texts convey images and meanings that over time become identified with Christmas. They help set a frame for hearing and responding to sermons, discussions of the birth narratives in the Gospels, interpretations of contemporary gift giving and so forth. Much of this "instruction" in the meaning and practices of Christmas may never take place in a formal educational setting. Instead, it occurs in and through the informal conversations of people in the congregation and community.

The movie industry is well acquainted with the pedagogy associated with events. The introduction of a major new film has all the characteristics of event education. Advertisements, promotionals, advance reviews, and CDs of the musical score are released well ahead of the first showing of the film. This "pedagogical activity" only unleashes a torrent of "learning" as those who attend to its possibilities anticipate the film, learn its story line, and become familiar with its songs. The public, in other words, is prepared to participate in the event of its release. The effectiveness of this process was dramatized for me recently by a colleague who explained that his daughters, who were not allowed to see a certain major film aimed at children, had nevertheless learned all the songs by memory—simply through their interactions with friends. This is the process of developing the vocabulary for the informal conversations I am describing.

In the preparation of persons for participation in the events of congregational life, those in teaching roles have the opportunity *to introduce formal vocabularies to inform and critique* the informal

vocabularies of people around congregational events. I am reminded
of a pastor who wanted to help children (and many adults) discover
that there are a number of ways of seeing the birth of Christ. He pro-
ceeded to help them compare and contrast the Matthew and Luke versions of the story. As they discovered that the Bible says nothing about
three wise men, that Matthew says nothing about shepherds, and Luke
says nothing at all about wise men, they had new information that
challenged the informal versions of the story they had heard and told.
This new information may have spilled over into conversations after
the conclusion of the worship service. It would probably not enter the
informal vocabulary of the congregation, however, until it had been
rehearsed and discussed often enough to challenge the more familiar
versions of the story.

CONVERSATION IN THE CONGREGATION'S CURRICULAR INFRASTRUCTURE

What does this conversational curricular undercurrent look like? It is,
in the first place, *polylogical.* I discovered the term "polylogue" while
reading Michael Joyce's exploration of the impact of hypertext on
pedagogy in his book, *Of Two Minds.* In this case polylogue involves
the possibility of layering texts and images through networks of computerized technology. I find the term useful for describing the dynamics of conversation in communities that embrace not only the diversity
of persons but also their various perspectives on texts, traditions, and
contexts in which they find themselves. In other words, I no longer
find dialogue to be an adequate model for our conversations.

Much attention has been given to the character of dialogue in discussions among educators on the dynamics of teaching and learning. It
dominates Paulo Friere's vision of the relationship of teacher and
learner with both the subject matter and the learning community. Nel
Noddings, a contemporary philosopher of education, probes the possibilities of dialogue in a different direction. She observes that it establishes the framework for an "ethic of caring" in the practice of teaching because it engages its teachers and students in an open-ended,
mutual, and reciprocal search for enlightenment or perspective. In his
study of teaching that responds to the diversity of learning styles and
cultural patterns in students, C. A. Bowers uses the word more de-
scriptively to account for the patterns of negotiated turntaking among

students and between students and teacher. He notes that in dialogue either party may introduce or change a topic. There is much overlapping of talk. Interruptions, digressions, and backtracking are tolerated as long as the parties involved continue to be engaged in the interaction.

In her study of the patterns of address by teachers, Elizabeth Ellsworth challenges the simplicity of most of this discussion in at least two important ways. She notes in *Teaching Positions* that the "dialogue" between teacher and student or between text and student is always trialogical. It involves not only the teacher and/or text with the student but the student's unconscious, which speaks back to the teacher and/or text through asides, by denying or forgetting, or through such feelings as fear, shame, pleasure, and doubt. I think it would just as likely include the teacher's unconscious as a fourth partner; clearly a polylogical rather than a dialogical exchange.

In this double-shadowed pattern of communication, the resulting conversation may well express, at times, elements of that which has been otherwise repressed in the interaction of teacher and student or student and text. Despite the appeal of the Buberian quest for mutuality in dialogue, in pedagogical situations it typically engages teachers and students in the power dynamics of authority structures in which the partners are really not equal. Students cannot enter collegially into dialogue with a teacher whose training provides a clear edge in the quest to know or with a text that carries the weight of tradition. The mutuality of dialogue may be disrupted by the intervention of the subconscious of either teacher or student. At this point we may discover another source to the not-remembering of students. It exists in the resistance of students to the formal and/or technical information conveyed by teachers and texts. Their resistance may originate from a lack of adequate preparation to encounter new information, the subconscious recognition of the challenge it poses to existing values and perspectives, or the realization that it insists on a response that violates the student's sense of personal or corporate identity.

In the embrace of diversity the limits of dialogue as a form of conversation become even more clear. With whom is any student or the teacher or a text in dialogue? This insight occurred to me while working through the corpus of Freire's works with a group of students in a doctoral seminar. What struck me with new force was the invisibility of the students, first in his *Pedagogy of the Oppressed* and then in other works as well. Even as he claimed interchangeable roles for teacher and student, the interaction of students with each other and with the teacher was invisible. They lacked both face and voice in the dialogic of his liberative pedagogy.

In the embrace of diversity the dynamics of the conversation among teachers and students is even more multifaceted and multidimensional than Freire imagined. We have a hint of this polylogical possibility in a comparison of different readings of the Exodus narratives to be found in commentaries that are available for use by teachers and students in congregations. The range of the theological views among the scholars creates multiple perspectives on the text. Perhaps even more striking is the influence of their racial, social, cultural, and religious heritage on their readings of the text. Jewish scholars and Christian scholars of northern European, African American, and Native American heritage each approach the text shaped in part by their historical and social contexts. Insights rooted in the particular ways of seeing in these contexts both illumine and obscure their reading. These differences may never be discovered if people only read or participate in discussions with others who share their own social, cultural, and historical experience. Unlike the apparent cleanness of dialogical interactions, this multiplicity of perspectives contributes to the messiness and the openness of polylogical conversations.

This brings us to a second characteristic of the informal conversation that forms the curricular infrastructure of congregations that embrace diversity. It involves the nurture of *empathic consciousness* on the part of both teachers and students. Without this capacity, teaching practices contribute to the oppression or marginalization of some students. Empathic consciousness funds the possibility for interactive mutuality and reciprocity among teachers and students. But it is driven by the recognition that in the embrace of difference none of us will ever be able to appreciate or understand fully the perspectives or approaches that others take to a question or issue. This is the kind of knowing that occurred in one of my classes when students from both African and European heritages read Robert Warrior's commentary on the Exodus and *recognized* their own inability to grasp fully how the identification of Native Americans with the Canaanites being expelled from their land challenged their own relationship to that text. Empathic consciousness, in other words, humanizes the contentiousness of our encounters with the differences among ourselves. It creates the conditions for reconciling and transforming conversation and confounds our tendencies to demean, suppress, or dominate that which is unfamiliar.

This leads me to a third characteristic of the conversational infrastructure that nurtures remembering in the teaching and learning in communities of diversity. It is located in the capacity of teachers and learners to participate in an ethos of *collaborative critique*. There is in the literature considerable discussion on the reciprocity required in the mutuality of critique, when the give-and-take of critique is shared. As a metaphor of interaction, mutuality, like dialogue, conveys an image of two parties. So we think of teacher and students, or student and student. In polylogical understandings of conversation that image is not adequate to the task of engaging the views of the multiplicity of others we meet—even in a congregational educational event. The danger for the education of a congregation occurs whenever any person or group assesses the contributions of others through the lens of their own cultural, theological, or social experience. When this happens, those involved run the risk of idolatrizing their own heritage and often of demonizing the views of others.

The starting place for collaborative critique occurs in the recognition that conversation is polylogical. It includes multiple partners, who are seeking to hear truth in the wisdom of others. In this process, an empathic consciousness deepens and sensitizes our hearing and speaking with each other. When it is missing, we slip into another exercise of power in which one person or group exerts dominance over another.

The practice of collaborative critique encourages diverse participants in a congregation or teaching and learning group to move beyond the taken-for-granted vocabularies of their informal conversations to see how their views are perceived by others. It illumines possibilities for strengthening their informal conversations in their differences with each other. It undergirds the capacities of people to enter into political negotiations with other folk in diverse groups around issues and problems that matter deeply to all involved. It helps to create an environment in which teachers and learners might consider transformative actions in their lives and their congregations or communities.

CONCLUSION

I began this chapter with a question that persists in the minds of teachers: Why don't they remember what I teach? Typically questions like this one have been addressed in the educational literature as the problem of the teacher. The issue, I contend, is much deeper and more profound. Certainly effective teaching can improve student remembering. But if the context of the teaching/learning interaction does not reinforce or sustain that effort, the chances of remembering are quite remote. Students remember what is important to them. Just as significantly, they remember what is important to the communities with which they most identify. This insight, I contend, has been lost in the current debates over education, especially, perhaps, in the debates that occur in religious communities.

Without diminishing the attention given to the roles of teachers and students, the multifaceted processes of learning, and the agency of the school and curriculum resources, religious educators also need to attend to what I am calling the infrastructure of communities of faith that support and sustain our religious education aims. That infrastructure is increasingly fragile. The consciousness of the pluralism of culture, ideology, and practice—both religious and secular—that characterizes the period of history in which we live calls for a flexibility and responsiveness that does not exist in the institutions we have inherited. The explosion of knowledge renders judgments about what should be taught to extend the identity and vocation of a congregation into the future difficult. The challenge before congregational education, therefore, has little to do with how to deny or avoid the dynamics of pluralism in the congregation, but how to embrace it as a gift to be honored and nurtured.

I therefore suggest that the infrastructure that nurtures and sustains congregational education is not so much institutional or ideological as it is relational. It takes form and is given momentum through the informal conversations of the congregation—those building blocks to the interconnectivity of diverse peoples. The pace of contemporary life in most of our communities, however, negates the practicality of conversation as a source of congregational coherence. The places have to be created. The times have to be chosen. The relationships have to be nurtured. I believe those places and times already exist in the calendars of every congregation—in the events that most distinctively give them shape and purpose. If congregations choose to focus their education around these events, each becomes a catalyst to a moment of conversation. The repetition of events over the years provides occasions to recall, renew, and expand on their learnings from prior events.

The model is in the Passover meal—the annual rehearsal of the story of the Exodus from Egypt in which a child asks the question that prompts the telling and the retelling of the story. It is not just any story. It is the story that includes every Jewish child who participates in this practice. It is not just the telling of the story. It is the conversation that recalls prior times when the story was told, seeks to interpret its significance for the situation in which those telling the story find themselves, and anticipates future times and perhaps different circumstances when the story will be told again. Although the not-remembering of a group of ninth graders raises questions about the adequacy of their religious education, the challenge is much more profound. If they do not remember, who will tell the story to the next generation?

5

Candles in the Darkness

KENNETH O. GANGEL

With a booming economy and the decorations of prosperity gilding the Western world, humanity has crossed the mythical boundary of another millennium with hopes that miracle-working technology will provide even greater progress and hope for the future. But as the stock market in 1999 reached for 12,000, the world languishes in tribal warfare, erupting around the globe with frightening regularity as hundreds of thousands of refugees huddle in epiphytic squalor hoping to live another day. Billion-dollar missiles destroy cities while in other cities thousands of homeless search garbage cans for food.

Children and teenagers have become a marketing fixation and among their many expensive purchases are automatic weapons used to kill classmates and peers. Twenty-five-year-old millionaires race their fingers across laptops, buying and selling stocks while street gangs control large segments of most urban territory. Viewed from an economic perspective, these are indeed the best of times for many. Measurements of righteousness, however, suggest that the moral miasma into which we find ourselves sinking may indicate the worst of times.

SOCIAL LANDSCAPE

Meanwhile, our global population tops 6 billion. Twenty-one cities around the world claim a population of over 10 million; during this next century, India will surpass China as the world's most populous nation. One-half the population of Africa's continent is under fifteen years of age. In the United States, the generation of children younger than eighteen has grown from 69.5 million three years ago to 70.2 million today—and the baby boom continues.

We have talked for years about the impact of the baby boomer generation, and its impact cannot be denied. But the so-called millennial generation has already left its fingerprints all over public and private life—crowded schools, sky rocketing sales of toys and children's magazines, growing demand for pediatricians, and a voracious appetite for marketing to children, who now influence more adult spending decisions than baby boomers ever dreamed about.

The umbrella of social climate covers a boundless variety of issues religious educators must address, including controversial and emotional problems such as abortion, euthanasia, genetic engineering, pornography, ecology, the media, and many more. All of them contribute to the breakdown of the family. In the forty-year time period of 1960–1999, illegitimate births increased more than 400 percent causing some to consider it the most important social problem of our time. According to Michael Novak, "Children born out of wedlock tend to have high infant mortality, low birth weight (with attendant morbidities), and high probabilities of being poor, not completing school, and staying on welfare themselves. As a matter of public policy (not to mention biblical morality) it pays for society to approve of marriage as the best setting for children, and to discourage having children out of wedlock."

The problem complicates itself when we recognize that most unwed mothers are teenagers. Every sixty-four seconds a teenager mother gives birth, and every five minutes a baby is born to a teenager who already has a child. Teenage mothers of infants fathered by adults are not a new problem in our society but now the teens no longer marry the biological fathers. Indeed, as we cross into the new millennium, 65 percent of teenage mothers are unmarried and facing a cycle of poverty and welfare dependency.

No religious educator could fail to weep for and minister to single parents, particularly mothers (90 percent of single-parent homes have no father). The backbreaking, spirit-crushing burdens of raising children alone while working full-time for unconscionably low wages represents another injustice of our time. We seem to have no sensitivity to the ultimate communal results of individual suffering. Daniel Patrick Moynihan could hardly be confused with the radical right, but his warning thirty-five years ago turns out to be eerily on target: "From the wild Irish slums of the nineteenth century Eastern seaboard, to the riot-torn suburbs of Los Angeles, there is one unmistakable lesson in America history: A community that allows a large number of young men to grow up in broken families, dominated by women, never acquiring any stable relationship to male authority, never acquiring any rational expectations about the future—that community asks for and gets chaos. Crime, violence, unrest, disorder—most particularly the furious, unstrained lashing out at the whole social structure—these are not only to be expected, they are nearly inevitable." Any religious education in the third millennium that does not offer strong support for families, in whatever form we find them, must be rated deficient in both nexus and praxus.

RELIGIOUS CLIMATE

With respect to religious commitment, one hardly knows whom to believe. Attendance at evangelical seminaries, and now more recently Catholic seminaries, continues to grow. Prayer breakfasts and megachurches abound. The number of Christians is growing at about twice the rate of the world's population. But according to George Barna, only 28 percent of people in the United States, when surveyed on the statement "the Christian churches in your area are relevant to the way you live today" agreed strongly, with another 38 percent "agreeing somewhat," leaving more than a third in disagreement. More shocking was the finding that so-called born again Christians only strongly agree at 41 percent and regular attendees at 34 percent. The problem appears to be continental. From 1945 to 1975 the exposure of Canadian young people to religious groups on a regular basis dropped from 60 percent to 35 percent, and by 1995 the number had plummeted to 26 percent.

We struggle with the rapidity of change, which challenges our ability to keep up with the complex transitions in sociology, anthropology, and theology with which we work. The groups we must deal with five years from now will be very different from those we know today. As the high-loyalty sponsor generation exits the religious scene, we feel the loss of their presence and their charitable giving over the past half century.

More nonsense was proffered in the name of religion during the last quarter of the twentieth century than in all similar periods since Simon Stylitus came down from his pole. Capitalistic economy caters to consumer desires, offering convenience and a staggeringly high level of living. The marketing craze has consumed churches and religious organizations, which often crassly recruit "customers" by telling them what they want to hear instead of a genuine message from God. I agree with Thomas Oden when he claims that the Babylonian captivity to novelty tempts all modern reflection, a bewitchment from which all mainline denominations have suffered for two centuries. I harbor no fantasies that religious colleges and seminaries can provide some curricular fix for social and religious deficiencies. Perhaps the greatest long-range solution lies in the modeling role of educational leaders in pulpits, classrooms, and study groups around the world.

ESSENTIAL CORE

My own faith community requires a recapturing of biblical gospel and refocusing on biblical teaching and preaching. In its Easter issue of 1999, *Newsweek* reflected on "2000 Years of Jesus." Editor Kenneth Woodward, whose theological perceptivity equals or surpasses that of many seminary professors, comments that the early church "bequeathed to Western culture a God Who revealed Himself definitively in the person of Jesus, and who continues to redeem the world by the work of the Holy Spirit. . . . To a world ruled by fate and the winds of capricious gods, Christianity brought the promise of everlasting life. At the core of the Christian faith was the assertion that the crucified Jesus was resurrected by God and present in the church as "the Body of Christ."

Herein rests the central theme of the Christian message, a core of belief around which Christians have created tomes of denominational particularity. Other faith groups will select other cores, to be sure, but Christian religious educators who want to function vibrantly in the social and religious climates of the third millennium must proclaim allegiance to the essentials of life-changing truth rather than the externals of marketing paradigms.

Yes, candles glow in the darkness—lights that have shined, albeit often dimly, for thousands of years of Judeo-Christian heritage; lights that point upward rather than outward, that signify a world in the ultimate control of its Creator, distant though he sometimes seems to our frail and fearful hearts. And in this new decade, which lengthens its aqueous shadow into a century, he has not left himself without witness in the world. From the call of Abraham to the present hour, the God of heaven reveals his name and message through people willing to proclaim it, people we call religious educators, whose prayers and pedagogy affirm the reality of truth and grace.

Shaken by depression and two world wars, the church has turned to such people in the past half century for hope and nurture to cope with the increasing darkness of the ungodly culture. Parents and pastors, professors and practitioners have proclaimed the faith with clarity and conviction. And never were they more needed, never their message more appropriate, than in a time when the lubricious idolatry of greed threatens to choke the life of faith.

NARROWED FOCUS

But how do we, who hold the torch and pass it to others, protect and perpetuate that light? What should we build into disciples and students so they too can stand in the unbroken line of those who have committed themselves to the godly nurture of others? I hope in these few paragraphs to describe the essential nature of religious education for the future, isolating some unique particularities that set it apart from secular education. Admittedly, I work with a certain bias which not all readers will accept. In *Fides et Ratio*, Pope John Paul II set forth the argument of the complementary relationship of faith and reason. I find such a position appealing while holding that in such dialogue faith must ultimately arise as the stronger companion.

BIBLICAL IN AUTHORITY

Those who know my writings over the past three decades would expect me to plant my pulpit on the platform of authority. In the postmodern scene all the familiar players—reason, tradition, revelation—have marched off the stage. The rejection of universal truth and absolute moral principles has broken the ideals that formerly linked us together and has left us with tribal loyalties that serve only to divide us. Standing against a secular education with virtually no remaining commitment to authoritative underpinnings, I call religious educators to return to the theology of David.

> The law of the Lord is perfect, reviving the soul. The statutes of the Lord are trustworthy, making wise the simple. The precepts of the Lord are right, giving joy to the heart. The commands of the Lord are radiant, giving light to the eyes. The fear of the Lord is pure, enduring forever. The ordinances of the Lord are sure and altogether righteous. They are more precious than gold, than much pure gold; they are sweeter than honey, than honey from the comb. By them is your servant warned; in keeping them there is great reward. (Psalm 19:7–11)

Two thousand years ago Jesus called the people of his day back to the truth and authority of the Old Testament text. Five hundred years ago Luther and Calvin echoed that call for both testaments. Religious education that captures the hearts and minds of twenty-first century people must anchor them to God's message of eternal and absolute truth. Our infatuation with modernity has led us to believe that only new philosophies and new methodologies can capture the contemporary mind. But C. S. Lewis called this the "chronological fallacy," the idea that ideas are wrong just because they are old. We must measure truth neither by age nor by the energy level of those eager to expound it. In my view, *the cutting edge difference between secular education and religious education rests in an appeal to divine revelation, the word of the living God, incarnate and inscripturated.* It would be a dangerous riffle in this forum to argue hermeneutics; I limit my appeal to the recognition of a simple yet basic standard—if there is a God and if God has spoken in history, the most important aspect of religious education is to discover what he has said and what humanity must do about it.

Permit me to narrow my focus to my own faith community for just a few lines. Though the gospel has always been transcultural, Christians have frequently been tempted to adapt so dramatically to their cultural surroundings that they fade into the scenery of the world and become scarcely noticeable. To be sure this behavior, often results from sincere motives a desire to contextualize the message or appear relevant to the times, this behavior, reflective of Renaissance and Enlightenment thinking, characterizes much of modern Christianity—hooked on futurism, movements, groups and slogans. Yet New

Testament believers knew nothing of programs and paradigms; their hallmarks were unity and generosity, as the historian, Luke, reminds us.

> All the believers were one in heart and mind. No one claimed that any of his possessions was his own, but they shared everything they had. With great power the apostles continued to testify to the resurrection of the Lord Jesus, and much grace was upon them all. There were no needy persons among them. For from time to time those who owned lands or houses sold them, brought the money from the sales and put it at the apostles' feet, and it was distributed to anyone as he had need. (Acts 4:32–35)

Descended spiritually from people who penetrated the mists of Greco-Roman culture and sent the gospel around the Mediterranean world, across oceans, and over enormous mountain ranges, too many of us have become, in this third millennium, people who have returned to ancient religious symbols—*our* place, *our* time, *our* building, *our* priests.

All religious faiths honor some form of proclamation, from the bold advances of evangelism to the quiet welcoming of interested seekers. But in the biblical formula, building the people of God precedes any other passion. Religious educators, standing on the foundation of biblical authority, serve God by developing people of faith into people of unity, mutuality, and generosity.

THELOGICAL IN DERIVATION

The role of theology, according to Anselm of Canterbury, is to declare, deepen, explain and express the truth of God's word. Serious religious education becomes Anselm's *fides quaerens intellectum*, "faith seeking understanding." In recent years the debate has raged over the relative importance of the noun or the adjective. Do we teach religious education as a subset of the broader field of education which, therefore, affirms its foundation in the social sciences? Or is it primarily defined by its adjective, whether "religious" or "Christian"? I have consistently argued the latter. I see our discipline as the normal affiliate of a theological curriculum, informed and enhanced by the social sciences to be sure, but finding its veracity and vision in theological foundations.

The Nature of Truth

And the more definitive the theology, the more committed the process. Cam Wyckoff once told us that religious education consists in teaching and learning as modes and means of commitment to value, whereas Christian education consists in teaching and learning as modes and means of response to revelation. I find that distinction useful, though I would question the quality of a religious education that focuses on values that have not been formed by theology.

In churches and classrooms, theological educators must have a highly developed biblical awareness, enabling them to integrate Scriptural truth with the realities of contemporary life. For many of us, God's revelation—personal, written, natural—stands as the foundation for a theology of learning. We carry a two-edged sword. With one razor edge we slice through specialized academic disciplines and with the other, sharply apply biblical answers to academic and cultural questions.

Such an integrative process provides clear understanding of the nature, source, discovery, and assimilation of truth. Theological educators affirm that all truth is God's truth, by which they simply mean all genuine truth can ultimately be traced back to God as its source. And since the God of revelation is also the God of creation, the true relationship between natural and special revelation begins in epistemological quiddity.

Yet so much of what passes for theology today takes its cue from sociological pragmatism, ignoring or perverting authoritative biblical sources. The very process of education lends itself to a superficial pragmatism in which many become "methodologists," as though crucial questions about the nature of God, the nature of man, and the relationship between them can be handled with neutrality. When technique becomes the center of educational process we find ourselves handling only the shadows of truth, only occasionally in search of a theology. Modern secularism affords neither lesser nor greater threat to biblical truth than Roman paganism; indeed, the similarities are striking. One needs no obsession with evil spirits to see Satanic footprints all over the path of contemporary culture.

The Nature of Humanity

In education, the significance of anthropology is preceded only by epistemology, and both must be viewed through theological eyes. Whatever one's hermeneutic of the early chapters of Genesis, their significance in understanding human nature can hardly be discounted. In the final and greatest creative act, the one becomes two. We see the birth of the first human community, characterized by harmony with nature and unity with each other, and the two recognize their completeness and interdependence. Sadly, rebellion altered their relationship with God and forced them into disharmony with nature and disunity with each other.

Though different faith communities approach image anthropology from widely varied directions, we can hardly move forward with a philosophy of education until basic theological components yield a sufficient worldview. Some regard creation in God's image as rational and moral capacity, community, or even dominion (Genesis 1:26, 28). Seasoned religious educators avoid speculation in anthropomorphic domains which argue gender and body parts. Instead we refresh our thinking with the theology of the restored image, although, as some have put it, the image of God has not been erased in humanity, but it certainly has been defaced. Humankind retains the capacity to demonstrate God's likeness, to make moral decisions, and to sincerely seek and find truth. Image anthropology acknowledges not only the tarnishing of sin but the restoration of dignity and sanctity of life. Since all persons have the potential to be fully conformed to God's likeness, all human life is valuable. Sin has prevented the world and its people from fulfilling creative ideals, but in redemption God offers dignity to the dishonored and deliverance to the oppressed.

How do we teach restored imagery as a lifestyle? As finite human beings, we cannot ultimately understand God, who is as all powerful, has complete knowledge, and is present in all places at all times. But many other attributes of God do find expression in humanity— sacrificial love, unconditional forgiveness, a justice that knows no favoritism, and a choice of moral and ethical values in line with our religious belief system. From such a combination of epistemology and anthropology, we teach our students to develop a worldview.

FOCUSED IN WORLDVIEW

A striking piece of research appeared just a few years ago. A religious educator at a church-related college discovered that students on that campus seemed to be less principled in moral decision making than their non-Christian counterparts. Just one project to be sure, and quite possibly offset by many contrary studies, but a reminder of the essential holism of religious nurture. It seems to me that crucial decision points—those choices that produce lifelong behavioral effect—are informed by a person's underlying worldview (weltanschauung).

Purpose of Worldview

Worldview comes from long-range thoughts, and is not confined by the need for instantaneous responses. It influences decisions to choose kindness and patience instead of pushing to be first and best. The kind of functioning adults most religious educators want to produce have woven their moral and spiritual lives into a worldview based on ethical and righteous values.

To be sure, core beliefs are anchors, but not all beliefs are core. Religious educators carry the awesome responsibility of helping people develop a worldview that leads to responsible life choices. When built upon the biblical and theological foundations already emphasized, such thinking is distinguished by the integration of natural and special revelation into human learning and experience.

Implications of Worldview

Such a worldview hardly demands uniformity in political, religious, or economic choices. However, it does seem to find itself in conflict with the communal nature of creation, the earliest disavowal of intellectual monasticism. The biblical record of fall and redemption carries at least three major implications for religious educators seeking to build a truly revelational worldview. First, we reject dualism, any separation of the mental, emotional, and spiritual elements of humanity from the physical or corporal parts. Second, we come to some understanding of the image theology discussed above, able to grasp God's revelation and speak with him through prayer and meditation. Third, we grapple with the educational implications of a humanity tarnished by the stain of the fall.

Principles of Worldview

Yet another important dimension of worldview is its holism, the holy unity of biblical living. The Puritans completely rejected a division of life that called some parts of it more sacred, and therefore of higher calling, and some secular, carrying less importance. Our contemporary world needs reacquaintance with the view that every dimension of life is sacred. God's people bring salt and light to the world; they affirm and encourage the dignity of all life, an affirmation that God is interested neither in ethnic nor gender boundaries in his redemptive call, certified by empty cross and empty tomb.

In *The Contemporary Christian*, Anglican cleric John Stott offers good advice when he says, "We must not marginalize God, or try to squeeze Him out of the non-religious section of our lives. We must remember that our vocation (i.e., God's calling) includes these things. It is in these that we are to serve and glorify God." Those who hold special leadership roles do not carry responsibility to do the work of God's people but rather prepare those people to do so. One needs no special applicational magic to see religious educators equipping their students for life tasks far greater than final exams or graduation. Our ultimate purpose finds reality in kingdom living, not academic honors.

Biblical and theological religious educators promote a worldview that rejects contemporary reincarnations of nineteenth-century Unitarian pantheism. The God of creation and revelation, not nature nor humanity, forms the ultimate worship point.

Practice of Worldview

We must also affirm that bibliocentric education extends to all areas of life. It relates to every activity, even in a crassly secular society. A religious education that speaks openly about integrating faith and learning assumes the accompanying responsibility to demonstrate how that philosophical posture takes flesh and spirit in the lives of students at all times and in all places. Learning unrelated to life fares no better than faith without works. Our distinctive worldview centers in a truth we do not create but discover. We experience it formally or informally and, based on our understanding of special revelation, we ascertain with divine assistance precisely how truth fits into life.

The aloneness of the first human brought the creation of the second and we learn early in the ancient text that we were created for community and relationship. As the triune God lives in eternal and loving relationships, so he created us for eternal and loving relationships. Educators who serve in highly visible worlds know how much easier it is to preach patience in public than to practice patience in privacy. Although North American society thrives on individualism, most significant religious ministries function because of relationships. Applied to questions of axiology, the image of God in human community grows and glows as Kingdom people display godly, loving relationships and interdependent team ministries.

Yet the relational implementation of worldview hardly takes place in a vacuum. The leadership of its educators transcends the impact of its placement and politicians in nurturing a kinder and gentler society. The survival of the world hangs tenuously on the rationality of its leaders. Yet we are forced to question the rationality of many of those leaders, and with no small amount of evidence.

As we practice godliness in the secular community, we are often wrongly accused of irrationality. But I feel inclined to argue that religious educators are our best hope for rationality in an irrational age, and the laborious but essential process of blending faith and learning qualifies us to face such a challenge. Sadly, the knowledge explosion appears to have left socially damaging fallout in much of secular education. Its godlessness, often irrationally but passionately proclaimed, threatens the Western educational scene with no less force than Greek idolatry mustered over 2,000 years ago. As much as we talk about cooperation with other disciplines (a posture that I applaud), we surely recognize a form of spiritual warfare that requires us to activate Paul's challenge to "demolish arguments and every pretension that sets itself up against the knowledge of God" (2 Corinthians 10:5).

I am firmly committed to the view that although biblical faith is properly experimental and inescapably subjective, it is anchored in logic and history. In my view, its interpretation of reality is the only one that can be rationally validated, a body of belief that requires the disciplined use of our intelligence and the full employment of our cognitive powers. Serious educators prepare people for honest interaction with persons of different ideologies. Genuine tolerance acknowledges legitimate claims to truth without insisting on acceptance of antisocial and even bizarre behavior. In my view, such tolerance can only be corrupted when people seek to settle an issue by force. The practice of a biblical worldview invites interaction that, in itself, attests freedom and calls all humankind to pursue the quest for truth.

A holistic worldview does not just happen; effective communicators deliberately design it through a theological philosophy that calls us to bring culture and truth into close union without fearing that culture will destroy truth. Such an exercise in intellectual and spiritual development appears to require at least three steps: knowing the Scriptures intimately, studying the culture diligently, and analyzing events and issues theologically.

SPIRITUAL IN VALUES

According to Albert Einstein, "the essential purpose of education is to decide for oneself what is of genuine value in life, and then to find the courage to take one's own thoughts seriously." But in the process of deciding for oneself, a host of voices clamor for attention and, to a greater or lesser extent, influence value choices. The scores of teachers who will read this book represent a major component of that influence. What values do we want religious education to reinforce in children, youth, and adults? What role does biblical axiology play in our view of the workplace? Recreation? Relationship to the poor and oppressed?

Enemies of Spiritual Values
School systems that insist on teaching a value-laden curriculum which ignores the existence of a final meeting outside humanity produce students for whom naturalistic humanism becomes the final answer. Control by a totalitarian state and a misguided globalism that reconstructs national histories only complicates the problem. Add innumerable pornographic sites on the Internet, video games that train children for violence, destructive television programming that defies theistic values, and we reap a spiritually numb culture.

We find ourselves back at the doorway to epistemology. What we used to call "situation ethics" has now been codified as a social law of tolerance. Sociology texts commonly proclaim some form of the eleventh commandment of the postmodern world: "Everything is right somewhere and nothing is right everywhere." The cultural fact of pluralism thus becomes a relativized absolute in a culture that rejects absolutes. Educational systems draw the illegitimate conclusion that, since there is no justifiable way of choosing among the variety of views and values in the world, truth must therefore be merely opinion and goodness whatever draws the majority vote.

We cannot create self-esteem by dumbing down educational standards. We cannot create an awareness of cultural diversity by regarding all lifestyles as equally valid even when they violate biblical standards. We cannot achieve social tolerance by affirming that any behavior is acceptable as long as it makes sense to its advocates. And we cannot produce values clarification by teaching the undulant ichor of contemporary neopantheism.

Foundations of Spiritual Values

To be sure, the word "spiritual" includes a variety of meanings. I use it to describe how religious educators practice their calling as a means of receiving and referring God's transforming grace. Teaching spiritual values means applying truth to life in such an effective way that people in our churches and schools allow the heavenly Parent to produce a devotional lifestyle in their daily tasks.

And let us never concede that spirituality must function under a numinous coat of mysticism. The central issues of spirituality are also the central issues of theology, and spirituality in religious education stems from our epistemological base, as I have argued in earlier paragraphs. Religious educators do not create truth; that is God's domain. But we must approach the challenge with a careful balance between open-mindedness and unchallenged doctrine. Unwarranted dogmatism that offers regimented indoctrination to learners finds no serious place in a distinctly Christian classroom. Teachers and students who wish to develop their minds and spirits in a biblical world and life view must learn to think spiritually about surrounding culture.

The spiritual integration of faith and learning rests on their appropriate relationship. Certainly it never becomes an accomplished ideal but an eternal quest. At best, we point to some position along the journey and trust by God's grace that it will be more advanced than positions at previous points of evaluation. Integrating faith and learning with spirituality falls within the boundaries of that magical word "liturgy"—both worship and service.

COMMUNAL IN RELATIONSHIPS

The latest and best thinking in leadership strongly rejects the imperial mentality that characterizes much of ecclesiastical life. Corporate researchers speak with passion about the decline in trust and respect for professionals and the flattening of hierarchies throughout all human systems. Such attitudes, coupled with the failure of personal responsibility, have forced organizations to turn to a new focus on communal relationships of quality. Writing in the provocative book *The Community of the Future*, Margaret Wheatley and Myron Kellner-Rogers tell us that, "clarity at the core of community about its purpose changes the entire nature of the relationships within that community. This type of community does not ask people to forfeit their freedom as a condition of belonging. It avoids the magnetic pole of proscribing behaviors and beliefs, it avoids becoming doctrinaire and dictatorial, it stays focused on what its members are trying to create together, and diversity flourishes within it. Belonging together is defined by a shared sense of purpose, not by shared beliefs about specific behaviors."

To be sure, in religious education "shared beliefs" hold higher priority, but the communal emphasis is as old as Adam and Eve. We find within the intricate web of intimate relationship the best and most difficult platform from which to reflect the image of God. It is hardly accidental that the New Testament requires relational capability in the family before men and women are qualified to exercise leadership in the wider community of the church.

My son recently finished his doctorate with a dissertation centering on spiritual development on Christian college campuses and discovered that nothing matches faculty influence for the quality of spiritual formation and the development of campus community. On college and seminary campuses, only faculty can actually translate mission and vision into reality. And what faculty do on campuses, other religious educators do in churches, schools, and a host of organizations committed to developing communal relationships based not on models of group therapy but on models of both Testaments, which proclaim the oneness of God's people. Interesting, isn't it, how the culture wars of today stand in such stark contrast to the formula of the early church, a formula that could revitalize any congregation of any size from sickness to health in a matter of weeks:

> Be completely humble and gentle; be patient, bearing with one another
> in love. Make every effort to keep the unity of the Spirit through the
> bond of peace. There is one body and one Spirit—just as you were
> called to one hope when you were called—one Lord, one faith, one
> baptism; one God and Father of all, who is over all and through all and
> in all. (Ephesians 4:2–6)

EXCELLENT IN APPLICATION

Today, as never before, religious educators must strive for excellence, setting the standard rather than just meeting it. In the world of higher education, obsessed with reconstructing history and deconstructing language, many campuses are approaching an intellectual climate of dingy nihilism. In such a social environment Kingdom people not only proclaim truth and values but make every effort to ensure the quality of proclamation.

Excellence is a malleable concept; John Gardner compared it to a Rorschach test. At the human level, it must be viewed comparatively, but religious educators traffic in the ultimate excellence of God. In one genuine sense, the closer one comes to God, the more excellence one achieves. We could very well say of our students and parishioners,

> And this is my prayer: that your love may abound more and more in
> knowledge and depth of insight, so that you may be able to discern
> what is best and may be pure and blameless until the day of Christ,
> filled with the fruit of righteousness that comes through Jesus Christ—
> to the glory and praise of God. (Philippians 1:9–11)

Excellent religious education is described not only by the sophistication of its techniques but by outcomes in the lives of its students. Since God expects only the faithful utilization of what he gives us, the practice of excellence becomes a stewardship of doing the very best we can with the resources he has provided. Learning grounded in faith and truth should produce a constant series of inner renewals made possible by a continuing experience with God through His Word. In many struggling churches and schools, economy is important and even laudable. But economy must give way to efficiency which in turn surrenders to excellence, a satisfactory position on the growth scale commensurate with God's gifts and call at any given point in the life of a person or a ministry.

For religious educators and their students, the motivation of excellence must center in the glory of God. Together we and our students play a symphony of godly living that denies the one-note monotony of which many often accuse us. Through prayer and meditation, we ask God to allow his Spirit to choreograph our lives. But, in the midst of a confused and chaotic society, burdened by the sin of human inadequacies, how can people genuinely glorify God? Both Old and New Testaments offer multiple answers: by loving one another, by fulfilling God's will for our lives, by acknowledging God's presence in all we do. God also condemns our focus on ego, and, in the biblical perspective of excellence, he provides the pattern while spiritual maturity sets the purpose.

COMPREHENSIVE IN SCOPE

Sociologists tell us that life patterns are more enduring than lifestyles. The former develop from values and tend to resist the erosion of time, while the latter flow with the tides of society, particularly variable economics. Perhaps we have not made this distinction carefully enough, erroneously thinking that life patterns and righteous values resist all the changing dynamics of the modern world. But families continue to disintegrate and the most repugnant and obnoxious lifestyles form a moral petechia on public display. Abuse of children, women, and the elderly continues unabated in most societies of the world. Brutality and slavery arising from ethnic or religious causes mark our world at the beginning of the twenty-first century. Surveys show us that the culture considers religion irrelevant but demonstrates an enormous appetite for supernaturalism, though many give nary a fillip whether they choose demon or angels.

To many, religion seems a bad habit, a legacy of less enlightened times that society should outgrow. Our obsession with tolerance has brought with it a tolerance for evil and ugliness unparalleled in Western culture until the modern era. My point centers in the necessity for religious educators to move beyond content and out of the comfortable pockets of our own traditional suits. Like Paul in Athens, we must speak to the marketplace where we find it, in a voice that articulates truth and faith in a language and idiom understandable to the uninitiated.

In the face of communism's collapse and capitalism's confusion, religious educators as the servants of the servants of God proclaim peace in his name and reject the use of human power to dominate and influence the world. Territorial growth or control ought to be odious to a people engaged in building a kingdom not of this world. In my view, the best of religious education in the twenty-first century will call God's people back to a pilgrim mentality, a rejected yet victorious remnant that can live beyond the boundaries of a sin-cursed world. Our new emphasis should be not on denominational distinctives but on a global ecclesiology of the redeemed. This transcultural message for a multicultural world moves forward as we keep one hand tightly grasping the message of God's truth and the other graciously open to those who need to know him and hear his message of redemption. Oppressed by paltry dictatorships of every ideology, we say with the early disciples, "Thy kingdom come."

Holding on to a model of effectiveness in achieving our mission, rather than successes measured by our peers in secular education, can only serve to remind us that we have been historically called by God to spiritual and eternal purposes. We are not a group of negative whiners and victims but a cadre of spiritually minded educators committed to the activity of the mind and the heart. May our teaching produce a harvest of truth and faith.

COMPETENT IN LEADERSHIP

In recent decades we have seen significant professionalization in the field of religious education. Large multistaff churches often include several pastors in charge of various educational programs. I applaud that kind of emphasis and have worked nearly forty years to encourage it. But professionalization does not come without drawbacks. One dilemma facing many churches in the new millennium is the absence of comprehensive oversight and orchestration of educational programs. Specialization has led to a lack of coordination, and the problem seems compounded by the size of a ministry.

But the greater problem of professionalization and specialization rests in a decreasing rather than increasing involvement of lay leadership. The genius of the church in New Testament times and since the Reformation has rested in the involvement of lay leadership. And this is hardly an evangelical Protestant perspective; Nathan Jones clearly sees it in Catholic education. "As the laity assume responsibility for ministry and mission, it is incumbent on the ordained priest, not to suppress the charisma of others out of fear that laity are trying to take over the clergy's necessary place, but to integrate and coordinate them through a *ministry of leadership* . . . ordination presumes ministry, but ministry does not demand ordination."

Somehow religious educators must activate leadership in both lay and professional areas, making cooperative ministry teams possible. The people of God should reject monarchial leadership in favor of the cooperative mutual service of people who have bonded to God and one another. As Robert Greenleaf once put it, "We have mistakenly confused leadership with ego display, covert manipulation, and an overuse of coercive power."

The deficiency arises from our failure to grasp a clear and distinctive biblical model of servant leadership, both modeled and commanded by Jesus. Too many pastors, missionaries, presidents, professors, and educators have bought into an autocratic model of leadership that is old covenant in theology, political in style, and outdated even in the best current secular literature. The fact that it sometimes works does not alter its incontrovertible opposition to biblical truth. In my opinion, more people are hurt in religious vocations by oppressive leadership styles than by inadequate salaries, inferior facilities, or indifferent students.

Meanwhile the melody of shared leadership rings through almost all contemporary secular leadership literature. In *The Community of the Future*, Marshall Goldsmith tells us, "The traditional standards of leadership that may have been acceptable in the past will not lead to success in the future. The leader of the community of the future will face much greater challenges in retaining members. The leader's success in adapting to the new world of the community of choice will be a huge factor in determining the community's success and long-term prosperity."

If we cannot protect and care for people in ministry, we don't deserve positions of leadership. And if we cannot produce caring leaders, we should not call ourselves religious educators. Jesus' description of himself ought to characterize us and all those whom we teach: "Come to me, all you who are weary and burdened, and I will give you rest. Take my yoke upon you and learn of Me, for I am gentle and humble of heart, and you will find rest for your souls. For My yoke is easy and My burden is light" (Matthew 11:28–30).

We light our candles and collectively ask God to let them shine in the darkness. For many, the campus becomes a parish. On the larger scene, however, the components come together with greatest where and when God's people gather for worship and learning—churches, synagogues, temples, and a variety of assembly halls. One could argue that religious education for the future must be congregational in ecclesiology.

Our candles lighting the darkness illumine the appalling ignorance and superficiality found so often among the people we serve. Can we turn back the tide of amusement and entertainment beating against the shores of worship and learning? Can we recapture a spirit of prayer and proclamation and use it to batter the spirit of apathy? As I think of the gathered groups we serve, I am reminded of the words Peter used to describe believers: "living stones, built into a spiritual house to be a holy priesthood and offering spiritual sacrifices acceptable to God. . . . A chosen people, a royal priesthood, a holy nation, a people belonging to God, that you may declare the praise of Him who called you out of darkness into his wonderful light."

The publisher of this book has taken steps to ensure that these chapters do not further divide us. I applaud that goal, and in these paragraphs I have attempted to design what I would consider a revitalization of the broader discipline of religious education while dutifully speaking to my own faith group as well. The task reminds me of Francis Schaeffer's distinction between allies and co-belligerents; some of us may never become the former but should certainly stand together as the latter. Schaeffer's distinction finds practicality in simple words: "The world . . . will very quickly understand the difference of our differences from the world's differences if they see us having our differences in open and observable love on a practical level."

As I bring these paragraphs to a close, I sense the enormity of the task. But that only extends the boundaries of opportunity. The darkness of our culture needs the light we bring. Religious educators working through a biblical worldview will extend themselves to build whole people, not just brains and hands. Like us, the people we serve represent a fallen but forgiven community needing to live out redemption in relationships. Philosophical platitudes do not sustain effective religious education; our task requires the impact of life on life by means of truth on tongue. Modeling, not moralizing, will produce the eternal results for which we all pray, for which our candles burn.

6

Building on the Past

GABRIEL MORAN

Anyone who proposes to make predictions about the future should know something about the recent past. Although anyone can describe how things will be or should be in the new century, the realistic possibility that things will turn out that way is a different matter. The most important question here is what lines of development already exist that suggest a basis on which to build in the future.

This question is especially relevant for religious education, most of whose history was in the twentieth century. What has been built so far is rather fragile and fragmentary. Before there can be vigorous growth in religious education, there is underbrush that still needs to be cleared away. Nevertheless, what has been done by our predecessors deserves the respect of our study, even as we try to better their work.

I begin with a premise that seems to me self-evident: religious education is the meeting place of religion and education. How they should meet can be endlessly debated, but I wish to give equal weight to the two components. Religious education should be neither education's view of religion nor religion's use of education. Instead, religious education should be a genuine confrontation of these two important dimensions of human life. Religion ought to be challenged by its encounter with education. Likewise, the configuration of education ought to be open to fundamental change by the challenge that religion offers.

Because religious education is a synthesis of religion and education, it cannot be any stronger than either of its components. If either education or religion is severely limited, the weakness will be evident in religious education. Conversely, any progress in either the religious or the educational area presents an opportunity for religious education. Thus I propose to look at the two building blocks of religious education to identify recent limitations, and possible progress in each area.

This chapter has four parts: (1) the recent past of religious education, (2) the current religious outlook, (3) educational reform, and (4) the future of religious education.

RELIGIOUS EDUCATION: A CENTURY

During the past few decades I have often said that the Religious Education Association was founded about a century too early. The time is now drawing near when my statement can be confirmed or disproved. That is, the Religious Education Association, which was founded in 1903, has had a tenuous existence right from the start. Whether 2003 will be a good time for a second beginning of that organization depends in part on what has been learned in its twentieth-century experience.

Religious education, of course, is not the same as the Religious Education Association. But that organization, at its origin, represented the great hopes of the people who were responsible for the first widespread use of the term "religious education." (The earliest use of the term I have found was by Unitarians in the 1860s; in the seventeenth century the words "religious" and "education" come together a few times but not as a single term with a specific referent). What was announced at the beginning of the twentieth century was not a new organization but a new *movement* that would bring the forces of education and religion into a dynamic new relation.

As inevitably happens when any group lays claim to a vision that will change the world, the background and assumptions of the founders exercise a greater constraint than they are aware of. Nevertheless, some moments of history are opportune for a breakthrough to new language and new institutional forms. The beginning of the twentieth century was a time of great religious upheaval and grand educational expansion. In 1903, when four hundred religious, educational, political, and business leaders met to found the Religious Education Association, it seemed to the people in attendance that there was evidence of history being on their side. They listened to a keynote address by a young professor named John Dewey on the exciting possibilities of the new field of psychology.

Almost immediately, however, the religious education movement found it impossible to keep all the parties under one organizational umbrella. Among Jews, not surprisingly, all but the most liberal minded distrusted an organization that had Christian trappings and Christian leadership. A bigger blow, from the standpoint of numbers, was the unwillingness of the Roman Catholic Church to participate. Instead, Catholics founded the National Catholic Educational Association and had little to do with the Religious Education Association until the 1960s. Just as important a drawback to a religious education movement was the absence of the conservative wing of U.S. Protestantism. In other words, "religious education" became a name for liberal Protestant education during the first half of the twentieth century.

In the second half of the twentieth century, this meaning of "religious education" became qualified in two ways. First, as liberal Protestant education lost much of its energy and influence, Roman Catholics, who had made some use of the term since the 1930s, began to use the term regularly in the 1960s. Unfortunately, the term most often had a narrow meaning as a synonym for the Confraternity of Christian Doctrine, or parish-based programs, in contrast to Catholic schools.

The second major change was in England, where "religious education" had migrated from the United States through statements at missionary conferences. In the 1940s, political and religious leaders in England (and Wales) made a careful decision to use "religious education" for describing a mandated function of the state school. Archbishop William Temple was the individual most responsible for the term's adoption at the end of World War II. He thought "religious education" was appropriate for a combination of the school's Christian worship and a study of religion that would not be limited to Church of England concerns.

The aims of the religious education movement in 1903 still strike me as worth pursuing or at least discussing: (1) a cooperation among Catholic, Protestant and Jewish educators (2) a bridging of the gap between the state school and the religiously affiliated school and (3) the professionalizing of instructional efforts in church and synagogue; that is, if some people need special training for academic instruction, they should be adequately prepared and appropriately compensated for their work

Any new formulations of these three aims must examine the limitations in the statement and the execution of those earlier aims. Unforseen events can cripple the best laid plans. For example, the economic depression of the 1930s had a profound effect on the aim of professionalizing religious education. By that time all three of the association's aims were encountering trouble. Twenty-five years ago, in *Interplay: A Theory of Religion and Education,* I compared the Religious Education Association to the U.N. flag, which has little force except the hope of future cooperation; the comparison seems to me even more appropriate today. Like the United Nations, the Religious Education Association needs probing as to why it is so severely limited in its ability to achieve its lofty aims.

The developments noted above in the Roman Catholic Church and in England and Wales are at the least symptomatic of the weakness of the religious education movement in the twentieth century. The Catholic Church took over the term "religious education" with such enthusiasm that Catholics often sound as if they own the term. "Religious education," instead of being a venture to which Catholics contribute becomes the name of one element within the Catholic Church's education. The logic may make little sense, but the reality of numbers can override logic. For some of its international conferences the Religious Education Association has had barely two hundred participants. Compare that to the Catholic Diocese of Los Angeles, which has an annual "religious education congress" with over twenty thousand participants. My point is that convincing anyone about what should be done in religious education is inescapably tied to how many people use the term. If religious education is ever to flourish, its meaning cannot be separated from the existing work and loyalties of large numbers of people.

The British experience of "religious education" during the last sixty years is not something that the United States is likely to imitate. But it is an approach that needs to be studied and understood by those of us in the United States. If there is a desire to professionalize religious education, there are lessons to be learned from the British experience. The difference between the United States and England on this point is profound. Whatever "religious education" means in the United States, it is *not* a subject taught in state schools. This difference can be a problem in communication and understanding. Nevertheless, a conversation about the difference can be a helpful reminder that one country or religious body cannot dictate the meaning of "religious education."

RELIGIOUS RESOURCES

Religion as a human phenomenon is probably as old as the human race. Religion in the plural—religions as a set of institutions—has been with us only since the sixteenth century. For the Greeks and Romans, for Augustine and Aquinas and Calvin, there was true religion and false religion or, more simply, there was religion and superstition. Thomas Aquinas, for example, could take over Cicero's definition of religion as "true service to God," a part of the virtue of justice. The idea that there are many "world religions" was unthinkable.

The plural "religions" was first used in German and then in English in the second half of the sixteenth century to refer to the many "Christian religions." That usage was replaced in the seventeenth century by the categories of natural religion and revealed religions. In modern times, historians, philosophers, anthropologists, and sociologists have presumed it a simple fact that there are institutions called "religions." The people in these groups regularly rebel against being thrown into this generic classification. A Jew will say that being Jewish is not a religion; being Jewish is a way of life. A similar sentiment is expressed by Buddhists, Muslims, and Hindus. The "religionless Christianity" of the 1960s was only one striking example of what has regularly occurred in modern Christianity: the contrast between the Christian faith and the religions of the world.

This protest is understandable. People do not like to think that their own deepest beliefs and practices are merely a subset of a category created by modern scholars: "Other people may have religion but God chose us and we are obeying God's commands." Thus the Jew does not live in a world of Judaism and other religions but in a world of Torah/Halakhah, which stands in contrast to religions. The Christian says that "Christ is unique"; therefore, faith in our Lord and Savior Jesus Christ is set in contrast to mere religion.

Scholars outside these groups become impatient with this protest; they think that the Christian, Jew, Muslim, or Buddhist should stop resisting and should accept what is obvious: Christianity, Judaism,

Islam, Buddhism, and the rest are religions. But this obvious solution is only half a solution. There are times when it is acceptable and even advantageous for the Jew, Christian, Buddhist, or Muslim to work within the idea of religion. Being able to have a conversation under a common rubric can reduce misunderstandings and conflicts. There might even be positive understanding and insight arising from comparison.

The danger for the world lies in the half of the problem for which this is no solution at all. Only persons who actually practice a religious way of life-accepting the beliefs, moral code, and rituals of a tradition-will grasp that being a Christian, Jew, Buddhist, or Muslim is not experienced as "having a religion." Thus an education in being religious will have a different character from the modern study of religion.

Two different problems are entangled here. The first is that the secular-minded person needs to respect the religious experience even if he or she does not share in it. The second is that people in one religious group have to respect the fact that other people can have a comparable though contrasting experience of their own. In the first case, an educator has to realize that "religion" is a helpful but not a comprehensive basis for understanding the lives of Jew, Christian, Buddhist, or Muslim. In the second case, an educator has to realize that, while formation into the practices of one religious way of life is educational, the educator can no longer speak and act as if there were not a plurality of religions.

The vitality of the religious and religion at the beginning of this new millennium would astound the intellectual leaders of the early twentieth century. They assumed that the force of religion was spent or at least that it was being rationalized. That is, religion would now be explained in the same way as is politics, economics, or geology. Christianity, which had laid claim to being the most advanced religion, seemed to be fighting a rear-guard action to preserve some of its general philosophy and rational code of conduct. The term "Judeo-Christian" was coined in the United States in the 1890s to refer to these general principles. Since there is no Judeo-Christian religion, the discussion of "the Judeo-Christian tradition" was a convenient ploy for seeming to take account of religion while not having to contend with its practice.

The liberal wing of Protestantism continued to speak confidently at the turn of the twentieth century but the difference between modern science and liberal Christianity was becoming indistinct. In both Europe and the United States, Christian scholars attached their hopes to a modern theory of progress, helped by advances in the sciences, including an evolutionary theory of biology. The world was becoming more enlightened, and a "Christian revelation" was thought to be a culmination of "natural religion."

A contrasting approach to modernity was taken by Protestant Christians who came to be known in 1920 as the "fundamentalists." They were intent on defending the Bible's authority against the undermining effects of archeology, history, and biology. This Christian movement flourished in the first quarter of the century, especially after World War I. The fundamentalists' patriotic fervor and their suspicion of German intellectuals put them in good standing. Flush with success, they decided to have a showdown with the "progressive education" of the 1920s. The chosen site was Dayton, Tennessee, where a biology teacher named John Scopes was charged with teaching evolution. He was convicted of the crime (a judgment later overturned), but fundamentalism suffered a humiliating defeat at the hands of the news media.

I would vote for the Scopes trial as the most important moment in the twentieth-century religious history of the United States. "Almost everything about the Scopes trial has been misrepresented," wrote Garry Wills, "and it is the 'educated' part of America that accepted the distortion." Seventy-five years later, the religious picture of the United States still depends upon stereotypes created at that trial. Fundamentalists went underground or, more exactly, they disappeared from national politics and the national news media. Then in the 1970s, they reappeared. During the 1976 presidential campaign, *Newsweek, Time,* and the television networks reported on "evangelical" or "born again" Christians as if they were a strange new tribe that had just been discovered somewhere in the South Pacific.

During the past twenty-five years, the religious and the religions have been a force to be reckoned with by politicians and the news media. Religious stereotypes surround all religion but particularly the evangelical voice. On some issues, especially abortion, evangelical Protestants have joined forces with their traditional opponents, Roman Catholics. The news media are relentless in their disparaging of any conservative voice in religion. Stereotypes are, of course, an exaggeration of something that is real. In this case, conservative Protestantism suffered fifty years of isolation from the educational mainstream. Much of the resurgence of religion is resistant to education, except on its own narrow terms. This situation is not a healthy one either for religion or education.

While Protestant Christianity was rising from the South, other religious groups were also showing that they were far from moribund. The Roman Catholic Church, which many people had dismissed as intellectually stagnant, made remarkable changes in the 1960s. The Second Vatican Council (1961–1965) was, among other things, a coming of age for the Roman Catholic Church in the United States, both in its intellectual contribution to the worldwide church and in its being accepted within the political structure of the United States. The Vatican, since its condemnation of "Americanism" at the turn of the twentieth century, has been concerned with the emergence of a distinctive Catholicism in the United States. The reverberations from the Second Vatican Council, both in the United States and around the world, have probably only begun.

In the United States, the 60 million members of the Roman Catholic Church now hold considerable power in a country that once feared Catholic immigrants as superstitious subversives. Things have changed so rapidly that Catholics have not had time to think out their new place in the country's religious and educational arrangements. Because of its unyielding stand on abortion, the Catholic Church is regularly portrayed as mindless and reactionary. But for many Catholics there is a consistency in opposing all death-dealing politics, including capital punishment, war, and euthanasia. The concern for vulnerable life extends to the government's policy toward the poor and oppressed. As social welfare was being subjected to devastating cuts, the U.S. Catholic Conference was the most powerful and determined voice of opposition. The growth of the Catholic Church in the United States and its thoughtful stands on some social issues constitute a story that is inadequately reported in the news media.

Probably the most significant religious story in the last third of the twentieth century was the rise of Islam. The Muslim resurgence is a worldwide phenomenon that has only slowly become visible within the United States. However, the U.S. government has been forced to recognize the new strength of Islam in international clashes. Similar to fundamentalism in the United States, Islam had never disappeared but it had dropped from the awareness of New York and Washington. The United States had assumed that the shadow of Islam was being rapidly overcome by the blessings of Western enlightenment. That assumption began to be challenged by Muammar Gadhafi's revolution in Libya during the late 1960s. The changing perception in the United States reached near hysteria during the Iranian revolution of 1979–1980.

During the hostage standoff with Iran, the saying around Washington was that everyone in the government was speedreading the Qur'an. United States officials suddenly realized that they had no idea what moved the world's half billion Muslims. The inroads that Muslims had made in the United States, especially among African Americans, had passed unnoticed or had been dismissed as a racial cult. Very slowly throughout the 1980s and 1990s the United States has had to come to grips with the fact that Islam is one of the world's great religions. Like the other religions, it can be a great force for good or it can be dangerous.

There is still an appalling ignorance in the United States concerning Islam. Hollywood's treatment of it, which has never been good, has gotten worse since the disappearance of the Soviet Union as chief supplier of movie villains. I meet college professors who do not know the difference between Arabs and Muslims (They are surprised to hear that most Muslims are not Arabs or that most Arab Americans are Christian.) The entrance of Muslims into Jewish-Christian dialogue is a benefit to the understanding of all three religions. Securing a place for Islam in the public life of the United States is one of the great challenges of the new century. I look forward optimistically to that development.

EDUCATIONAL REFORM

Education, like religion, is as old as the human race. Education in the specialized form of school has existed since the spread of literacy. In ancient times, the teaching of "letters" was provided only for a select few people. Jewish and Christian religions gave impetus to the spread of book learning. The Talmud says, "When man is led for judgment he is asked: Did you fix time for learning?" The Christian Scripture was a key element in the invention of the codex, or book. The church called its collection of writings "the book," or Bible. Nonetheless, until modern times most of the Christian population had little schooling. Education occurred in the family, the church liturgy, and apprenticeship for work.

The worldwide emphasis on education in school is a story of the nineteenth and twentieth centuries. The movement for universal ("free and compulsory") education was for the most part an admirable and welcome development. Even the poorest child now had some access to the tools of literacy. However, it did skew the meaning of education in two ways: (1) education became identified with a single age group, namely, children between the ages of about six and sixteen and (2) education became identified with a single form of teaching, namely, instruction in the classroom.

At the turn of the twentieth century, schools had been given a messianic mission. John Dewey in 1897 concluded his "Pedagogic Creed" by saying that "the [school]teacher is the true prophet who ushers in the kingdom of God." Believing that the school was "infinitely religious," Dewey echoed the widespread belief that the school was going to replace the church. Many people seriously believed that crime would be "virtually abolished" by the school.

In 1893 Terrence Powderly predicted that "the citizens would become so educated and refined that the confinement and punishment of criminals will occupy but little of the thought and time of the men of 1993." Edward Ross, in his influential 1901 book, *Social Control*, wrote: "Underneath the medley of systems we find an almost worldwide drift from religion toward education as the method of indirect social restraint." Aassuming that education is a replacement for religion makes religious education simply inconceivable.

What was at first called the "common school" eventually took over the term "public education." Schools for instructing children in their letters were given the task of forming the public life of the nation. Horace Mann, the chief architect of the system, presumed the modern distinction between two kinds of religion: a natural religion, which was a generalized Christianity, and revealed religion, a sectarian addition to the pure religion of nature. The common schools, in Mann's words, "were to teach the one, indivisible, all glorious system of Christianity." At the same time, the schools were to avoid "the discordant sounds of religious debate."

During the late nineteenth century Jews put up with this generalized Christianity in the schools. They made good use of free academic

instruction while they supplied a Jewish education in home and synagogue. Roman Catholics opted to pour their limited resources into
building an enormous school system. This system of parochial and
diocesan schools was, and still is, called "Catholic education." That
fact is indicative of how much the Catholic Church was caught up in
imitating "public education" even while fighting it. The church found
itself competing financially and academically with "public education,"
instead of being able to have a catholic education that would include
instruction in the practice of Catholic Christianity, combined with participation in the tax supported education of the public.

Horace Mann's deadening language of natural and revealed religion
set the direction of state supported schools for more than a century. In
the 1960s, the U.S. Supreme Court removed much of generic Christianity, including Bible reading and mandated prayers. However, the
Court's attempt to encourage the schools to deal appropriately with re-
ligion-that is, for teachers to teach it and students to study it-was
mired in convoluted language. The Supreme Court, like the rest of the
country, had no ready-made language to describe how the schools
should deal with religion. Terms and phrases such as "religious education," "religious instruction," and "teaching religion" were assumed to
be beyond retrieval for describing the proper work of a public school.

Artificially contrived phrases were employed that guaranteed there
would be no serious challenge to the curriculum of a public school.
For example, the Supreme Court borrowed a distinction from the
1940s between "teach religion" and "teach about religion." An educational discussion might have ensued about how these two aspects of
teaching relate to a single process. Instead, their separation became an
unchallengeable dogma. "Teaching about religion" was declared to be
the only category for discussion. Not surprisingly, the idea has never
attracted many people. In 1987 the Association for Supervision and
Curriculum Development issued a report entitled *Religion in the Curriculum*. The document assumes without any discussion that "religious
education" and "teaching religion" in the public school are unconstitu-
tional. The document's proposal to put religion into the curriculum
can never be effected so long as "teaching religion" and "religious education" cannot be uttered in the school.

As the twentieth century wore on, the messianic expectations for
the common school became muted. But all the hopes having been
placed on the common school, there was no other way to discuss

"public education." The entire burden of educating the public had been placed on the shoulders of teachers in the tax-supported elementary and secondary schools. John Dewey, as noted above, was one of the early apostles of the common school as redemptive. Dewey, in surveying the recent past from the vantage of 1900, saw the collapse of the home, the church and apprenticeship as educationally effective forms. Only the school offered redemption. But in 1937, the seventy-eight-year-old Dewey concluded, "It is unrealistic, in my opinion, to suppose that the schools can be a *main* agency in producing the intellectual and moral changes which are necessary for the creation of a new social order."

In the first two decades after World War II, the United States continued and even accelerated its commitment to state schools. Four years of college was increasingly assumed to be the normal pattern. In the 1930s, one out of every ten students went to college. By the end of the century, six out of ten students did so; and the president of the United States was calling for ten out of ten. But in the 1950s the seemingly solid system began to show cracks. The GI Bill, which brought millions of older men into the child-oriented schools, had effects that no one had foreseen. The feminist movement, which had been put on hold during the 1940s and 1950s, exploded with new life in the 1960s. Issues of age, race, and gender emerged, along with changes in transportation, communication, and the environment. At century's end, the country was still trying to come to grips with all these developments.

The actual workings of education have been in a drastic shift since the 1960s, even though most of our educational language is still stuck in the late nineteenth century. I suspect that in the future the period 1860–1960 will be seen as an aberration in the history of education, that is, the era when instructing children in schools was equated not only with education but with public education. Even more strange, it was the time when these schools for children were thought to be a replacement for religion (or a replacement religion). It is not a disparaging of these schools to say that schools are not designed to do the work of religion and that schools for children can never be the sole instrument of a public education.

At the turn of the twentieth century, there were already voices warning against placing an insupportable burden on schools for children. The "adult education movement" had begun with a vision of

what education for the whole community might mean. The leaders of
this movement predicted that by the end of the twentieth century
schools for children would have been absorbed into community learning centers. These visionaries of 1900 would be disappointed at the
subsequent narrowing vision of "adult education." The movement
failed to change the language of 1900, which is still with us for the
beginning of a new century. The adjective "adult" has acquired various synonyms (such as "continuing" or "lifelong") to be put before
"education." But every library, college catalogue, and political agenda
contrasts adult education with (real) education, that is, schools for
children. Many worthwhile experiments and reforms in education
have been undertaken, but they are weighed down by inadequate educational language. The exclusion of religious education from lifelong
and lifewide education of the public is one of the serious inadequacies
of educational language.

RELIGIOUS EDUCATION: POSSIBILITIES

This final section is not a prediction of what religious education will
be in the new century. Instead, I have tried to find developments in
twentieth-century religion and education that suggest what might happen. My interest is to state what realistically could be, and in my judgment should be, the meaning and practice of religious education.

   A religious education movement has a better chance of succeeding
in this coming century than it had in the century just ended. The messianic hopes of what Emile Durkheim in 1900 called "a purely rationalistic education" have dimmed. At the same time, religion, much to
the surprise of its expectant undertakers, shows no signs of dying. The
secular world may now be ready to engage religion if only for the sake
of trying to get peace. Most of the wars in recent decades have involved religion, but religion can also be a great moral force. The nineteenth century wanted to keep the Christian moral message while getting rid of Christian beliefs and rituals. There is perhaps a better
realization today that the integrity of the religious community has to
be respected if the religion is to contribute to the public good. From
the religious side a serious engagement with the best of education is to
be hoped for.

   In summarizing the following material, I will use the four characteristics of religious education that I wrote about in *Religious*

Education as a Second Language. Religious education is (1) international, (2) interreligious, (3) inter-institutional, and (4) intergenerational.

In each of these four cases, the need is not simply for diversity but for interaction among the diverse elements. The most fundamental diversity and interaction is within the aims of religious education itself. As the discussion of religion suggested, education has to include both the understanding of religion and the practice of a religious way of life. The distinction between these two aims, as well as their interaction, should find expression in each of the following characteristics.

International

In the second half of the twentieth century, a global interaction truly began. The jet plane, the television, the computer, and other recent inventions have brought nations into closer proximity. The results, so far, have been mixed. There is a "new order," but its shape and authority are not yet clear. The nation-state is quite possibly withering away but national characteristics, especially language, will be here for decades, if not centuries.

Religious education is always practiced locally, but its context will be increasingly international. Speaking with someone from a different nation or culture about religious education is always difficult, exciting, and surprising. How to translate "religious education" into German, Russian, Hebrew, Japanese, or Arabic must be addressed before we can converse on a common topic.

Even within the English language, the term can have quite different meanings. I noted in the first section that England adopted the term "religious education" in the 1940s to cover worship and instruction in the schools. In recent decades, the term has usually been the name of the curriculum subject. This meaning of religious education can be found in Canada (including Quebec), Australia, New Zealand, Ireland, South Africa, Zimbabwe, the Netherlands, Scandinavia, and other places. We may think that other countries are strange, but it is the United States that stands out as different. The peculiar configuration of religion and education in the United States has its strengths and weaknesses. International conversation is difficult, but we in the United States need to be reminded that "religious education" cannot be pursued under the exclusive auspices of church and synagogue.

When the Religious Education Association was founded, it immediately declared itself to be "international," that is, it included Canada and the United States. That was a tiny step but to its credit the organization has taken its Canadian-U.S. partnership seriously. The same cannot be said about many U.S. organizations. They are not oblivious of other nations, but they expect them to join in ventures on U.S. terms. Since 1989 this problem has in some ways gotten worse, but the U.S. dominance is likely to be very temporary. Big international conferences on religious education would be premature, but exchanges by individuals and groups can and do go on.

Interreligious

A religious education involves dialogue about religion itself. Countries throughout the world are now confronting a plurality of religions within their borders. An increase of diversity is almost certain to continue. The United States often claims to be the world's leader and model in accepting religious diversity. And, in fact, the U.S. Constitution tolerates some religious groups. One of the glories of U.S. history is the political freedom that the United States has provided for the Jews. (Among other immigrant groups, about half of the people who came here went back home; nearly all the Jews stayed.)

The United States, like the rest of the world, still has a long way to go in accepting and understanding religious diversity. Protestants, Roman Catholics, and Jews have been able to reach a living arrangement in the United States. The religious idea of "America," with its origin in biblical imagery, can embrace Christians and Jews. Nearly 90 percent of the population calls itself "Christian." For those of us who are Christians, that statistic may be wonderfully encouraging. For much of the world, however, the United States is overbearingly Christian, especially in its missionary outreach and its messianic zeal, which often seem determined to make the world "American."

The Christian forms of religious education need to be practiced within a greater religious diversity than generally exists in the United States. Of course, we all start wherever we are. Most of us will not experience a Christian education within a Buddhist or Muslim culture. Nevertheless, we can become increasingly aware that the human race is entering a novel period in which our own religion is understood and practiced in a continuously closer relation to other religious peoples, whose religions we have to respect and try to understand.

The main point here is not that everyone should become an expert in Shinto, Sikhism, and Hinduism. The first need is to understand and to practice one's own religion. But the diversity of religion and the task of interreligious education includes one's own religious commitment. "Christian" can refer both to the practice of a religious way and to a religion. Sometimes Christians (Jew, Muslims, and so forth) think they can escape "having a religion" by being anti-institutional or non-institutional. However, one cannot divest oneself of what the modern world calls "a religion." Religious education has to offer the opportunity to understand that religion as a step toward reforming its institutional aspects.

Being religious is similar to speaking a language. A person can speak a language without studying any of its rules. The best way to learn the rules of one's own language is to study another language. At the university where I teach, a professor of Islam told me that his classes were filled with Jewish students who wished to understand Judaism. Strange as that may seem, it makes sense; Judaism and Islam are structurally very similar as religions. If we already speak a language, then learning its rules can improve our speaking. But before one acquires the ability to speak a language, learning rules can actually interfere with speaking, as most adults find out when they try learning to speak another language. Eventually these two processes should help each other: speaking a language and understanding language. Similarly, practicing a religious way of life and understanding religion (one's own in comparison to others) are distinct activities that can interfere with each other. Eventually, these two aims of religious education can reinforce each other.

The emergence of Islam as a full participant in religious dialogue within the United States should be a very helpful contribution to the interreligious character of religious education. There are already more Muslims than Jews in the United States although no one could guess that from public policy and discussion. Islam will change the dynamics of existing Jewish-Christian exchanges that tend to run along set paths. Islam is the first serious challenge to the biblical assumptions that have shaped the colonial and national periods of U.S. history. Like Protestant fundamentalism, Islam does not bow down to modern enlightenment. Unlike fundamentalism, which absorbed seventeenth-

century science, Islam has a very different history, which includes a
rich medieval heritage of science, medicine and art. The practice of
Islam challenges many of the assumptions that Christians and Jews
bring to the understanding of religion.

Interinstitutional

All education requires cooperation between institutions. The two
aims of religious education highlight a contrast within education itself. The simplest way to align the aims of education with institutions
is to say that the community teaches the individual to practice a way
of life; in contrast, a school, with its classroom instruction, teaches
the individual to understand academic subjects. Thus, in religious education the community or congregation would teach the practice of a
religious way of life; the school would teach the understanding of religion. However, in today's world the picture is more complex on
both sides.

Community practice includes formation in the home, the experience of leisure activities, and the practice of liturgy. Especially within
the last of these components there can be an academic element. The
Catholic Church calls this kind of teaching "catechizing," an ancient
name for a needed practice. While the retrieving of this element since
the 1960s has been advantageous, catechizing is often equated with
the whole of religious education. A proper situating of catechetical instruction within the liturgy is indispensable for the internal life of the
Catholic Church and its relation to other institutions.

On the other side of the community/school divide, a "school" can
mean diverse things. In the United States, we describe a person at-
tending university as going to school (people in other countries find
this language amusing). But then we also use "school" as a main division of the university. We use "school" for almost any kind of trade or
occupational training. We also use it to refer to a group of scholars in
any field who think alike. "School" is of course used for primary and
secondary units of our educational system. When we are not referring
simply to the buildings, we probably assume that "school" means a set
of experiences similar to whatever was our own early experience. At
the turn of the twentieth century, "school" generally meant a room
with students and a teacher. Today the classroom still exists, although
it is often overlaid with a lot of technology. But the school is likely to
include sports, arts and work experience. Thus, to talk about school as

part of education is ambiguous. The secular schools that young people attend today usually include a community formation with its own "liturgical" experience.

The institutional configuration of religious education is therefore varied and somewhat confusing. Schools not only teach young people to understand academic matters. Schools also shape the lives of young people. Schools are not only for children and adolescents (with post-adolescents included if school is assumed to include college). School, at least the instructional aspect of school, should be available for children who are still sometimes classified as being of "preschool" age. At the other end of the age spectrum, a class or a course of study can bring excitement to an urban community center or a nursing home. Some of the best students I have ever had in the classroom were in their seventies or eighties. But school, even the most complex suburban system, cannot be asked to do the whole job of education.

Despite the great variety of people's lives, there are some educational institutions that affect nearly everyone. I noted earlier John Dewey's dismissal of home, church, and work as educational agencies; Dewey's view was a disastrous misreading of history. The family, for better and worse, remains the most formative educator. Church, synagogue, and mosque have to pay more than the standard lip service to the parent as educator.

Preparation for a job and work experience itself are as important as ever for education. Many bored young people are in high school and college classrooms because they do not have a good alternative. The United States needs to invest in apprenticeship programs that are not just for students who are assumed to be lacking in academic skills. Preparation for one's life's work involves a combination of classroom teaching and teaching on the work site. Volunteering to work with people who are in need can be one of the most effective forms of religious education. For young people, this kind of work is often coordinated by the school.

The church remains a powerful educational influence for its own members and beyond. Judged by the numbers who participate in voluntary organizations within the United States, the church leaves every competitor in the dust. How well a particular congregation educates has often depended on one person. In the Catholic Church the priest is often unprepared to carry out educational work. A revolution in the making is reflected in the following statistics: while the number of men preparing to become priests has been in steep decline, the number of people in theological schools preparing for nonordained ministries rose from 10,000 in 1985 to 30,000 in 1998. Within the next decade or two this revolution will become apparent. The educational possibilities of parish education will be transformed. The result is unpredictable, but a great range of creativity will certainly be unleashed.

Some classroom instruction in religion would be helpful for everyone. Catholic schools could receive a bonanza of support from the widespread adoption of vouchers, a movement that is now having an impact. Catholics, as well as other religious groups, have to be concerned that their good fortune is not at the expense of children and parents who are stuck with a worse public system. Perhaps for the first time since the 1840s, the country has to rethink what a "public school" should mean. I am not sanguine about politicians getting beyond their standard pieties on education or the vested interests in our current schools being willing to entertain system shaking change. Nevertheless, the pressure is coming from many quarters: charter schools and vouchers, television and computers, changes in family structure, work, religion, race, and gender.

In the past, people interested in developing religious education may have been unmindful of "public education" as part of the puzzle. But an adequate religious education in the future cannot neglect what "public education" means. It should include the civic, artistic, and welfare aspects of community life, as well as religious concerns. City and state governments have no business trying to provide a religious formation, but neither should they be doing things that are antagonistic to religious practice. Tax-supported schools for young people, which contribute to but are not equivalent to public education, should include courses in religion. A public school with religion in its curriculum is the more public by that fact.

Intergenerational

The last characteristic, which refers to interaction across the age divisions, overlaps the interinstitutional pattern. Depending on age, a person tends to be assigned to one institution: the home in infancy, the school in youth, the workplace in adulthood. Associating an age bracket with an institution may be inevitable, but no group should be encapsulated in one institution and segregated from people older and younger. A child may best be at home but it needs interaction with grandparents, as well as with parents and siblings. A young person, whose major commitment is to schoolwork, still needs interaction with infants and grandparents, perhaps through doing volunteer work. A person retired from a job can be an invaluable asset for infants and parents at home, for teenagers in school and for young adults at their jobs.

The key word here is "interaction". Education in churches often duplicates the age segregation of society. Thus there may be preschool workers, Bible school teachers, youth ministers, and adult educators. Interaction across the generations does happen within these categories. A Sunday school teacher who listens to students and learns from teaching is engaged in intergenerational education. Nonetheless, job descriptions and budget lines can be a major restraint on learning across generations. Whether or not job titles are changed, there has to be regular attention to ways of crossing the age divisions instead of just just settling into them.

Interaction across the generations is important for all education but preeminently for religious education. The first great moment of religious education is being born; the final one is dying. We start to learn a religious way of living at the moment of birth. As infants and small children, we learn from all the generations before us. When we go to school, we should be able to learn to understand religion and very probably we will eventually learn to rebel against religion. We need academic teachers to help us understand religion. And as we rebel against religion, we need the example and testimony (probably at a distance) of an older population that remains faithful to religious practice. When young adults become parents, they find themselves in "inter-generational dialogue," that is, talking with their children. What they often need is dialogue with their own parents. These older parents can be of special help with infants and teenagers when society's superficial barriers are broken through.

It might seem unnecessary or even unwise to name as "religious education" all the different aspects of education that I have described. It certainly is not necessary to be always intruding the term "religious education." Nonetheless, those of us who teach courses in religion need to recognize that it is a complex field of study that has to be set in cooperative relation to the study of history, art, and science. In addition, the teaching of religion ultimately has a relation to the actual practice of a religious way of life. Those of us whose work is shaping the life of a Christian, Jewish, or Muslim congregation cannot neglect the community's relation to issues of economic justice, aesthetic life, and environmental concerns. The congregation cannot cope with such issues without help from a study of religion.

7

A Black Christian Pedagogy of Hope: Religious Education in Black Perspective

ANNE E. STREATY WIMBERLY

I leave you hope . . . I leave you love. . . I leave you racial dignity.

> From the last will and testament
> of Mary McLeod Bethune

BACKGROUND

Hope has historically been the energizing core of black Christian faith and life and a necessary central theme of religious educational endeavors. Yet, much has happened throughout the years of black people's sojourn in the United States that demands our critical consideration of the theme of hope and its potential as a religious educational emphasis in the third millennium. An important aspect of this criticality is the recall of uses of the theme along black people's journey as a basis for my proposal of a black Christian pedagogy of hope for this new era.

Two basic assumptions underlie my insistence on recalling black people's past religious educational emphasis on hope and on my proposing hope as a central theme in the third millennium black church, albeit it from a revisionist perspective. First, hope has been and must continue to create transforming experience and action in black life. Second, in order for black Christians to continue to grasp the meaning and power of hope in action for our lives, religious education must focus on hope and must draw from experiences of hope-building in the past and on present life.

The Hope Agenda in the Black Exodus Event

The exodus of black people from slavery in 1865 affirmed the faithfulness and promises of God about which black forebears taught throughout their experience of bondage. Yet the imagined "promised land" into which black people entered called forth a challenge to ongoing hopefulness. In the Reconstruction years following slavery and into the twentieth century, black people struggled profoundly with the realities of oppression. And, amid emerging and interconnected difficulties of black people's public, communal, and personal lives, black churches were challenged to create a responsive religious educational agenda. Such an agenda became directed toward reaffirming God's faithfulness and toward helping black people develop new approaches to hope in action that could address their existential situation. This agenda was implemented most powerfully in congregational worship in which the language and symbols of hope came forth in ritual, sermon, music, prayers, and testimonies. Moreover, planned educational and social outreach programs, as well as home and school religious teaching, contributed to a comprehensive pedagogy of hope, although it was never identified as such.

The Hope Agenda in and after the
Black Freedom Movement

The black freedom movement of the 1950s and 1960s became a capstone era of hope in action that was carried out by an unlabeled pedagogy of hope. The movement centered on teaching black youth and adults God's value of their humanness, tools of nonviolent resistance to human degradation, and skills of political involvement to assure a hopeful future. The hopeful future was encapsulated in the publically articulated dream of a beloved community in which all God's people would dwell in a land of peace, justice, and safety.

But with this movement's abrupt end, a new set of challenges emerged as black people grieved the loss of the prophetic leadership of the movement's leader, Martin Luther King Jr. Black faith communities faced the pedagogical question: What do we now teach about hope, nonviolence, and justice? Moreover, another challenge was posed by the entrenchment of larger society in competitive, materialistic, and individualistic values into which black people also became enculturated. The pressure to compete, the desire for material gain, and heightened emphasis on self-interest and self-gratification became black people's alternative way of being in the world, in contrast to the historical black communal ethic by which cultural issues were addressed.

On top of emerging values, a deepening societal bent toward violence emerged that tended to beget violence in myriad forms. Violence also began to explode in pockets within the black community. In the waning decades of the twentieth century, a sense of powerlessness began to creep in, and serious questions began to be raised about the ability of the black church in general and existing religious education paradigms in specific to reverse the troubling trends.

In "An African-American Pathway to Hope: Belief Formation through Uses of Narrative in Christian Education," which appears in the summer 1996 issue of *Religious Education*, I identified a pervasive hopelessness that currently exists in the black community, particularly among our youth and the poor. Hopelessness is couched in persons' despair at being unable to imagine a positive and realizable future that differs from the present. In their important book, *The Black Church in the African American Experience*, C. Eric Lincoln and Lawrence Mamiya contend that the hopelessness of black people stems from continuing fractures of life in an era of depleted humanitarian concern.

Vincent Harding's masterful work, *Hope and History: Why We Must Share the Story of the Movement*, also refers to an explosive hopelessness that is fueled by unrealized notions of material success and other expressions of American values and the American dream. Black young people follow the lives of millionaire athletes and popular entertainers, build fantasies of life on these heroes, and shape understandings of life from lyrics of rap and pop music. Many succumb too easily to destructive self-hatred or violent, damaging life options in order to live out their fantasies, not realizing that they have embraced a false and distorted hope. At the same time, many black youth and adults alike continue to set goals, move into situations of accomplishment, and show through their lives racial pride and progress.

Yet, even amid this positive frame, we grieve unseen progress, set-backs revealed by racial epithets that are hurled at black people, inci-dents of unfair treatment and brutality directed at black individuals, and other difficulties in the lives of black people across the various ages/stages. Hopelessness is being fueled by a pervasive sense that black people are powerless to arrive at a positive and lasting existence within larger society and within the black community. The cry re-sounds within the troubled existence: What dare we hope for? Is there no balm in Gilead?

Hopelessness is a profound challenge to us all in the new millen-nium. There is an urgent role for black churches to mirror Richard Wright's poetic description that appears in *112 Million Black Voices:* the church must be the place "where we dip our tired bodies in cool springs of hope." This role is not a new one; but it must become a *re-newed* one with focused attention on hope-oriented Christian religious education for the sake of present and future generations. In the third millennium, black churches must be hope-inspiring places in which people engage earnestly in a broadly conceived black Christian peda-gogy of hope. But what ought this pedagogy encompass? What is its intent? What are its content, processes, and contexts?

TOWARD A BLACK CHRISTIAN
PEDAGOGY OF HOPE

Underlying a black Christian pedagogy of hope is the view of an eter-nal hopefulness on which Christian faith stands and toward which black churches must teach. The pedagogical intent is to bring black people to new awareness of the nature of this hopefulness and how we may activate it in everyday life. Such a pedagogy builds on black peo-ple's historical belief in God's faithful nearness and activity on our be-half, and in God's empowerment of us to bring about relational whole-ness and hope-oriented living Likewise, the pedagogy emphasizes the biblical narrative of God's promises and the values of forebears who anticipated the possibilities of God's mission and sought to act on these potentials.

A black Christian pedagogy of hope assumes that hope oriented liv-ing is not an automatically known state of being or action in life. Black churches must teach, and we must learn what hope is and what it means to undertake hope in action. A black Christian pedagogy of hope proposes that an important aspect of the learning process is the intentional exploration of historical and contemporary biographies of black people. Biographical material serves as essential content through which we become privy to imaginative acts of hope in tough times. Through biographical material, we are enabled to consider our experiences of trouble, adversity, and terror that block hope, to give voice to feelings surrounding these experiences, and to engage in what might be called constructive "imaginative futuring."

But a black Christian pedagogy of hope must also entail our discovering God's favorable activity on behalf of black people and our envisioning how, under God's guidance, we may move toward a different future away from the one that present struggles in our communities and larger society would predict. Also, a black Christian pedagogy of hope must include black people's reflection on and affirmation of the normative conditions, based on biblical texts, that help us to "see" where we are, where we need to be headed, and how we may put hope into action. Through this form of Christian religious education, we are to come face-to-face with what it means to participate with hope in life and to orient our lives in a way that results in our contributing to our own and others' wholeness.

In short, I propose that black Christian religious education over the third millennium must entail a pedagogy of hope that emphasizes a historical, relational, and hermeneutical religious educational method. This pedagogy must use biography, reflection, interpretation, imagination, and decision that results in black participants' "rebiographing" or reframing their lives in the direction of God's hope-filled mission of human wholeness.

Historical Biographical Method

We have seen within the black community a waning significance of black history, particularly among the young, which has resulted in the loss of contact with models of hope in times of difficulty and suffering. This ahistorical or history-revoking posture prevents black people from being taught and nurtured by the Christian heritage stories of black people who would not sit down, give up, or compromise on the goal of liberation and human wholeness over the centuries of slavery (1619–1865). Because this posture dismisses the past by absolutizing the present and future, we fail to discover the presence and activity of the God of hope in our forebears' lives. Therefore, we do not anticipate this same presence and activity in the present and future. Moreover, this posture deters our learning the qualities of Christian hoping that appear in the narratives of black slaves and late nineteenth- and twentieth century post bondage forebears. We do not become privy to these forebears' reliance on the God of hope, to their commitment to be courageous disciples of Jesus Christ, and to their persistent endeavor to achieve human dignity.

What is so desperately needed in the third millennium is a historical biographical mandate. Indeed, a black Christian pedagogy of hope must begin with the intentional engagement of black Christian education participants with historical biography as a central means of capturing meanings of struggle, resistence, spiritual determination, and hope in the midst of life's difficulty and suffering. Vincent Harding's book, *Hope and History*, promotes the uses of historical biography as a passage from the present to the past that affords us a firmer grasp of the future. Harding states that, in the passage from our present troublesome and racially fractured times to past eras of struggle, we become open to discover the powerfully human dimensions of hope. We move back and discover a way to move forward from the days when black forebears transcended fears, overcame weakness by singing "we are not afraid" even as their knees quivered, and decided that it was right to live and die for more than a private agenda.

The value of moving backward lies in the discovery of new meaning that this movement promotes. New meaning becomes possible because historical biography is not a static representation of life; nor is it a dead entity. Indeed, in Mario Valdes' edited work, *A Ricoeur Reader: Reflection and Imagination,* Paul Ricoeur is credited with the important insight that inherited discourse and activity of the past *discloses* new meaning. This perspective is an exceedingly helpful one for a black Christian pedagogy of hope inasmuch as new meaning points to the establishment of hope. Specifically, moving backward into historical scenes of life is a hope-disclosing and hope-building effort, since this movement affords us opportunity to reinterpret our lives through imaginative participation in what was past but is alive in the present.

Who may lead this historical biographical aspect of the pedagogical process? We will need to assure the presence of twenty-first century griots (storytellers) and to develop the griot's narrative art in ongoing generations within our faith communities. Black preachers, teachers of organized religious education efforts, other adults, especially elders and parents, and older youth are among those whose narrative skills must be hewn and offered in such environments as worship, church school, Bible study, retreat, community center, and home. The griot must be the prominent religious education leader in the third millennium.

The roles of the griot. The role of the griot is exceedingly critical to the historical biographical method. The griot guides the listener into creative acts of learning hope in the present and future by the griot's knowing and recalling past stories of hope. Actually, in the historical biographical process, the griot becomes a spiritual guide and agent of hope. In this role, the griot is, first, the *poetic historian.* In the forward to Harding's book, *Hope and History*, Lerone Bennett Jr. describes the *poetic historian* in terms of one who has personally experienced the shaping effect of the God of hope and the history of our forebears. Because of this experience, the griot/guide *testifies* to choices that have helped and continue to form her/his own biography.

Second, the griot/guide becomes the *artistic storyteller* who seeks to draw the listener into active participation in an experience of hearing, feeling, and seeing images of history to the degree that listeners are evoked to self-discovery and the ability to see the present and future differently. The intent of the biographical moment is for listeners to become full participants who enter the image and for the image to enter them. Thus, for example, the telling of Harriet Tubman's dangerous but relentless and courageous treks northward to freedom with her precious passengers on the clandestine underground railway becomes the griot/guide's and the listeners' own experience. In this way, the idea of hope is being born and the nature of hope in action is being formed. In his description of the process, Bennett says that such images of history can evoke trembling or a sense of awesome awareness of the power of hope.

Third, the griot/guide is also the *interlocutor* who invites the participants to raise and answer questions that emerge from biographies of the past. In this role, the griot/guide challenges the participants to struggle with potential current and future meanings of answers to the questions. The *interlocutor* may also be an interrogator who poses the questions, for example. Based on the biography, what dare we hope for? Can we sing the Lord's song in a strange land? Is there no balm in Gilead? But, the *interlocutor* continues by nudging participants toward bringing some closure to historical biographical meanings, paradoxes, and applications to contemporary life.

Assuring the role of the participant. Although the role of the griot is critical in the historical-biographical method, the investment of participants beyond that of listener is also of pivotal importance. Whether in church or community environments, a challenge in implementing a black Christian pedagogy of hope will be to respond to the evolving new age of unidirectional learning styles. People are increasingly involved in one-way communication in which human response is either diminished or nonexistent. For example, TV and movies involve whole families in a receptive, passive, and entertaining mode with little or no personal face-to-face feedback. Moreover, cyberspace machinations, of which e-mail, Internet, and video games are part, require individual action and control without benefit of personal face-to-face response. In these situations, the thoughts of others are neither sought nor shared. It is difficult to develop interactive and reflective skills that are important for processing divergent trends of thought, for dealing with human feelings, for arriving at resolution of conflicts, and for forging understandings of both individual and communal hope. The participants' role of *listener* opens the way for *dialogue partnership*.

As a means of building on the undirectional and entertaining focus of communication, black religious educators will also find helpful the use of a dramaturgical emphasis. Through incorporating this emphasis, however, our intent is to move beyond simply entertainment. Inherent in this emphasis is our engagement of persons in the role of *participant observer* and *critic* in a process of *aesthesis* or artistic activity that brings expressive present reality to what young people typically regard as "those things, people, and places back in ancient times."

Bernard Reymond, in his paper "Theatre and Practical Theology," which was presented at the 1999 International Academy of Practical Theology, asserts that the theatrical dimension takes us beyond written texts and in the direction of "scenic production." This production evokes a process of recognition in which participant observers see their own personal stories in the drama. The participant observers are enabled to see their own image in a "mirror." Moreover, theatrical producers and actors become involved in symbolic meanings and play that put them in touch with parts of existence through which they may see analogous relationships to their own lives.

Specifically, in a black Christian pedagogy of hope, the dramaturgical emphasis may rely on actual real-life dramatizations, movie versions, specially created videos, or multimedia enactments of historical events and stories of Christian exemplars. Some black churches are already moving in this direction, particularly with live drama that sometimes replaces sermons followed by congregational interaction. In this way, congregations become *participant observers* who are invited to visualize and dialogue about new meanings and hope as well as the nature of hope in action in history and in their own lives. Some black families carefully select videos with historical significance around which to engage family members in discussion.

Another objective is to move participants beyond the position of *participant observer* and to the role of *dramatists* who themselves reenact the historical events and stories. In this way, the participants become the producers and actors and, in an important sense, become the griots/guides. Through their taking on production and acting responsibilities, participants enter the historical events or stories and grapple critically with the content, meanings, obvious and hidden messages, cultural cues, and ways of making all of these aspects come alive. Even though there is what Reymond calls a necessary "distanciation" between the producer, actor and a dramatic production, the producer and actor nonetheless become engaged in a symbolization process that entails connecting aspects of the past with the present. It is essential, though, that these connections become the topic of dialogue in which the *dramatist* or the producers and actors serve either as the primary *interlocutor(s)*, or serve in the interlocutory capacity with an assigned griot/guide.

In the language of Paul Ricoeur, the meaning that is disclosed through dramatic participation in life has to do with seeing order in life. Dramatic participation and the re-enactment of biographies of significant exemplars connect us with significant hopeful plots that can take our lives in new and hopeful directions. Drama discloses the fact that life moves on like the unfolding of a plot with setbacks; nonetheless, life always moves toward a hopeful end. Dramatic participation contributes to what might be termed *emplotment* as persons discover that their lives either already re-present or can re-present the same meaningful direction that is represented in the biography.

Contemporary Biographical Method

In my two articles on the faith community as listener in the era of cyberspace, which appear in the fall 1997 issue of *The Journal of the
Interdenominational Theological Center*, I draw attention to the increasing pull away from direct person-to-person, face-to-face communications in deference to machinated communication. Moreover, I
draw awareness to children and adults alike who bemoan the unavail-
ability of others willing take the time to enter honestly in conversation
with their full selves, which includes their ears, eyes, and bodily ges-
tures. The increasing techno-mediated ways of communicating, alongside the demands of obligations and rampant individualistic values,
have made us vulnerable to being nonreceptive, unresponsive pres-
ences in face-to-face relationships in our day-to-day environments. Indeed, we have become susceptible to a loss of hope for covenantal relationships in which love of God and love of neighbor is demonstrated
in direct person-to-person, face-to-face storytelling and storylistening.
Hoping is severely curtailed when people cannot voice their stories
and when there is no invitation to people to consider where God is at
work in their lives.

An added significant point here is that true learning involves people's full participation in human relationships rather than in their with-
drawal from relationships. Building on the insights of Paul Ricoeur,
new meaning and thus hope are apprehended through people's participation in ongoing community, past and present, and in their hearing
the voices of others.

Bringing contemporary biography to life. Michael Nichols' book,
The Lost Art of Listening, brings to our awareness the imperative need
for our recovery of auditory sensitivity, or hearing through the heart.
This sensitivity does not occur happenstance; it must be learned. The
third century black church must be on the forefront of providing
telling and listening skills and the context for practicing the skills.
One black pastor related to me that, in response to the tremendous
need for rebuilding church and family cohesiveness, designated worship services are entirely devoted to shared story around particular
topics. The pastor functions as a guide who introduces the topic with
which the community is concerned.

As guide, the pastor facilitates cross-generational story modeling,
first by previously chosen volunteers and then by volunteers; guides

cross-generational responses from the congregation; and introduces and comments on selected scriptures, drawing small groups throughout the congregation into conversation on meanings of the biblical material for everyday life. The pastor calls for cross-generational responses before the entire congregation; proposes applications of Scripture in life situations during the coming week; and invites family members not only to identify their own personal actions or life responses to biblical passages but also to use the congregation's shared story process in the family. As part of the experience, songs are sung and prayers are offered.

The pastor indicated that this approach to worship has enlivened the congregation. The creative use of contemporary biographical has created a tangible hope within the congregation that relational distances between individuals and generations can be addressed and that people can envision in the context of sharing as well as commit to identified ways of being and doing in family and community. In the African context of Zimbabwe, similar use of the contemporary biographical method takes place in cross-generational meetings of small groups that are formed through the subdivision of congregations into sections. I believe that this kind of interactive teaching/learning worship experience offers to us a creative model for hoping in the new millennium. Indeed, in a black Christian pedagogy of hope in third millennium, black churches will need to address relational issues by recognizing, first, that both church and family contexts offer opportunities for face-to-face contemporary storytelling and storylistening processes through which we build interactive and hoping skills.

Second, the contemporary biographical method in the black Christian pedagogy of hope must include a space for both the lament and celebration to surface in dialogue with others and Scripture. In both church and community environments, the contemporary biographical method is a religious educational means of discovering one another's lament through our sharing stories of distress, adversity, terror, and hopelessness that often go unsaid and unheard. This methodological emphasis allows us to learn the permissability of wailing or lamentation and to build a vocabulary for wailing before God through uses of Scripture. Using this method, we help people to become acquainted with the laments of the Hebrew psalmists and to take on the role of third millennium psalmists who cry out to God in the presence of caring listening others. The intent is also for people to learn that the God of hope hears and is present often in the listening other. The method is also aimed toward black people's connecting with Scripture in order to consider what Walter Brueggemann in his book *Hopeful Imagination: Prophetic Voices in Exile* calls the entertainment of an alternative world that is not yet visible.

At the same time, through the contemporary biographical method, space must be afforded for people to hear one another's experiences of relief, well-being, and accomplishment and to learn meanings of celebration by engaging in celebratory responses of laughing, hugging, dancing, singing, praising God, and praying. Teaching and learning the nature of hope entails our looking at positive aspects of contemporary biographies of black people that can overtake internalized negative images and messages about black life, at-risk behaviors, and negative qualities. And, linked with Scripture, contemporary biographies also offer opportunity for us to question the veracity of personal views and society's claims about our lives and to arrive at the recognition of the reality of God's affirming activity and renewal of the human spirit.

Third, the contemporary biographical method must take into consideration what I call the "relationality of contexts." This consideration is based on the realization that black people's stories of lament, celebration, and social critique are now (and will continue to be) told in pop culture and through popular media, particularly through music. While some of the gospel music that is heard in the public domain is attempted in black church worship, there remains a prevalent bifurcation of "churchly" functions and the functions of popular culture. Stories contained in rap, rhythm and blues, and other "soul music" are typically relegated to the public space and are not brought into the realms of religious education and critical theological discussion. Consequently, discussions of anger, despair, pessimism, and social critique that often form the content of the stories do not occur; and theologies of hope cannot be broached. Neither is it possible to enter into critical dialogue on beliefs about God that are explicitly stated or implied in these public expressions. The emphasis on a relationality of contexts would intentionally bring the content of stories from popular culture into critical dialogical efforts.

Fourth, the contemporary biographical method must make room for the spontaneous generation of symbols or people's unplanned and Spirit-led encounters with hope-producing images and symbols in the faith community. The implementation of a black Christian pedagogy of hope must make room for the surprising work of the Holy Spirit. There must be a willingness on the part of guide and participants alike to pay attention to people's cry for and the presence of the numinous. This attentiveness requires the teacher/guide's release from the safety of preplanned processes. Stated another way, there is a quality in a black Christian pedagogy of hope that cannot be planned for but will be missed if adherence to a predetermined plan of action is paramount. We might say that the pedagogy includes "planning" for the unplanned.

I am reminded of a discussion among members of a religious education group on the topic of the direction of their lives during which a participant had great difficulty in seeing a hopeful future. The planned group discussion of who God is in our lives and of God's activity and promise was problematic for the participant. The participant recoiled into what seemed to be a voiceless presence. But, when we stopped the discussion and gently invited the participant's response in whatever way the participant desired, we discovered this person's summons to what Brueggemann calls hopeful imagination. The participant simply said "I cannot say in words what I feel or even what I think I know. I may not discover what I need to know in my own spoken language or the language of others. I need to dance it. I will have to dance what is inside me." What resulted from this person's dance was an extraordinary clarity of focus and a visit of the numinous. Through dance there evolved a "working through" of problematic blocks in life and hopeless images, of experiencing God's coming in the middle of uncertainty and shining a light on the darkened path, and of seeing and anticipating a future that is worth facing.

Special roles of the guide. Because of black people's continuing experiences of denigration and self-devaluation in larger society and because of the decline in receptive and responsive face-to-face relationships, the guide in the pedagogy of hope must be a *counter-cultural advocate.* This advocacy role will need to include guiding participants into what Douglas Steere in his book, *On Listening to Another,* calls "holy listening." This kind of listening requires the formation of a relational environment in which people see one another as gifts who are made in God's image. Moreover, the environment of "holy listening" models the kind of community in which relationships are clothed "with love, which binds everything together in perfect harmony" (Colossians 3:12).

Of necessity, the role of the guide requires knowing and imparting skills of openness to one another, genuine attentiveness, appreciation of one another's self-disclosures, awareness of the vulnerabilities that sharing creates, and follow-up inquiry. In this way, the advocacy role of the guide not simply encourages and fosters storysharing but opens the space for hope in action to occur.

In the contemporary biographical method, the guide must also be a *catalyst* for the participants' becoming consciously aware of and responsive to the importance of "holy listening"as well as for the participants' acknowledgment of and openness to Spirit-led "hopeful imagination." And the teacher/guide must continually be a *learning teacher* and *teaching model* who values others' offerings for the insights these offerings generate in her or him and models both the compassionate listener and ways of posing provocative questions of self and others that lead to clear understandings of hope and commitment to hope in action.

The Normative Framework and
Pedagogical Method

Across the years, Scripture has formed the normative basis for black Christians' hoping and has functioned as a rationale for the formation of a black liberation theology. The central role of the Bible in black Christian faith and life unfolded precisely because of parallels that black people have seen particularly between the Old Testament Exodus narrative, other Old Testament liberation texts, and our own lives. Moreover, black Christians have found ample grounds for hope and for a liberation thrust in the life and ministry of Jesus Christ.

However, we are seeing increasing numbers of black people, with and without church affiliation, who are unfamiliar with the Bible. In this group are individuals who are seeking encounters with Scripture, ones who have a fair amount of ambivalence about the applicability of ancient texts to current life, and ones who show no interest in Scripture. At the same time, there is extraordinary growth in numbers and popularity of Word churches, in which the whole of church life centers on teaching and preaching the Word which is the Bible.

Overall, there is little question among black Christians and in the black church about the continuing need for a biblically shaped and scripturally oriented community. However, the prevailing view in black Christendom is that Scripture must be translated into understandable and relevant contemporary cultural terms. In light of this mandate, the question must be raised: How, then, should the Bible function in a black Christian pedagogy of hope in the third millennium?

I want to propose here that, in the pedagogy of hope, Scripture must form the normative framework for critical reflection on historical and contemporary biographical material. The Bible must be a lens for critically reflecting on hope and hope in action in biographical exploration. And the Bible must be mined for perspectives that help us to decide our own views of hope and how we will act on hope. But what models may we use for this endeavor? In the following sections, I will propose revisionist views of two existing cultural models for the use of Scripture in a black Christian pedagogy of hope. These models focus on the use of Exodus and Exile themes in Scripture. I will also give brief attention to two alternate models. One alternate model has appeared in black theological explorations as a counter proposal to the Exodus and Exile models. The remaining one proposes a dual emphasis on the Exodus and Exile models.

The Exodus model. In his groundbreaking book, *Teaching Scripture From An African-American Perspective*, Joseph Crockett details an "Exodus strategy of education." Crockett's strategy guides participants in bringing sociopolitical issues to the study of Scripture. Participants are to envision how people can exit from inhumane situations and can exist in, as well as contribute to a more just and loving community.

The Exodus strategy begins with the disclosure of a personal or public issue, its source, decision-makers and agencies that have addressed the issue, and beneficiaries of decisions that are made. Analogies are then drawn between existing personal or public issues and similar issues in scriptural material. A particular emphasis in this analogical method is the discovery of beliefs and values that appear in biblical accounts of liberating action and must undergird human action in present difficult sociopolitical circumstances. The strategy then moves to the participants' formation of an exodus approach, including necessary beliefs and values, identification of and ways of addressing unjust public policies and practices. A concluding aspect of the strategy guides participants in reflecting on their Exodus-oriented actions.

Crockett's strategy provides one framework for a black pedagogy of hope for the third millennium. However, it is necessary to revise and append his strategy in a way that allows for the uses of my earlier mentioned historical and contemporary biographical methods.

The specific role of Scripture in the revisionist Exodus framework of the pedagogy of hope is to provide normative lenses for reflecting on biographical material. For example, participants would enter the Old Testament narrative of the Israelites' Exodus from bondage in Egypt and other Old Testament liberation narratives. Attention would also be given to New Testament narratives of Jesus' life, ministry, and suffering on behalf of outcasts and oppressed people as well as to texts that respond and give guidance to first-century Christians. The intent is to draw analogies between personal and public issues in the biblical narratives and in black historical and biographical material. The participants are to envision how the issues relate to human action.

Particular emphasis on beliefs and values has pivotal importance in a black Christian pedagogy of hope for the third millennium particularly because, even though our churches say that we need them, we often neglect to give focused attention to them. In his book, *Integrity*, Stephen Carter also makes forcefully clear that, in the busyness of our everyday lives, it is often exceedingly difficult to find the time to contemplate societal mores, moral questions, or the values that affect our judgments of right and wrong. But we must take the time, according to Carter, because our children and our families are hurting.

Crockett does not identify specific Christian beliefs and values. However, I want to propose that a revisionist Exodus framework for a black Christian pedagogy of hope must do so. By Christian beliefs, I mean that which we claim and can defend as true in our journey as Christians. By Christian values, I mean qualities of the heart, mind, and actions of Christians that are precious and esteemed because they reflect the heart, mind, and action of Jesus Christ. Christian values inform the behavior of persons and contribute to what Stanley Hauerwas calls "a community of character."

Of necessity, when guiding participants to enter into hopeful imagination of a world or just society that does not yet exist, we must ruminate, for example, on our beliefs about the following: Who is God? How does God act? What is God's intent for humankind? What is the value of human life? What is the responsibility of humans for one another? What is the specific summons or "call" to service by God to us? What is my part in the imagined world or society? These are kind of questions for teacher/guides and participants to pose and answer in the process of reflecting on biblical and historical and contemporary biographical material. The intent is for participants to reflect critically on answers to the questions that appear in biblical and biographical materials and on the impact of these answers for the participants' own answers.

I also want to propose eight Christian values that are essential in any endeavor to lodge the historical and biographical methods of a Black pedagogy of hope in the Exodus Framework. The significance of the values to be presented here lies in the profuse evidence of them in Steven Barboza's voluminous work, *The African American Book of Values*, which is a vast compendium of narratives, stories, and poems of black people. The values are as follows:

- *Vigilance:* conscious watchfulness for manifestations of God's liberating activity
- *Courage:* the ability to withstand the onslaught of trials and tribulations, based on our knowing God's sustaining presence with us
- *Tenacity:* the willful struggle to survive with dignity either quietly or through overt activities that support or engender human dignity
- *Faith:* confidence in the present and liberating God; generates hope and allows for the formation of an inner certainty of things unseen
- *Love:* the expression of one's devoted acknowledgment of and response to God's love and one's actualizing God's care that is shown in Jesus Christ. This expression includes care for persons and the environment and may also include what is known as "tough love," or confrontation that has the well-being of individuals, the community, and the environment at heart.
- *Integrity*: particularly in the way Stephen Carter uses it, refers to one's discernment of what is right and in God's will, one's acting on what is discerned and one's willingness to stand unashamedly with honesty and sincerity on that action
- *Community:* functions of persons as an extended family that seek the good of the whole family and the individuals within it
- *Respect:* an attitude and action of honoring another and showing kindness and consideration because another, like us, is a valued creation of God. This quality is especially shown toward elders

As was the case with Christian beliefs, the intent is for participants to enter into critical dialogue about evidences of Christian values that appear in biblical narratives as well as in historical and contemporary biographical material. Such a discussion would also include concern for conflicting values and the prevalence of values that counter Christian ones. An added importance of including Christian beliefs and values in a normative framework within which to explore biographical material in a black Christian pedagogy of hope lies in the goal of the pedagogy to form agents and models of hope.

The Exile Model. Shelby Rooks' article, "Toward the Promised Land," which appeared in an issue of *The Black Church* (a quarterly journal of the Black Ecumenical Commission of Massachusetts), proposes a diaspora perspective for understanding black life in America in the light of Scripture. Rooks' perspective builds on the Old Testament narrative of the Israelites' exile experience in Babylonia.

Crockett also focuses on the biblical image of exile in his proposal of an Exile Strategy for black people's study of Scripture in the black church. According to Crockett, this image provides a reference point for making sense out of the dispersion of African ancestors beyond Africa, of the [dis]placement of slaves across America, and of the subsequent ghettoization and marginalization of black Americans in the United States. Of particular note is the view that black people exited the era of enslavement and increasingly found themselves in exile-like circumstances and continue to experience exile-like experiences.

The goal of the Exile strategy is the participants' awareness of harmony and its absence in larger and local communities as well as of strategies to build positive relationships that result in harmonious living in community and with all creation. The identification and formation of Christian habits, or "habits of the heart," that reflect ethical behavior in communal relationships are also central to the strategy.

Crockett's Exile strategy begins with an invitation for participants to acknowledge the harmony or disharmony, wholeness or brokenness that exist in black life within the larger and local communities. The strategy proceeds to the discussion of "habits of the heart" that appear in biblical texts such as Abraham's response to God's call (Genesis 12); the Ten Commandments (Exodus 20:1–21); Old Testament narratives of Ruth, Ezra, Nehemiah, and Esther; the ethical command in Micah 6:6–8; God's requirement for human behavior (Matthew 5:7); Jesus' and the disciples' relational model (Luke 4:16–21; and the nature of Christian discipline (Paul's letters). Participants are also invited to consider their responses to the texts. The intent is for black people to fashion "habits of the heart" by seeing and feeling the heart of God. An additional step fosters specific exploration of the biblical narratives of the Israelites' Babylonian exile in order to prompt discussion of God's intent and activity in chaotic and defeating circumstances as well as of opportunities for the practice of "habits of the heart." Finally, the strategy invites reflection on connections between real life circumstances, "habits of the heart," and biblical material.

Crockett's emphasis on the formation of Christian habits has immense significance for a black Christian pedagogy of hope. Yet much must be added to his description of the normative framework wherein this formation is conceived. For example, Crockett suggests that there is a "seeing and feeling" dimension to fashioning the "habits of the heart." However, he does not make clear what this dimension entails. From a revisionist standpoint, I want to suggest that "seeing and feeling" are integral aspects of an imaginative process into which Scripture invites us; this imaginative process must precede any attention to the formation of Christian habits.

As part of a black Christian pedagogy of hope, participants must be invited to "see" in the biblical narratives of exile more than meanings of the exile in its original context. Through entering Scripture, we want to enable participants to "see," speak through, and speak about our own past and present biographies that reveal exile-like separation, marginalization, and broken-ness. We want Scripture to invoke people's ability to articulate deep feelings of despair and grief at exile-like circumstances that seem to go on interminably. And we want biblical narratives to prompt us to name positives that are occurring in the midst of chaotic circumstances so that we "see" God's heart in the form of God's hope-giving activity in our lives. Moreover, through exploring the exile narratives in the Bible, our intent is to help participants to "see" models of habits that allow us to survive constructively and with hope in exile-like circumstances.

In his provocative book, *The Prophetic Imagination*, Walter Brueggemann gives us some hints about using of Scripture to engage in a process of giving voice to "feeling." For example, he draws on the Old Testament prophet Jeremiah to illustrate the necessity of voicing grief and raising the theodicy question: Is there no balm in Gilead? (Jeremiah 8:23). Moreover, his presentation of the narrative of Jeremiah's ministry provides a model and an invitation for speaking of

God's grief for God's people in exile wherever the circumstance of exile occurs.

I am reminded of an occasion in a church school group when a group member's identification with Jeremiah resulted not only in her disclosure of her story of exile at her workplace but also in her expression of grief through deep sobs. Amid her crying, she restated Jeremiah's theodicy question. The group gathered around her and, for a time, was silent. The words that broke their silence were: We understand what you're going through. We know because we've been there. God understands too and God will not forsake you.

After regaining her composure, the group member wanted to apologize; but we urged her to accept our plea that she did not need to do so. What followed was a discussion about the controlled environment that most often circumscribes religious teaching/learning endeavors. The group made ever so clear that there must be room for the often unexpressed story and its concomitant emotion. Another key point is that Scripture has the power to energize our memory and to prompt our release of feelings. The guide must make room for this response in a black Christian pedagogy of hope. Doing so recognizes that hoping proceeds from our giving voice to exile-like experiences or to break through the "exile" that unheard stories and repressed emotions create. This aspect of the pedagogy also precedes any consideration of habits.

Again, with regard to habits, Scripture provides an important normative framework. In *The Prophetic Imagination*, Brueggemann suggests that the Bible discloses to exiles the nature of an alternative community and alternative consciousness that prods us to imagine the same for ourselves. Indeed, the intent in exploring biblical texts of this nature is to help participants to imagine the kinds of habits or behaviors that will criticize and finally dismantle the dehumanizing ethos of the dominant community. Both Old Testament narratives of the Judaean exile and New Testament texts of the ministry of Jesus provide lenses for reflecting critically on habits that both occur in and are warranted by historical and contemporary biographies. Moreover, teachers/guides may use these texts to encourage participants' imagination and practice of habits that help them to move through exile-like experiences with hope.

It is important to add here that underlying our attention to "habits of the heart" in biblical texts and in black biographical materials is the understanding that hope in action is somehow connected to moral practice. Black Christians' survival with hope in the third millennium will need to be linked to a black Christian pedagogy of hope that takes seriously biblically inspired moral judgments and behaviors. We will need this pedagogy to contribute to a new standing ground in exile-like circumstances and to affirm, for example, of God's promise to all exiles:

> [God] does not faint or grow weary; [God's] understanding is un-searchable. [God] gives power to the faint, And strengthens the power-less. Even youths will faint and be weary, And the young will fall ex-hausted; but those who wait for the Lord Shall renew their strength, they shall mount up with wings like eagles, they shall run and not be weary, They shall walk and not faint. (Isaiah 40:28b–31, NRSV)

Also underlying the use of Scripture in discussions of moral action is the realization that third-century Americans, including black Americans, must overcome the preceding "age of disruption" in which individualism resulted in private views of morality and the loss of a common frame of accountability. People in general have become confused about how to behave and about what is right or wrong to do. This state of affairs exists in black communal life as well. A black Christian pedagogy of hope must bring black people into dialogue about moral practice and must provide scriptural guides in order to connect people with a common moral tradition.

In his book, *Making Moral Decisions: A Christian Approach to Personal and Social Ethics*, Paul Jersild suggests that the habits of Christian moral life are the behaviors of believers who commit to live a responsible life in accordance with their understanding of the biblical story that culminates in Jesus Christ. However, Jersild also cautions that, given the complex nature of moral issues, unanimity among Christians about moral behavior is difficult to achieve. Moreover, we must recognize that emerging moral dilemmas that were unimaginable in biblical times may not receive decisive direction from Scripture. Thus, in any exploration about habits in a black Christian pedagogy of hope, agreement on every point is not likely to occur.

Nonetheless, in an authentic pedagogy of hope in the third millennium, we are obligated to address the issue of moral behavior and to do so from inside the unique circumstances of black people. Indeed, when we come from this inductive stance, we may "see" requirements for new demands for social critique within and beyond our communities. We may imagine new and important nonviolent responses to ongoing exile-like experiences. We may contemplate actions that contribute to healing of racial and other relational fractures. Our attention to "habits of the heart," or moral practice, signals our concern for hope in action, which exemplifies the heart of Jesus Christ and points to our commitment to the gospel's goal of human wholeness.

Importantly, moral behavior builds on and interacts with the values we hold. Consequently, an emphasis on "habits of the heart" in a black Christian pedagogy of hope that adheres to the Exile model must be linked with the values on which I have already focused on the Exodus model.

Alternative Models. William Jones' book, *Is God a White Racist*, criticizes both Exodus and Exile perspectives in favor of a "humanocentric" framework. Based on this perspective, a black Christian pedagogy of hope would deviate from a "theocentric" orientation, which emphasizes God's divinely authored liberating activity in favor of a limited God who must have human assistance to deal with the issue of theodicy or suffering. Building on this framework, pedagogical activity would center on participants' examination of biblical texts of terror and of past and present human suffering that has tended to persist with limited or no resolution. Moreover, participants would develop a black people's agenda for intervening in human suffering. Hope resides in the participants' vision of interventive action and responses to suffering that reflects the commitment to "bear one another's burdens."

A second alternative model promotes the dual use of the Exodus and Exile themes. This model responds to the heterogeneity of black people and the complexities of Black life. Pedagogical processes are based on the realization that Black people's experiences differ on the basis of education, social class, residential location, occupational status, family circumstances, and church affiliation. We face across the life-span the predictable crises that accompany maturation. In varying ways and at differing times, we confront struggles and triumphs that are associated with individually experienced life events, relationships, and the results of choices we make. These life experiences are also impacted by and interact with race and class struggles.

In a black Christian pedagogy of hope, the teacher/guide will need to bring participants into a discussion of these complexities in

Hope in Revealed Truth not exclusive to blacks, but better understood by blacks based upon experiance

historical and contemporary biographies. Moreover, biblical material that represents both the Exodus and Exile models must be brought into dialogue with the issues that are raised on the biographies. Uses of both models respond to the reality, for example, that at various junctures in individual family or local community life, black people may experience profound yearnings for liberation or for exodus from particularly troubling and ensnaring circumstances. Likewise, at differing times, individuals, families, or local communities may experience more profoundly a sense of exile. The key point here is that hope-oriented teaching/learning in the third millennium must take seriously the full range of black people's life experiences. And, in light of these experiences, we must intentionally engage participants in exploring critically meanings of hope and the nature of hope in action.

"VILLAGE" ORIENTED CONTEXTS FOR A BLACK CHRISTIAN PEDAGOGY OF HOPE

Much emphasis continues to be placed on the black church building and the church school as the loci for religious educational activity. However, a black Christian pedagogy of hope in the third millennium must be a multicontextual and an intercontextual endeavor. Challenges to hope and the potential for hoping exist in every aspect of black church life and in every segment of black community life. Consequently, application of the pedagogy of hope must take place not simply in the church but in homes, schools, workplaces, and other community sites. Importantly however, black churches, through our ritual life and planned teaching/learning endeavors, must serve as models, rallying points, disseminators, and nurturers of approaches to be used community locations.

Four specific views undergird the "village" oriented emphasis. First, the "village-forming" and "village-functioning" approach to teaching/learning in a black Christian pedagogy of hope derives from the awareness that, over the post-slavery eras, communal solidarity has given way to the larger society's individual, competitive values. The third millennium must be an era of reclaiming "village" values, which emphasize the coordinated efforts of community members in the various community locations.

Second, black families are critical relational contexts for adults and children to consider together the direction, goals, and quality of their lives, what is realistically possible for their lives and why, what is needed to reach stated goals, and how the Christian faith connects with these concerns. Black family life constitutes living biographies that can provide a rich basis for conversation and reflection when shared across the generations. This experience is enhanced when Scripture is used as a lens in ways which I have already described.

Of course, I recognize that there are instances of troublesome and even harmful black family situations. In such circumstances, positive engagement of a black Christian pedagogy of hope is questionable. But the point I wish to make here has to do with the broader understanding that black families have a significant role in the "village" with respect to Christian teaching/learning that is hope-directed and therefore wholeness-producing.

Third, music of pop culture, techno-media of the cyberspace age, and other written and visual media impact our everyday lives; and we have tended to accept these aspects of everyday life uncritically. A "village-forming" and "village-functioning" orientation challenges us to take time to critically assess the impact of these dimensions of life. A black Christian pedagogy of hope in the third century must include conversations within and across church, family, school, and community agencies about the values, behaviors, and images of black life that music and media convey. Attention must be given to how these dimensions contribute to or impede black Christian faith and life as well as our ability to hope.

Finally, whether at church, work, school, play, or community sites, we are teaching by what we say and do; and we are learning from what we hear and see. A black Christian pedagogy of hope must promote our understanding that the most powerful "curriculum" on hope is the life we live wherever we are. This "curriculum" of lived biography must be recognized, reflected on, and revised to the end that we as black people truly model hope in action.

8

A New Clue for Religious Education?

Cross-Disciplinary Thinking and the Quest for Integrity and Intelligibility

RICHARD ROBERT OSMER

Across the centuries, the teaching ministry of the church at its best has operated between two poles: integrity and intelligibility. By integrity, I mean the task of maintaining continuity with the revelatory events that brought the church into being. By intelligibility, I have in mind the ongoing reinterpretation of the Christian tradition in shifting cultural and historical settings. Both of these tasks are found in the New Testament and are explicitly related to its teaching ministry. Integrity is closely associated with the New Testament term *paradidomi*, "to hand on the faith." We find it in 1 Corinthians 15:3, where Paul writes, "I *handed on* to you as of first importance what I in turn had received: that Christ died for our sins in accordance with the scriptures, and that he was buried, and that he was raised on the third day in accordance with the scriptures." Here, we have the pole of integrity expressed in a paradigmatic fashion. It focuses on the task of handing on the Christian tradition from generation to generation in ways that maintain continuity with God's self-disclosure in Jesus Christ within the context of the history of Israel. This is a dynamic task; simple transmission and inculcation are not enough. In handing on the beliefs and practices of the tradition, the church points beyond

179

the tradition, inviting persons to enter or deepen a living relationship with the One of whom this tradition speaks.

The second pole within which the teaching ministry works is that of intelligibility, the ongoing reinterpretation of the Christian tradition in shifting cultural and historical settings. This too is found in the New Testament. It is particularly evident at those points at which the early church is beginning to move beyond its original context and address non-Jewish audiences. The prologue of John, for example, opens with a *logos* Christology that is heavily influenced by the intellectual resources of the Hellenistic world. Various epistles likewise draw on the household codes of the surrounding culture to describe the moral obligations and practices of Christian family life. Broadly speaking, intelligibility grows out of the catholicity of the church's faith, a universal thrust born of the church's confidence that the God in whom it believes is the Lord of all nations and is relevant to every aspect of life. It includes but is not confined to the cognitive challenges of new sociohistorical contexts. It also includes the task of embodying the faith in practices that are responsive to the opportunities and temptations of a particular time and place.

At its best, the teaching ministry of the church across the centuries has held in tension the poles of integrity and intelligibility. Even a cursory glance at its history reveals examples of church teaching in which this is evident, from the Nicene Creed's use of *homoousion* language to explicate the Trinity to Aquinas's use of the *disputatio* of the medieval university to structure his *Summa Theologica*. Maintaining this tension, however, has not been easy to achieve in twentieth century religious education theory. In the first part of this chapter, I will explore the difficulties Protestant religious education theory had in holding integrity and intelligibility in tension in relation to one theme: evolution. In ways that find analogues across many religious communities during this period, Protestant religious education theory engaged evolutionary thinking like a pendulum, swinging at one moment toward the pole of intelligibility and, at others, the pole of integrity. I will then temporarily leave the theme of evolution to describe the nature and purpose of cross-disciplinary thinking in religious education theory, arguing that it holds the "clue" to striking a balance between integrity and intelligibility as religious education enters the twenty-first century. Drawing on the framework and examples developed in this section, I will then return to the theme of evolution, examining its influence on the thinking of Howard Gardner and exploring how the evolutionary assumptions of Gardner's thinking might be critically appropriated in an explicit program of cross-disciplinary conversation in religious education theory.

EVOLUTION IN TWENTIETH CENTURY RELIGIOUS EDUCATION THEORY

Evolution in the Thinking of George Albert Coe: The Quest for Intelligibility

George Albert Coe, generally considered the dean of the religious education movement, was a proponent of evolutionary thinking from the beginning to the end of his career. His writing on this topic is far more sophisticated than is commonly realized, moving from an optimistic reading of evolution in his earliest writings to a highly nuanced position that was critical at points of the way evolution was portrayed by some of his closest dialogue partners. Throughout, Coe was interested in pointing to the important role religion plays over the course of cultural evolution, unwilling to cede this important scientific theory to those who portrayed religion as an appendage of an earlier stage of human evolution now being left behind. Broadly speaking, Coe's thinking on this topic passed through three phases: (1) evolution within the perspective of philosophical personalism, (2) evolution in dialogue with functional psychology and philosophical pragmatism, and (3) evolution within the perspective of a chastened personalism. In the space of this chapter, I can only take up in depth the second phase of Coe's thinking.

Coe first confronted evolution as a serious intellectual option during his college years. His acceptance of evolutionary thinking during this period was part of a decision to reject what he called a "dogmatic" approach to religion in favor of one that was empirical and scientific. Coe's studies under Borden Parker Bowne (the leading light of Boston personalism) led him to conceptualize the core of cultural evolution as the emergence of "the personal": the human capacity to reflect on and reconstruct these values by which life is given direction. This voluntaristic and axiological understanding of personalism would stay with Coe over the course of his entire career and played an important role in his encounter with functional psychology and philosophical pragmatism during the second phase of his thinking. This phase is marked by the publication of *The Psychology of Religion* (1916) and *A Social Theory of Religious Education* (1917).

Functional psychology was deeply rooted in evolutionary thinking, portraying human cognition, emotion, and action as adaptive activities responsive to natural and social environments. This functionalist perspective was an important part of Dewey's theory of education in *Democracy and Education* (1916), which portrayed the task of education as shaping the habits of personal and social intelligence, that is, as cultivating those dispositions, cognitive skills, and communicative competencies that enable humans to solve problems across all spheres of life. Education that nurtures these capacities represents the heart of the evolutionary process. It is evolution becoming conscious of itself, shaping its environment and affording greater adaptive competence over wider and more complex areas of life.

Coe was deeply influenced by the evolutionary thrust of these perspectives, but he also was critical, rejecting their reductionistic portrayals of religion as merely facilitating "adjustment" to the social and natural environment along the lines of evolutionary adaptation. In *The Psychology of Religion*, he argues that the most important role religion has played across cultural evolution is the threefold function of idealizing, unifying, and reconstructing the central values that human communities have held at different points in history. Coe portrays this ongoing "revaluation of values" as one of the higher functions of the self, allowing him to depict religion as closely identified with the emergence of "the personal" in both cultural evolution and an individual's psychological development. Aware that religion has not always supported the "revaluation of values," he projects an evolutionary typology in which religion is portrayed as functioning in different ways. Notably, it is the prophetic strand of the Judeo-Christian tradition that is described as embodying the revaluative function most fully, a clue to the way Coe conceptualized his own constructive work in *A Social Theory of Religious Education*.

In this book, Coe takes up Dewey's claim that education is "conscious evolution," leading him to describe modern religious education as the process by which religious communities self-consciously idealize, unify, and reconstruct the most important values of the emerging modern world. This leads him to reject doctrines like Original Sin in light of modern child psychology and to transmute the biblical theme of the Kingdom of God into the Democracy of God to create a social ideal more appropriate to modern political, economic, familial, and religious life. He commends educational practices that would support the ongoing revaluation of values in Protestant communities in the hope that they might support the personalizing trends of modern life, guiding the most recent stage of cultural evolution toward its unrealized potential.

During the final phase of his thinking, beginning after World War I, Coe would portray evolution in terms of a chastened personalism, rejecting a "too-easy identification of evolution with progress" in the *Motives of Men* (1928) and describing the personalizing trends of culture as a fragile twig on the larger trunk of evolution in *What is Christian Education?* (1929). Religious communities committed to the ongoing revaluation of values are now portrayed as creative minorities serving as the cutting edge of evolution and as likely to encounter strong resistance. Evolutionary thinking thus played an important role in Coe's work from beginning to end. Here, the pendulum swings far in the direction of intelligibility, as an important theory of modern science is engaged to shape Coe's understanding of religion in general and Christianity in particular.

The Critique of Evolutionary Thinking by Shelton Smith: The Quest for Integrity

The pendulum was to swing sharply toward the pole of integrity during the middle of the twentieth century in the work of persons like Shelton Smith, James Smart, Lewis Joseph Sherrill, and other religious educators influenced by the "theological turn" occasioned by Karl Barth, Paul Tillich, and the Niebuhr brothers. Shelton Smith's *Faith and Nurture* (1948) will be taken as representative of their attitude toward evolutionary thinking. Smith is best known for calling on the religious education establishment to "reckon" with the theology of Karl Barth. He was not himself a Barthian, however, being far more influenced by the thinking of Reinhold Niebuhr and identifying with that strand of Protestantism he called liberal evangelicalism. In the opening chapter of *Faith and Nurture*, he offers a critique of four tenets of liberal Protestantism, a critique that is aimed directly at the thinking of Coe and the religious education establishment in general: (1) divine immanence, (2) growth, (3) the goodness of "man," and (4) the historical Jesus. An overreliance on evolutionary thinking is present in each of these tenets, he argues.

Smith begins by pointing out that divine immanence had come to be closely associated with the idea of evolution in liberal Protestantism, virtually identifying God with certain historical or social trends emerging over the course of evolution. Coe's interpretation of evolution along the lines of personalism is offered as a case in point. Smith then notes the way the second tenet also is grounded in evolution, an emphasis on growth. Here, Smith has in mind two closely related ideas: the belief that religion develops toward higher and more complex forms over the course of evolution and a strong preference for growth/nurture models over crisis/conversion models in religious education. Once again Smith sees both sides of this tenet in Coe's work, citing his popularization of Bushnell's concept of Christian nurture as an example of the latter and his evolutionary interpretation of religion, of the former.

Smith then proceeds to the third tenet—a strong affirmation of human goodness—noting the ways it is grounded in popular concepts of Darwinian evolution. He again illustrates this tenet with Coe, noting Coe's preference for the optimistic assessments of modern psychology over the historic Protestant doctrine of sin and his belief that over the course of evolution "the beast" in human nature is gradually being "worked out." Even the fourth tenet—the importance of the historical Jesus—is viewed by Smith as intertwined with evolutionary thinking. Coe, Sophia Fahs, and other members of the religious education establishment, he argues, commonly draw on historical-critical approaches to the Bible to portray it an artifact of our evolutionary past, possessing the authority of a valuable classic but inherently revisable in light of contemporary knowledge.

One by one, Smith offers a theological alternative to each of these tenets, drawing heavily on the thinking of Reinhold Niebuhr, Emil Brunner, and others. In place of an exclusive emphasis on divine immanence, he offers a theocentric and eschatological understanding of the Kingdom of God. An unequivocal affirmation of human goodness is replaced by an anthropology that portrays humans as God's creatures, made in God's image but fallen and in need of redemption. Smith's discussion of redemption draws on the themes of justification by grace through faith and a Christocentric treatment of reconciliation. This allows him to affirm the place of both growth and transformation in the Christian life, advocating a complex understanding of Christian nurture that is based on the unique nature of the church as a community called into being and continuously sustained by God. While he does not offer an extensive discussion of the Bible and historical-critical approaches to its interpretation, throughout *Faith and Nurture* he uses the Bible in a postcritical fashion reminiscent of Reinhold Niebuhr, who treats the truth of Scripture under the category of myth and not history.

Those interested in maintaining continuity with classical Protestantism will find Smith's theology a welcome corrective to the thinking of Coe and liberal Protestantism generally. It is the pole of integrity that comes to the fore. Notice what occurs in this swing of the pendulum, however. All meaningful discussion of theories like evolution falls to the side. There is no sustained engagement of the natural and human sciences at any point in Smith's thinking. Descriptions of the changing function of religion in the modern period or of bio-psychological theories of human development in an evolutionary perspective drop completely out of the picture. It is not that Smith rejects the findings of science; he often assesses them positively in passing. But at no point does he enter into a sustained, critical conversation with these sources in his theory of religious education.

The swing of the pendulum back and forth between the poles of integrity and intelligibility within Protestant religious education over the course of the twentieth century points to issues of importance to religious education more generally. The rest of this chapter finds the "clue" to breaking free of the pendulum-like oscillation from pole to pole in an explicit program of cross-disciplinary conversation in religious education theory in the third millennium.

CROSS-DISCIPLINARY THINKING: A NEW CLUE

Broadly speaking, cross-disciplinary thinking in religious education theory is the use of a number of disciplines to describe the purpose, persons, processes, and practices of religious education. Persons working within the truth claims of a particular religious tradition attempt to bring these claims, articulated theologically, into conversation with those generated by other fields, e.g., the natural and human sciences, art, philosophy, and ethics. Even when religious education theory does not work with theology, defining the purpose of religious education in philosophical terms, for example, it necessarily engages in cross-disciplinary thinking as it turns to the tasks of describing the persons involved in education and commends certain educational processes and practices as those best achieving this purpose. While it is not important that all third millennium religious education theorists work in the same way, it is important that they articulate the methodological commitments that guide their cross-disciplinary work. In light of the complexity of this sort of work, it important to distinguish the different levels of thinking it involves.

Different Levels of Cross-Disciplinary Thinking

Intradisciplinary thinking focuses on an author's evaluation of various options in a discipline. In virtually all fields today, more than one viable, theoretical approach is present. In contemporary psychology, for example, psychoanalysis, cognitive psychology, and evolutionary psychology are potential dialogue partners of religious education theory. Even within a particular school of thought, a range of positions often is present. Contemporary psychoanalysis, for example, contains theoretical approaches based on classical instinct theory, object relations theory, and self psychology. One of the first decisions religious education theorists must make in cross-disciplinary work is evaluation of the perspectives within a particular discipline and choice of those to be engaged as dialogue partners in the construction of their theory.

Interdisciplinary thinking focuses on the role different disciplines will play in the construction of religious education theory. True interdisciplinary thinking operates in a manner that respects the integrity of each field and coordinates their use in a methodologically explicit fashion. This is to be contrasted with a naïve eclecticism in which concepts and research of various fields are taken out their original disciplinary context and placed in a completely different theoretical framework in a haphazard manner. There are many different models of interdisciplinary thinking that can legitimately be used in religious education theory, and several will be explored below.

Multidisciplinary thinking is based on the assumption that many disciplines are needed to comprehend complex systems. It focuses on human knowledge as a whole and the role different disciplines play in understanding complex phenomena. If interdisciplinary thinking focuses on an intense conversation between one or more fields, multidisciplinary thinking attempts to chart the larger landscape in which this more focused conversation takes place. Contemporary examples of this sort of thinking (cf. Kline, *Conceptual Foundations for Multi-Disciplinary Thinking*, 1995) typically do not employ a unifying philosophical system along the lines of philosophical foundationalism, relying on historicist accounts of the present state of human knowledge in which the disciplines are portrayed as evolving systems of knowledge whose boundaries are constantly shifting. Multidisciplinary thinking allows religious education theory to locate religious education as a discipline in relation to other fields, describing its unique contribution to human knowledge and practice as a whole.

Metadisciplinary thinking focuses on the nature of the disciplines: what constitutes a discipline sociologically, rhetorically, and epistemologically and the rational operations appropriate to different fields. In our contemporary, postmodern intellectual scene, the idea of a discipline has received serious challenge. Contemporary metadisciplinary thinking must take these challenges seriously, setting forth the status of the disciplines as forms of knowledge, intersections of power, and forms of rational communication and articulating assumptions that guide cross-disciplinary work at other levels.

Contemporary Models of Interdisciplinary Thinking

While each of these levels is important in cross-disciplinary work, religious education theory generally focuses on the interdisciplinary level, bringing into conversation a range of disciplines to describe the purpose, persons, processes, and practices of religious education. It may be helpful to explore several models of interdisciplinary work that were present in twentiety-century religious education theory.

Correlational models view theology and its nontheological dialogue partners as equally important in the interdisciplinary thinking of Christian religious education. To correlate is to show the relationship between two forces that are mutually influential. Accordingly, this model attempts to bring into a mutually influential relationship interpretations of the Christian tradition and interpretations of contemporary existence. In Paul Tillich's *Systematic Theology* (1951) the latter is portrayed as raising the questions with which a particular era is struggling and the former, as providing the answers elicited from the tradition. Lewis Sherrill adapted this interdisciplinary model in *The Gift of Power* (1955). In recent decades, correlational models have moved away from this Tillichian formulation. David Tracy and Don Browning have developed a revised correlational approach in which the questions and answers of both the human situation and the Christian tradition are brought into a mutually critical conversation—an approach used by Thomas Groome in *Christian Religious Education* (1980). Mathew Lamb and Rebecca Chopp have developed a revised praxis correlational model in which the emancipatory praxis of new social movements and the praxis of Christian communities enter into a process of mutual learning.

A *transformational* model of interdisciplinary thinking is found in the writings of James Loder, most recently in *The Logic of the Spirit* (1998). Here, theology and its nontheological dialogue partners are conceptualized as standing in an asymmetrical bipolar unity that is analogous to the Christological formulations of the Council of Chalcedon. The Chalcedonian pattern, as developed by Karl Barth and his interpreters, Thomas Torrance and George Hunsinger, is viewed as setting forth a grammar for interdisciplinary thinking in theology. The grammar consists of three rules that characterize the relationship between the human and divine in Jesus Christ: indissoluble differentiation, inseparable unity, and indestructible order. In the second person of the Trinity, the divine and human coexist without the reduction of one to the other, coinhere in an inseparable unity, and stand in an asymmetrical order, with the divine having logical and ontological priority over the human.

This grammar, by analogy, can guide religious education theory's interdisciplinary work. The knowledge given to faith is unique and not to be confused with other forms of human knowledge; they are to be differentiated. Nonetheless, religious education theory, to the extent that it works with theology, cannot carry out its work apart from human knowledge of the world; they are inseparably joined in a bipolar unity. Their relationship, however, follows a definite order that is asymmetrical, with theology retaining marginal control over other forms of human knowledge. Although the insights of the natural and human sciences are taken with the utmost seriousness—as readers of Loder's books know full well—they can only be appropriated by theology through a process of transformation. Their rootage in assumptions inconsistent with Christian theology must be negated, on the one hand, that their positive contribution to Christian religious education can be appropriated, on the other—what Loder refers to as the negation of the negation.

A *transversal* model of interdisciplinary thinking has emerged in the work of Wentzel van Huyssteen (*Duet or Duel?*, 1998). The term "transverse" means to lie across, as a pile of beams might lie across one another at odd angles. The term suggests a fluid and dynamic understanding of the disciplines in which they intersect at some points and move apart at others. Disciplines are viewed, not as hermetically sealed wholes but as evolving traditions in which boundaries, core concepts, and research instrumentalities are constantly changing. Moreover, all disciplines are viewed as inherently interdisciplinary, as transversing other fields, often in surprising ways. It would be expected, for example, that philosophical theology would overlap cosmology or evolutionary epistemology at certain points while sharply diverging at others.

Broadly speaking, this model attempts to chart a middle course between foundationalism and antifoundationalism, a position van Huyssteen describes as postfoundationalism. Four basic moves undergird this perspective. First, the basic resources of rationality are viewed as distributed across the human community, making the sharing and evaluation of knowledge across contexts possible. These resources include the species-wide biological mechanisms of human cognition and the hermeneutical, rhetorical, and narrative dimensions of all rational inquiry. Second, the locus of rationality is located in the judgment of the rational agent, not in the propositions, beliefs, or procedures of a disciplinary community. Individuals can disagree about issues of fundamental importance to their discipline and still be considered rational in that their position is based on good reasons. Third, such judgments are socially mediated, that is, are subject to the critical examination of a relevant community of peers. Fourth, rational judgments are deepened when the community of relevant peers is expanded to include the members of disciplines and cultures beyond the rational agent's original context. Such judgments have a much stronger chance of forming a "better estimation" of the truth (not to be confused with a "closer approximation") because they take into account a wider range of knowledge and perspectives in the construction of good reasons.

EVOLUTIONARY THINKING IN HOWARD GARDNER

Having explored different dimensions and models of cross-disciplinary thinking, I will now return to the discussion of evolution and religious education which I have described as swinging back and forth between the poles of intelligibility (Coe) and integrity (Smith) in Protestant religious education over the course of the twentieth century. An explicit program of cross-disciplinary work in contemporary religious education holds the "clue" to moving beyond this pendulum-like oscillation and holding in tension the tasks of integrity and intelligibility. In the final part of this chapter I illustrate one way this might be done by engaging the work of Howard Gardner, whose theory of multiple intelligences and recent theory of education are heavily dependent on evolutionary thinking.

Religious educators across religious, denominational, and theological lines have recognized the importance of Howard Gardner's work. Gardner exemplifies transversal interdisciplinary thinking at its best, moving adeptly across a number of disciplines in his unfolding corpus. I will briefly summarize the development of his work, pointing to the influence of evolutionary thinking, and then focus on his description of the purpose of education in his most recent book, *The Disciplined Mind* (1999).

The Development of Gardner's Work

Gardner is best known for his theory of multiple intelligences, a perspective in which he argues that the human mind/brain is best construed as composed of eight (possibly nine) relatively distinct forms of human cognition: linguistic, spatial, logical-mathematical, bodily-kinesthetic, musical, intrapersonal, interpersonal, naturalist (recently added), and, perhaps, existential (still being considered). He first set forth MI theory in *Frames of Mind* (1983). In the early chapters of this book, he works transversally, constructing his position by ranging across a number of fields to construct his position: neurology, genetics, evolutionary biology, philosophy of mind, and developmental psychology. This interdisciplinary work issues in an understanding of intelligence as "the ability to solve problems, or to create products, that are valued within one or more cultural settings" (p. x). This relatively simple definition looks in two directions simultaneously, toward bio-psychological potentials and cultural amplifications. Both are framed in an evolutionary perspective.

Intelligence as a differentiated set of *bio-psychological potentials* points to distinct information processing mechanisms located in different parts of the brain. These computational mechanisms of the mind/brain respond to different kinds of information, have distinct developmental histories, and are subject to different kinds of dysfunction. They have evolved over thousands of years and are analogous to mechanisms found in other species, something Gardner explores in his discussion of birdsong. These differentiated bio-psychological potentials are portrayed as *amplified* in diverse ways by different cultures, as well as by different domains and disciplines within each culture, something pointed to in the emphasis on problem-solving skills and culturally valued creations in Gardner's definition of intelligence. Both call attention to the context-dependent nature of intelligence: it can only be understood (and assessed) in relation to the meaningful roles and products of particular cultural settings. This culturalist side of Gardner's thinking also is formed transversally, drawing on a number of perspectives, from Langer's philosophy of mind to Goodman's symbol system approach to intelligence.

Of special importance to Gardner's conceptualization of the relationship between bio-psychological potentials and cultural amplification in his emerging theory of education is David Feldman's nonuniversal theory of development, first articulated in *Beyond Universals in Cognitive Development* (1980). Feldman portrays many areas of life which are learned by children, youth, and adults as developmental but not necessarily universal, as moving through developmental pathways that are culturally particular. Feldman conceptualizes cognitive development along the lines of a continuum, ranging from developmental processes that are *universal* and then moving through those that are *pancultural, cultural, discipline based, idiosyncratic,* and *unique*. Gardner and his colleagues first began to link MI theory to Feldman's nonuniversal theory of development during the 1980s in Project Spectrum, a research project designed to create "intelligence fair" and context-dependent assessments of preschool children. The perspective emerging during this period was to play a pivotal role in the development of the Teaching for Understanding pedagogy, which Gardner and his associates have formed more recently on the basis of a six-year collaborative research project involving schoolteachers and researchers associated with the Harvard School of Education and Project Zero.

The focus of this framework is the concept of understanding, defined as "the ability to think and act flexibly with what one knows" (Wiske, ed., *Teaching for Understanding* 1998, 40). A close link is now posited between academic disciplines and the development of understanding in particular areas of culture. Disciplinary-based understanding is portrayed as involving four dimensions: knowledge, methods, purposes, and forms. Development of understanding in each of these areas is seen as passing through four levels: naïve, novice, apprentice, and master. Disciplines draw on different blends of the intelligences and amplify them toward the knowledge, skills, and types of thinking/performing central to understanding in each field.

This framework lies at the heart of Gardner's most recent book, *The Disciplined Mind*, in which he sets forth an "understanding pathway" of education for secondary schools. What is new and important in this book is Gardner's focus on the perennial human questions of truth, beauty, and goodness, questions faced by all persons across the human community and now lying at the heart of his theory of education. Different cultures have evolved different ways of helping people think about these questions in a systematic fashion. This is the important role the disciplines have played across cultural evolution: the sciences focus on matters of truth, the arts on beauty, and the humanities on the good. Education in the disciplines at the secondary school level thus is not primarily oriented toward helping young people become disciplinary experts but toward helping them develop greater understanding of the ways a particular discipline addresses one or more of these fundamental human questions.

Evolutionary Thinking in Gardner's Work

Evolutionary thinking is an important part of this theory of education at several points. At the most obvious level, the teaching of evolution is offered as an extended example of the way disciplines like biology can introduce students to matters of truth as they are raised by the modern sciences. At a more fundamental level, evolutionary thinking seems to provide Gardner with the assumptions undergirding his understanding of the epistemological status of the disciplines at a metadisciplinary level. Unfortunately, he does not set forth this perspective in a systematic fashion, forcing us to tease out the implications of comments scattered throughout *The Disciplined Mind*.

Most contemporary theories of human evolution distinguish between organic and cultural evolution (cf. Wuketits, *Evolutionary Epistemology* 1990). The former points to the gradual emergence over millions of years of information processing mechanisms in organic life that eventuate in the human brain and nervous system, a position consistent with Gardner's MI theory. The latter points to the evolution of the human mind as it has developed in concert with the broader processes of culture and society, a position consistent with the "culturalist" side of Gardner's theory of intelligence. Broadly speaking, two very different perspectives on cultural evolution have emerged in recent years: (1) an affirmation of cultural and epistemological relativism (the "many cultures, many rationalities" position often found in multicultural education, cultural anthropology, neo-Aristotelian virtue theory, and rhetorical epistemology) and (2) an affirmation of distinct validity claims in differentiated life spheres (Habermasian neo-Kantianism and the critical realism of evolutionary epistemology).

Gardner's explicit rejection of skeptical forms of postmodernism and his defense of the epistemic value of the disciplines seem to place him in the second camp. His modest nod toward multicultural education seems to indicate leanings toward the first. By failing to develop a metadisciplinary perspective on cultural evolution, Gardner leaves us with many unanswered questions about the epistemological status of the disciplines and the claims they make about truth, goodness, and beauty. His theory of education is long on example and suggestive insight and short on theoretical justification. When I turn to religious education's dialogue with Gardner, I will point to the problems this creates, especially in his description of the purpose of education as the cultivation of disciplined understanding in the areas of truth, goodness, and beauty.

Let us take up the most consistent line of thinking in *The Disciplined Mind*—the critique of skeptical postmodernism and defense of the disciplines—and point to the gains that would follow a more fulsome explication by Gardner of his metadisciplinary perspective on cultural evolution. This line of thinking seems to indicate a position quite close to the critical realism of evolutionary epistemology, a position aptly captured in the phrase "the eye is attuned to the sun." Critical realism argues for various forms of correspondence between nature's intelligibility and human intelligence, not along the lines of the older "naïve" realism but to describe the way the evolving structures of organic life "fit" the ordered universe of which they are a part.

Capacities as fundamental as the eye's sensitivity to light have evolved in concert with our planet's relation to the sun.

If Gardner does, in fact, belong to this metadisciplinary position, it clarifies the epistemological status of the scientific disciplines in his theory of education. From the perspective of evolutionary epistemology, science represents a culture's systematic approach to its cognitive beliefs, yielding knowledge that evolves over time. Such beliefs are inherently fallible but nonetheless provide a realistic account of the intelligible universe as it is comprehended by the structures of human intelligence at any given time. Gardner's contribution to this discussion is to expand greatly the notion of human cognition involved in the quest for intelligibility.

Consistently, evolutionary epistemologists portray evolution as culminating in modern science, which is seen as drawing on the most adequate knowledge-gaining mechanisms humans have evolved to this point. Gardner's pluralistic account of the bio-psychological potentials of the brain/mind and his attention to disciplines beyond science like the arts and the humanities point to a significantly wider notion of intelligibility. How should the validity claims of these disciplines be construed? Critical realism makes sense when treating science but does not take us very far in the areas of beauty and goodness. Would Gardner accept Habermas's argument that the differentiation of the spheres of art and morality in modern societies point to distinct reasoning strategies and forms of validation in the disciplines that treat them? This position might be construed as compatible with Gardner's account of the brain/mind/culture, but we simply do not know where he comes down.

This opens to a further question: What is the place of religion in this multifaceted quest for intelligibility? Steven Mithen in *The Prehistory of the Mind* (1996) and Ian Tattersall in *Becoming Human* (1998) make convincing arguments that any adequate account of cultural evolution must address the crucial role religion has played. It was present at the very beginning of the cultural explosion 40,000 years ago marking the emergence of the "modern mind" and has evolved in concert with the brain/mind/culture across human evolution. Should it not be viewed as a legitimate part of the human quest for intelligibility? Should not the disciplines that articulate the truth claims of religious communities be taken as seriously as those dealing with science, morality, and art?

RELIGIOUS EDUCATION THEORY IN DIALOGUE WITH GARDNER

Gardner's failure to give an answer to these kinds of questions at a metadisciplinary level leaves religious education in the position of approaching his theory of education and its implicit evolutionary framework with caution. Although his theory of multiple intelligences and Teaching for Understanding pedagogy have much to teach religious education, we must proceed with care in accepting the purpose of education as described in his most recent theory. I will focus on this part of his project in the final section of this chapter, pointing to ambiguities in his description of the disciplined pursuit of truth, beauty, and goodness.

An Interdisciplinary Model

The first step we must take is to describe the interdisciplinary method informing our conversation with Gardner. The perspective adopted here draws on elements of Loder's and van Huyssteen's models. Loder is right in pointing to the double negation involved in asserting the distinctive truth claims of Christian theology as they are taken up in religious education theory, both negating the assumptions of its dialogue partners and reappropriating their knowledge in a transformed intellectual context. Van Huyssteen, however, provides important insights into the transversal nature of this process, saving us from idealized understandings of rational communication across disciplines. Interdisciplinary conversation is ad hoc, moving back and forth between the disciplines to discover areas of convergence and divergence in ways that cannot be determined in advance but are specific to the disciplinary perspectives being engaged at any given time. If Loder's transformation model provides the grammar of interdisciplinary conversation, van Huyssteen's transversal model can be seen as providing the pragmatics.

As we have seen, Gardner's description of the purpose of education in *The Disciplined Mind* focuses on the cultivation of deeper understanding of the perennial questions of truth, goodness, and beauty as they are treated by the disciplines of a community. While religious education has much to learn from his richly textured work, it cannot merely adopt his theory in an unreconstructed fashion. Here, Loder's recognition of an inevitable moment of negation in interdisciplinary conversation must be taken seriously. Evolution does not serve as the ultimate context of existence for the Christian community. Nor does this community posit the human search for truth, goodness, and beauty as a fully adequate description of the purpose of its education. It finds the guiding purposes of its education in the nature and purpose of the church, a community called into existence by God and given a unique task within God's world. This leads me to transpose Gardner's description of education as focusing on the perennial questions of human truth, goodness, and beauty into three perennial tasks of the teaching ministry: catechesis, edification, and discernment. This position has been described elsewhere and thus will be treated briefly here (cf. "The Teaching Ministry in a Multicultural World," in Stackhouse, ed., *Religion, Globalization, & Spheres of Life* 2000).

Gardner and the Tasks of the Teaching Ministry

Catechesis is the task of handing on the central beliefs and practices of the Christian tradition in a manner that invites persons to a relationship of faith or deepens the *faith* they already have. *Edification* is the task of building up the Christian community through the identification and nurture of the spiritual gifts of its members, equipping them for ministries of Christlike *love*. *Discernment* is the task of teaching the members of this community how to judge the circumstances of their life and world in light of God's promised future, enabling them to read the signs of the times in Christian *hope*. The human search for truth, beauty, and goodness is transposed into education for faith, hope, and love, the three most important dimensions of the Christian life.

Each of these teaching tasks of religious education, however, must be unfolded in dialogue with cognitive, ethical, and aesthetic understandings that are present in a culture at any given time. Faith, after all, deals in part with what we believe and faces the task of revising its beliefs in dialogue with the cognitive challenges of human knowledge—in the contemporary context, modern science. Love, similarly, is blind without an interpretation of the contemporary situation and the moral challenges it poses. Hope often discovers its most important dialogue partner in art that evokes new ways of seeing the world. In each case, tasks defined in terms of the nature of the church necessarily engage the resources of the culture in which they are carried out, holding integrity and intelligibility in tension. In the following description of each task, the challenge of evolution as posed by Gardner's theory of education will serve as an example of how this might take place.

In catechesis, the church hands on its beliefs and practices in ways that invite persons to faith or to deepen the faith they already have. While faith most fundamentally is a relationship of trust in the God of grace revealed in Jesus Christ, it includes beliefs about God and the world in relation to God. These beliefs have been revised across the centuries through an encounter with human knowledge originating outside the circle of faith, including theories like evolution. In revising its beliefs in light of evolutionary thinking, the church must be careful to distinguish between the metaphysical commitments often accompanying this theory and the "science" of evolution.

Gardner's commitment to evolution as paradigmatic of the search for truth is a case in point. He is unclear about the extent to which he is committed to metaphysical materialism and whether this should be taught along with the theory of evolution by natural selection. Some contemporary proponents of evolution like Richard Dawkins are less reticent. They frame evolutionary theory within the assumptions of materialism and are dismissive toward religious alternatives. Such metaphysical beliefs cannot be proved by science and are not a part of science proper. Ultimately, they are a matter of faith.

Materialism asserts that the only things that exist are material things in space and that there is no purpose or meaning in the universe. As theologians like Arthur Peacock in *Theology for a Scientific Age* (1990) and Keith Ward in *God, Chance & Necessity* (1996) have pointed out, evolutionary thinking based solely on materialism has enormous difficulty explaining how the finely tuned universe giving rise to organic life could have evolved through chance alone. How likely is it that our universe would produce life, a universe that exploded at a relatively small epicenter 15 billion years ago, giving rise to space and time, the elements of hydrogen and helium (through which the stars were formed) and, ultimately, carbon (as the stars exploded), the basis of all life forms. The probability of organic life— much less human life—emerging out of such an evolutionary process is extremely slim. The hypothesis of an intelligent force guiding and sustaining this process from beginning to end is surely as believable and rational as a strictly materialist account relying on exclusively on random evolutionary permutations.

Taking this step—finding grace at the heart of the universe and viewing the unfolding processes of evolution as sustained by God's continuous creation—remains a matter of Christian faith. It cannot be "read" off evolution, as Coe often contended. It finds its reasons for this reading of evolution in the gracious God disclosed in Jesus Christ and moves from this clue to the meaning and direction of creation as a whole. Nonetheless, it will offer an account of creation, human uniqueness, and God's providence that takes account of science's descriptions of the origin of the universe and the emergence of organic life. Catechesis that educates Christians toward this sort of belief faces a far more challenging task than merely handing on the stories of the Bible or the received traditions of the church in an unreconstructed form. In dialogue with evolutionary thinking, it will find ways of teaching the Genesis stories of creation that are nonliteralistic and communicate the theological meaning of these stories in a manner that describes God's work in and through the processes of evolution. Individuals' construction of such complex beliefs takes time and will necessarily involve the cultivation of disciplined understanding in catechesis far beyond childhood and early adolescence.

Gardner's treatment of education toward goodness focuses exclusively on the role of history in providing examples of human good and evil. He is reticent about commending any normative moral framework. While this is might be viewed as a concession to the pluralistic nature of American society and the difficulties this creates for moral education in its public institutions, I believe Gardner's reticence reflects ambiguities inherent to his commitment to evolutionary adaptationism. Evolutionary theory offers no clear guidance about the "moral lessons" it has to offer. Is the moral imperative an affirmation of the survival of the fittest, as many social Darwinists have claimed? Or is it found in kin altruism and other forms of cooperative behavior detected among higher primates by evolutionary biologists? Or it an affirmation of the entire range of moralities found across cultures and history, a form of relativism found among many proponents of cultural evolution? Gardner leaves us guessing. None of these positions, moreover, represent an adequate description of education toward goodness from a Christian perspective. The first move must be one of negation of Gardner's description of this task.

Education toward goodness in religious education finds its center in the perennial task of edification: the identification and nurture of spiritual gifts that equip the members of the Christian community to pursue ministries of Christlike love. Does this focus on love at the heart of edification mean that religious education has nothing to learn from modern theories of evolution? I believe that the answer is no and that Coe points to aspects of evolutionary thinking important to contemporary religious education.

Coe, as you will recall, pointed to the changing function of religion in the context of modernity. Today, we might cast this in terms of developments like institutional and cultural differentiation, trends first noted by sociologists like Max Weber and Emile Durkheim and developed more recently by Habermas, Berger, and others. In modern societies, religion no longer has the all-important function of binding together and legitimating the moral norms of different life spheres. It is one social system among many. In modern Western democracies, it is viewed as a part of civil society, the network of associations and relationships located between the private sphere of the family and the fully public spheres of the polity and economy. Civil society is the sphere in which different cultural communities and individuals have the freedom to pursue widely different values and patterns of life.

These developments, broadly speaking, are a part of cultural evolution. Religion's changing function in differentiated modern societies has led some ethicists to recast the Kantian distinction between the right and the good in social terms (cf. Benhabib, *Situating the Self* 1992). The right concerns the spheres of law and public morality; the good concerns the particular moral convictions of different communities and individuals within the open space of civil society. While not unproblematic, this distinction provides a useful way of distinguishing two sorts of tasks in the teaching ministry of edification, both of which are governed by its love ethic. On the one hand, edification focuses squarely on the nurture of Christian goodness, offering stories, models, practices, and relationships that cultivate the vision and virtues by which individuals and congregations carry out explicit forms of ministry in the name of Christ. On the other hand, edification also focuses on cultivation of a public morality among its members, teaching them how live with tolerance in civil society and work for justice in the political and economic realms. While space does not permit further explication of these two tasks, enough has been said to indicate the way cultural evolution can be taken into account in the church's interpretation of its context without abandoning a substantive description of the love ethic standing at the heart of its moral education.

This brings us to the third task of education described by Gardner: development of understanding and competence in the pursuit of beauty. Over the course of his entire career, Gardner has given special attention to the arts, studying his own children's "artful scribbles" and arguing forcefully on behalf of the arts in public education in the face of shrinking budgets. Communities that do not cultivate a disciplined understanding of beauty in its education, he argues, are in danger of allowing the media-based standards of popular culture to completely capture the imagination of its young. This perspective is a welcome corrective to the narrowly utilitarian focus of much contemporary education.

Once again, however, we are left with unanswered questions embedded in the evolutionary frame informing Gardner's theory of education. Does he advocate a pluralistic understanding of beauty in which the standards of each evolving culture provide the pathways to disciplined skill and understanding of the arts? Or does he advocate a particular understanding of aesthetics? These questions remain unanswered in *The Disciplined Mind*, and we must turn elsewhere to gain clues to Gardner's underlying theory of the arts. In *To Open Minds*, Gardner offers an extended comparison of arts education in mainland China and the United States. He criticizes Chinese education for its overemphasis on imitation of the classics and the acquisition of performance skills in a rote fashion. He reveals a strong preference for American progressivism's emphasis on the element of personal creativity in artistic performance, arguing that experimentation during the early years is the seedbed of mature creativity and is to be encouraged. Only the nurture of such creativity, he believes, keeps alive the dynamism at the heart of living traditions of art.

Is this an adequate aesthetic for religious education? I believe not. Progressivism's overwhelming emphasis on the element of individual creativity in artistic expression severely underestimates the world—disclosive power of art—its capacity to reveal the world in which everyday life is embedded and to project new possibilities. Many contemporary aesthetic theories (especially those of critical social theory) portray art as evoking new ways of seeing the world with the potential of opening up new ways of living. Here, religious education finds important clues for its third teaching task: discernment.

Discernment focuses on teaching the members of the Christian community how to judge the circumstances of their life and world in light of God's promised future. It is both animated by and oriented toward Christian hope. More than any contemporary Protestant theologian, Jürgen Moltmann in *The Theology of Hope* has drawn attention to the utopian potential of Christian hope. He describes the church as a community that lives out of God's in-breaking future, placing it in a permanent, creative tension with the world as it is. The church is neither world negating nor world conforming; it is genuinely utopian, projecting imaginative alternatives that animate concrete engagement in the present. That which its seeks to discern is God's will for the present viewed through the lens of God's promised future. Here, aesthetics is appropriated to the task of evoking a new way of seeing the world, a creative task that may redirect the processes of cultural evolution toward possibilities that otherwise might go undetected and undeveloped.

In its pursuit of this task, religious education may find Gardner's theory of multiple intelligences more helpful than his theory of aesthetics. Education of the imagination toward a new way of seeing may best proceed not by a direct assault on the logical and verbal constructions of modern scientific worldviews but through exposure to and participation in artistic performances appealing to musical, visual, and bodily-kinesthetic forms of intelligence. Art's capacity to bypass the language and logic of everyday life and evoke new understanding of this world by appealing to intelligences frequently neglected in daily life may well be the key to teaching discernment. Religious education might creatively use music, sacred space, literature, and the electronic media to open the imagination to possibilities of transformation that would be rejected out of hand if presented as a moral harangue or coldly theoretic analysis. Teaching that nurtures hope, that longs for and works toward God's promised future, may well be the most important task before the church in our rapidly globalizing era.

CONCLUSION

In this chapter I have argued that an explicit program of cross-disciplinary work holds a new "clue" for religious education theory as it begins its progress in the third millennium. The treatment of evolutionary theory in twentieth century Protestant religious education was portrayed as oscillating like a pendulum between the poles of intelligibility (Coe) and integrity (Smith). Cross-disciplinary work, in contrast, holds the promise of allowing religion education theorists to hold these two poles in tension, articulating the theological and philosophical commitments of a particular position, on the one hand, and developing this position in dialogue with the cognitive, ethical, and aesthetic resources of the human community, on the other. The commitment to an explicit program of cross-disciplinary work in religious education does not entail that all theorists will work in the same way. It does entail, however, their articulation of the methodological commitments informing their work. Such articulation, I believe, would facilitate conversation across differing theoretical perspectives, clarifying the level of cross-disciplinary work (intradisciplinary, interdisciplinary, etc.) on which such perspectives disagree and pointing to the kinds of argumentation needed to justify a particular position. In our pluralistic, postmodern context, such clarification of points of difference and agreement, and not consensus across the field, is the goal toward which religious education should strive.

9

Practical Theology and Transformative Learning

Partnership for Christian Religious Education

BARBARA J. FLEISCHER

The cultural milieu in the United States at this turn of the millennium includes a conspicuously expressed hunger for "spirituality" in all forms and a longing for deeper sources of meaning. Television shows and films highlighting angels and God-themes top the ratings, and business texts include in their titles and contents explicit references to soul, spirit, and community. Ironic as it may be (though quite understandable in a "secular" society that seeks to keep religious language and sentiment out of its public, educational, and commercial systems), contemporary culture is experiencing a large-scale bubbling up of interest in books, films, and activities related to the sacred and the spiritual. Distrust of religious institutions and doctrine notwithstanding, U.S. Americans are struggling with their compartmentalized secular/sacred dichotomies and are not easily giving up either side of the dualism. While other Western countries do not contend with as solid a firewall as the United States has constructed between religion and public life, they do experience the continuing diminishment of religious life as the organizing principle of daily life rhythms, a wedge between religion and the rest of life fueled largely by post-Enlightenment developments in philosophy, science, and commerce.

203

The field of religious education from its inception has sought to heal the rift between the religious and the educational, the sacred and the ordinary dimensions of life. As such, it has been a counter-cultural movement in the West with its insistence on bringing the religious into conversation with the educational in language, forms, and methodologies and on developing a field that is interdisciplinary and therefore dialogical at its core. At the founding of the Religious Education Association in 1903, the mutuality of the religious and the educational were named explicitly as humanizing partners, and the task of bringing the ideals of each sphere of inquiry into dialogue with the other was hailed as a worthy purpose for the new field.

The short history of the field of religious education has shown that not every conception of education and religious thought is compatible with the dialogical character of religious education. Indeed, true dialogue involves the risk of change, and religious systems that claim to be inherently unchanging or authoritarian offer little opportunity for further conversation. Similarly, educational systems that seek simply to impart and measure the acquisition of predetermined sets of information offer little room for the novel and the emergent that issue forth from exploration and dialogue. Although there is an inherent tension between being true to one's own tradition and remaining open to new perspectives, some stances in both religion and education seem to be too stiff to allow for the sway of mutual enhancement.

As I imagine the possible future of religious education, and particularly Christian religious education, I would like to explore the interplay between two specific paradigms of religious inquiry and educational methodology that seem to be quite compatible with the dialogical nature of religious education: *practical theology* and *transformative learning*. I will first explore each, paying particular attention to the assumptions and characteristics that undergird each model's openness to dialogue, and then examine the interplay between the two approaches. From this exploration, I will further examine the avenues and directions that may open as the most fruitful for the future of religious education as a whole, and Christian religious education in particular, in the third millennium.

MY SOCIAL LOCATION
AS A RELIGIOUS EDUCATOR

For the past thirteen years, I have been involved with both the on-campus and extension graduate programs of the Loyola Institute for Ministry (Loyola University New Orleans). My earliest work was almost exclusively with the extension program (known as "LIMEX"), which offers pastoral studies and religious education courses in various locations across the United States, Canada, the United Kingdom, and Switzerland. My religious education praxis has been that of assisting Christian learning communities, composed of ten to fifteen students, engage one another in conversation to reflect critically on both course content and their life and ministry or religious education experiences. As I became aware of the expanding literature on practical theology and transformative education, I found that both models fit well and further informed our collective religious education praxis. Practical theology offers a model of religious reflection that draws learners and educators alike into attentive listening, dialogue, and engagement, not only with the discipline of education but with the whole of life. Transformative models of education foster interdisciplinary dialogue as a pathway for expanding and generating new paradigms of interpreting and living in the world. The interplay of the two offers a prime example of how religion and education can be mutually enhancing and also offers some possible contours and directions for the future of religious education. Indeed, the praxis approach that lies at the heart of each paradigm is the key, I believe, to full partnership between religious and education.

PRACTICAL THEOLOGY

Practical theology has undergone several shifts of meaning in the past two centuries. The nineteenth-century sense of practical theology viewed it primarily as one discipline among many in Christian theology. Edward Farley's history of the term in his essay "Interpreting Situations: An Inquiry into the Nature of Practical Theology" (in *Formation and Reflection* by Mudge and Poling) notes that practical theology was first used to designate a subspecialty of theology when it distinguished moral theology as practical application, separate from speculative theology. Later, "practical theology" came to include all "applied" areas of theology, such as homiletics, liturgical presiding, and pastoral care. This sense of "practical" was in contrast to the "theoretical" specialties of theology. Some nineteenth century schemas also included Christian religious education under this rubric of an "applied" practical subspecialty of theology, a conception that was later rejected by the nascent Religious Education Association.

In more recent decades, practical theology has named a major shift in the understanding of the theological enterprise itself, one that recognizes praxis as the core reality of religious being-in-the-world. Praxis breaks down the separation between theory and practice and acknowledges that every theory or concept springs from human experience and every action involves a guiding theory or set of assumptions. Practical theology is radically centered on work toward the realization of the reign, or shalom, of God and calls for a continual rhythm of action and reflection. Accordingly, practical theology in this mode has been called "praxic theology" by Bernard Lee, a leading theologian in the field. It does not name a subspecialty of theology but rather a new mode of envisioning and entering into the theological and religious enterprise itself.

This sense of theology as practical wisdom in service to the reign of God reappropriates a Judaic and early Christian view of religious reflection, dialogue, and living. In Jewish and early Christian communities, the purpose of pondering scriptural texts and entering into religious dialogue was not to develop an articulate theoretical description of reality. Rather, prayerful dialogical reflection provided a pathway for the community to encounter the holiness of God and so be transformed into a people of justice and compassion. The Hebrew and Christian Scriptures attest to God's actions in the world on behalf of the oppressed and marginalized. Entering into the holiness of God meant being caught up into God's pattern of justice and care. For the people of God, reflection on God's action in history and their own right action flowed together in a continual cycle of deepening conversion and empowerment to act with holiness. Religious reflection was thus both communal and practical in the sense that it continually pressed the people into engagement with the world.

As Christian theology became more influenced by Greek categories of being and eventually entered the university sphere as an academic discipline, it became more theoretical and "schooled." Thomas

Groome points out in his essay "Theology on Our Feet: A Revisionist Pedagogy for Healing the Gap between Academia and Ecclesia" (in *Formation and Reflection* by Mudge and Poling) that the split between the academic study of theology in universities and religious reflection in church communities seems to have grown even wider in the twentieth century. The reason for the split, he contends, is largely the "theory-to-practice" mind-set that treats reflective activity separate from action. His central thesis is that if theology is to become truly practical, it must develop a different educational praxis, one that does not pit theory against practice but rather integrates the two.

Aristotelian Roots of Theory versus Practice

Bernard Lee traces the roots of both the pedagogical and religious split of theory from practice back further to Aristotelian thought. (See, e.g., his analysis in *The Future Church of 140 BCE.*) For Aristotle, what was most sublime in the human person was the person's rationality and capacity to contemplate the good, the beautiful, and the true. Through this appreciative understanding, the person mirrored the divine Mind from whom all beauty, goodness, and truth flow. Thus the highest kind of knowledge that a human could develop was *episteme*, an appreciative understanding of the elegant abstract principles that underlie all reality. The kind of knowing involved in this level of knowledge is *theoria*, the root for our English word "theory." Aristotle's *theoria*, however, does not connote the "practical" dimension of theory that our English word does today (e.g., Kurt Lewin's oft quoted phrase that "there is nothing so practical as a good theory"). *Theoria* involved pondering life and its beauty for the joy of fulfilling our rational humanity. This was the highest kind of knowing, the ultimate privilege of the philosopher.

Questions such as "what is the nature of God?" or "what is the nature of the relationship of the Father and the Son?" that occupied so much of the Christian religious discourse of the fourth and fifth centuries take their root paradigm from this Greek emphasis on *theoria*. Knowing the underlying nature of reality was seen as the most pressing issue facing the human community, and pursuing contemplation in a way that shunned activity in the world became an exalted mode of Christian living.

After *episteme,* the next most important category of knowledge in the Aristotelian framework is *phronesis,* a kind of "practical wisdom" for ordering society and functioning as a wise citizen. The kind of knowing that develops *phronesis* is *praxis,* which involves reflective action in the world. *Phronesis* is the cumulative wisdom that both directs and results from reflective and intentional action to develop a healthy society and political order.

Bernard Lee points out that, unlike the Aristotelian schema that places *episteme* at the summit of human knowledge, the practical theology paradigm centers its discourse on questions of *phronesis* and *praxis.* Both Judaic and early Christian religious discourse lean heavily into questions such as "who are we called to be because of how God has acted for us in history?" Israel's remembrance of God's liberational activity in the Exodus event is not a pondering of abstract first principles; it is a covenantal, relational thanksgiving to the God who acts on their behalf. Similarly, Sunday worship for Christians recalls the liberating revelation of God's action in the resurrection of Jesus and the healing mission of Jesus in the world to which all Christians are called by virtue of their baptism. The emphasis on praxis shifts religious sensibilities away from a contemplative mode that shuns worldly action to an integrative mode that acts reflectively in the world in light of biblical themes of justice and compassion.

A third kind of knowledge in the Aristotelian classification remains to be explored; it is *techne,* or what U.S. Americans might call "practical know-how." *Techne* refers to the kind of craft knowledge involved in making things such as tables or clothing. *Poiesis* names the kind of knowing—skills development—involved in *techne.* Our English word "technical" finds its root in this Greek concept of knowledge.

U.S. Americans and, indeed, the whole "first" world has been focused on *techne* since the Industrial Revolution and the discovery that through science, humans could exert unprecedented control over the natural world (a control that is now beginning to reveal its disastrous ecological consequences). Questions such as "what are the best techniques for overcoming disease, developing transportation, heating homes, and entertaining ourselves?" have become both a preoccupation and full occupation for many contemporary people. The field of education has also centered much attention on identifying the "knowledge and skills competencies" that any educational approach should produce. As Irish author Joseph Dunn has pointed out in *Back to the Rough Ground,* such educational questions are clearly in the realm of *techne* rather than *phronesis* and often thwart efforts to move education toward the full pursuit of wisdom and the goal of wise *praxis* in the world. Technical concerns are crucially important in accomplishing the social vision developed through *phronesis* and *praxis*. However, if producing predetermined knowledge and skill outcomes becomes the sole focus of education, educational interactions will diminish into functional activities that may orient students away from larger questions of what the human community is ultimately doing and creating together. Bernard Lee points out that while *techne* is a necessary component of practical action in the world, it must remain at the service of *phronesis* and *praxis* if it is to center on action on behalf of the reign of God.

An Experiment in Practical Theology

In 1992, the Association of Graduate Programs in Ministry (a consortium of programs housed in Catholic institutions of higher learning) took up the challenge of forging a new way of envisioning the theological enterprise and shaping a dialogical approach to religious education. The association adopted practical theology as the paradigm for graduate programs in Christian religious and ministry education:

> The Association of Graduate Programs in Ministry (AGPIM) recognizes and supports the emergence of a new theological paradigm in graduate education for ministry. This theology, commonly referred to as practical or pastoral theology, is a mutually interpretive, critical and transforming conversation between the Christian tradition and contemporary experience. Historical, hermeneutical, and sociocultural analyses are integral to this method of theology. Pastoral or practical theology takes place in a community of faith, implies a spirituality that is both personal and liturgical, and is directed towards individual and social transformation in Christ.

The praxic character of this paradigm in theological education calls for a revision of the classical theory-to-practice approach in both religious discourse and educational methodology. At the Loyola Institute for Ministry, the practical theology paradigm shapes our curriculum (to include a number of courses that involve dialogue with the social sciences, natural sciences, and education) as well as our educational designs and conversations. Students are encouraged

to put course content in dialogue with their life and ministry experiences and engage one another in disciplined conversation. Such an
emphasis toward a dialogical educational methodology, however,
would not have been possible in graduate education for ministry
without a major change in the way theology itself and religious discourse were envisioned.

In Catholic circles, serious attention to practical theology in the
twentieth century was launched at the Second Vatican Council, especially with the last document of the Council, the *Pastoral Constitution
on the Church in the Modern World* (1965). That document was addressed "to the whole of humanity" and called for all to become adept
at reading "the signs of the times" in order to transform the social
order. All are called to form a society that is "founded on truth, built
on justice, and animated by love; in freedom it should grow every day
toward a more humane balance" (§ 26).

The document acknowledges that the action of God's Spirit is not
limited to any one religious group but rather "fills the earth." The
church, then, must be prepared to listen and learn from the wider culture as well as speak its wisdom. The document explicitly calls for
learning from other disciplines and particularly emphasizes the important role of the "secular" sciences, especially psychology and sociology. Reflection on a wide range of human learning is encouraged and
indeed required in order to read the "signs of the times" and address
issues of pressing concern facing the entire human community and the
whole earth.

This stance of radical commitment to the reign of God in history,
affirmed by the Second Vatican Council, had already been
established in many mainline Protestant churches, especially among
those churches who were most influenced by the Scripture scholarship of the nineteenth and twentieth centuries. The turn to biblical
images of the reign of God meant a turn to a religiosity engaged in
community and compassionate action; that is, a shift to practical theology. Historical and cultural studies, not only in Scripture scholarship but also in other areas of religious inquiry, have noted the intimate relationship between faith and culture and have shown how
that relationship has played out in various times and places. Such
scholarship has also helped move religious discourse to a practical
theology mode.

Mutually Interpretive, Critical, and Transforming Conversation

A key characteristic of practical theology is its mutuality and dialogical character. With a debt to David Tracy, the Association of Graduate Programs in Ministry described the heart of practical theology as a "mutually interpretive, critical, and transforming conversation between the Christian tradition and contemporary experience."

In *Blessed Rage for Order,* David Tracy set forth the basic task of any contemporary theology as that of deciphering and relating two sets of interpretations: "the Christian tradition and contemporary understandings of human existence" (p. 23). *How* these two areas are interrelated distinguishes various approaches to the Christian theological enterprise. In Orthodox and neo-Orthodox positions, the Christian tradition speaks and the culture is expected to listen; theologians reflect on the Christian tradition to address issues arising in human experience but do not allow the Christian tradition to be challenged in much depth by the culture itself. Orthodox interpretations of the Christian tradition remain buffered from contemporary challenges or shifts in interpretation. The liberal and radical theological positions, on the other hand, use the insights of the sciences and modern world as the ultimate criteria of theological affirmations. Thus, if science asserts that miracles are impossible, theologians should reinterpret their biblical exegeses accordingly. Tracy offers a balance between these two positions with a model that requires a dialogical approach and calls for a *mutually* critical correlation between interpretations of human experience and interpretations of Christian revelation.

Tracy suggests that the truth claims of all interpretations must be judged in terms of the internal coherence of the reflection, the disclosive power of the interpretation to provide resonant meaning, and the appropriateness of the interpretation in light of Christian texts, symbols, and the full tradition. His model thus centers the discernment of religious action in the world within a broad multidisciplinary conversation involving mutual critique in its interpretive framework. The model is inherently praxic because it involves reflection on human experience as well as on the wisdom of previous ages; it is transformative because it is broadly dialogical and therefore insistent on openness to new perspectives.

The question Tracy raises on how the Christian community relates its theological formulations with wider cultural insights mirrors in many ways the tension that the field of religious education has experienced throughout the twentieth century in connecting religion and education. The Religious Education Association early in the twentieth century called for a model in which the ideals of the educational enterprise would inform religious discourse and the ideals of religious worldviews would inform education. The brief history of the field has shown that one or the other discipline tends to dominate. Tracy's work on a conversational mode of interrelating insights from the Christian tradition and other interpretations of human experience coincides with the original ideals of the religious education community, which sought to forge a genuine dialogical partnership between religion and education. What seems to be clear is that *praxic* modes for both religious reflection and education are needed to sustain a true conversational partnership.

Historical, Hermeneutical, and Sociocultural Analyses

The AGPIM statement on practical theology asserts that "historical, hermeneutical, and sociocultural analyses are integral to this method of theology." All three forms of analysis are relatively new to the discipline of theology and are rooted in nineteenth- and twentieth-century developments in the social and natural sciences. For example, advances in cultural anthropology, linguistics, and sociology have heightened awareness regarding cultural differences and contextual meanings through which scriptural, archeological, and other data might be interpreted. Darwinian and other scientific discoveries about the emergent nature of our universe and planetary life have also created a familiarity with the notion of developmental processes in the world around us. These insights, in turn, have helped to forge the development of an historical consciousness that views Christian history and tradition not as a static set of revealed truths but rather as a human–divine conversation that continues to unfold in many languages, experiences, and cultural patterns. Each time-bound community develops its salient interpretations relative to the pressing questions of its culture and circumstances. Thus the questions of Greek-minded Christians in the fourth and fifth centuries differ in language categories and contexts from those of destitute Latin American base communities in the twentieth century. Yet both groups share much in common in faith and heritage. Historical and hermeneutical analyses are important to help each community situate its own Christian story within the ever-expanding horizon of other Christian histories and traditions. Each story lives within a larger cultural and linguistic pattern, and these must be uncovered to reveal the full breadth of meaning embedded in each layer of Christian historical development. Learning the Christian story in a community seeped in practical theology becomes an everwidening and exciting historical journey. The full, vibrant texture of the Christian tradition comes alive as community members search their roots with hermeneutical and sociocultural sensibilities. With each reflection, new aspects of the tradition come to light; the Christian community is always a learning community.

Sociocultural analyses also assist practical theologians in reading situations and cultures, so that they might join with others of good will in addressing the root issues underlying social and ecological ills of our day without engaging in the cultural devastation that has too often the been the case in Christian missionary efforts. As Edward Farley points out, practical theology requires a hermeneutic of situations—an interpretation of what is salient in our current realities. Again, the social sciences loom large as partners to religious reflection in discerning holy courses of action.

Communal Spirituality and Social Transformation

The last section of the AGPIM description of practical theology states that "pastoral or practical theology takes place in a community of faith, implies a spirituality that is both personal and liturgical, and is directed towards individual and social transformation in Christ." The statement points to the wholistic character of practical theology—study is joined with prayer and is rooted in a worshiping community of faith. Faith and critical reflection, reason and appreciative awe move together in a deepening, reflective spirituality that empowers both the person and the community of faith to act maturely on behalf of the gospel. Reflection on sacred texts is not limited to rational forms of critique; the whole person is engaged. Attentive silence begets word born of Spirit, and the worshiping community expresses its rich understandings of the Christian faith in praise and thanksgiving. From these moments of acknowledged gratitude, the community arises again, refreshed to live its joy in Christian service.

The social transformation that results is mutual. The community works toward a transformation of the social order according to Christian values, yet it is itself transformed as it encounters the Spirit in the challenges and questions of the wider culture and in its own reflective rhythm. The Spirit is already at work within the culture, the earth, and emerging universe and draws all into ever-deepening holiness.

Implications for Religious Education

Religious education in the twenty-first century has the major task of conveying the relevance and credibility of religious discourse and a religious worldview for a generation that is scientifically sophisticated, preoccupied with technological developments, increasingly indifferent to dogmatic formulations, and yet hungry for authentic spirituality. The contemporary culture's overwhelming enphasis on *techne* emphasis of contemporary culture has contributed to the longing for a wider, deeper vision of life but does not readily lead to the kind of questions that generate reflective wisdom. The *praxis/phronesis* focus of practical theology offers a new key and a shift in paradigm from *techne* concerns. Rootedness in a praxis mode of questioning and acting presents religious educators with a way forward for relevantly connecting contemporary life experiences with the full breadth of Christian vision, wisdom, and experience.

If religious education is to help people become integrated and develop spiritual wisdom and sensibilities, it will need to honor their human experience and help them put that experience into conversation with the insights and hopeful vision of previous ages. Such a movement toward human development and spiritual integration will also require overcoming the dualisms that have plagued the Christian tradition for centuries: culture versus faith, science versus religion, community versus the individual, and contemplation versus action. A religious education rooted in practical theology offers a path toward mature Christian development that is needed to respond to the cultural realities of the emerging millennium. Through ongoing rhythms of action and reflection and a sustained, mutually critical conversation between the deep Christian story and its present contextual realities, the Christian person and community exercise faith through engagement in the world. Such a faith will also be open and affected by the critiques of religious thought and religious organizations brought to it by its wider culture.

So far we have focused on the "religious" dimension of religious education. I would now like to explore educational paradigms that are rooted in *phronesis/praxis* approaches and propose that these educational models seem to be most amenable to an interplay with religious values. The mutually informing and critical conversation ideals set forth by the Religious Education Association in 1903 foreshadowed the later emergence of "practical theology" precisely because it was naming the kind of dialogical and multidisciplinary movement that a praxis rhythm requires. It also shared some of the major philosophical roots that led to the development of practical theology. What has impeded the development of religious education has not been the infeasible character of the field's ideals but rather the kind of knowing that has been emphasized in both religious and educational paradigms. The theory-to-practice mode that honors theory (or orthodoxy) first and then moves to practice later can quell reflection on experience as a possible starting point or conversation partner for developing guiding principles. Similarly, educational and moral approaches that solely emphasize preset behavioral "outcomes" and seek to develop the best techniques for reinforcing and shaping those learner outcomes often miss the larger questions that develop a truly reflective wisdom and capacity to discern unchartered courses of action. Certainly, all forms of knowing are important to human living. However, the primary framework emphasized in any system of religious discourse or education will determine which questions loom largest on the horizon. My central thesis is that a mode of praxis is needed in models of both religion and education for a truly mutual partnership and conversation between the two disciplines to emerge.

TRANSFORMATIVE MODELS OF EDUCATION

The natural educational partners for practical theology are those transformative models of education that also flow in an action-reflection rhythm of praxis and move toward both personal and social transformation. Paulo Freire in Brazil, for example, viewed education as a praxis of liberation (e.g., Freire's *Pedagogy of the Oppressed*). Working with the oppressed poor of Latin America, Freire's communities began with a clarifying examination of the social realities in which they found themselves. This *conscientization,* or development of critical awareness regarding experiences of injustice and their underlying causes, then opened the way for other educative actions, especially action on behalf of social transformation. Freire rejected what he called the "banking" concept of education that sees humans as accounts into which a teacher "deposits" new information that the student is expected to receive and memorize. Education for Freire centered on people's questions and problems related to their social and political realities; it involved praxis, people's actions and reflections upon their world, with an aim of transforming the social order into a more just and harmonious pattern.

Although Freire's educational methodologies arose out of his deep concern for addressing the embedded injustices and suffering he encountered, he also cautioned about too easily imitating the approaches that worked in his Brazilian context. Studying *about* the oppression of others does not lead to a liberative praxis unless the people themselves are conscienticized about the constraining bonds they experience in their own contextual realities. These bonds can be more subtle forms of alienation and dehumanization, such as those prevalent in wealthy countries like the United States, and may thus require different educational approaches for *conscientization* to occur.

A praxis-oriented educational paradigm in the United States that has received considerable attention and empirical research is the "Transformative and Emancipatory Learning" model proposed by Jack Mezirow (e.g., Mezirow's *Fostering Critical Reflection in Adulthood: A Guide to Transformative and Emancipatory Learning*). The model emphasizes a process of critical reflection on one's experiences and underlying interpretative assumptions as a means of reformulating what Mezirow calls "meaning perspectives," or networks of underlying assumptions that coalesce into one's worldview. The result of such learning is a fuller development of one's personhood and a greater capacity to act with integrity. The learners' search for more adequate frameworks of interpretation and their critical reflection on meaning perspectives challenge constraining assumptions that have been uncritically accepted and inherited from the surrounding culture. This transformation leads, according to Mezirow, to a broader and more integrative understanding of one's social realities and experiences. Acting with integrity is seen as a vital element of such "emancipatory" learning.

Caution Regarding Instrumental Learning

Mezirow points out that learning in most traditional societies centers on acquiring the normative outlook and skills needed to negotiate one's livelihood and fit in with established customs. Education often serves the purpose of passing on such traditions in order to preserve them and does not challenge their sources of authority or underlying assumptions. What the learner tends to assimilate uncritically are habits of perception, memory, thought, feeling, and problem-solving. These in turn become the meaning perspectives that frame the acquisition of new information. Unless such underlying perspectives are brought to light and critically examined, they will continue to guide the questions, surface reflections, and actions of adults in the society. Transformation of social structures ultimately requires some form of transformative learning that challenges underlying meaning schemes and allows new patterns to emerge creatively.

Drawing upon Habermas' domains of knowledge, which hearken back somewhat to Aristotelian distinctions, Mezirow distinguishes between instrumental learning, which emphasizes the acquisition of technical knowledge, and communicative learning, which centers on values and meanings. The *techne* concerns of instrumental learning focus education on learning how to perform a task or manipulate the environment in some way; the learning is geared toward specific task results and involves skills, however complex they may be. Mezirow acknowledges that instrumental learning has its place but maintains that it should take its direction and energy from the meaning and values that a community intentionally chooses. In many ways, the emphasis on instrumental learning in contemporary Western societies springs from the unexamined meaning perspectives that currently dominate.

Technical or instrumental learning is highly amenable to operationalized and preset measurable results and an accompanying empirical demonstration of acquired competencies. More difficult to preset as goals and therefore measure empirically are the results of a transformative conversation; measurement may determine that a paradigm shift has occurred, but the direction of the new framework cannot be predetermined before it is birthed. The educational shift is creative and emergent. The questions one asks using one set of meaning perspectives (e.g., for measurement of learning outcomes) may be vastly different from the questions considered to be most significant with new meaning perspectives. Transformative learning is not focused on the linear acquisition of a set of information or skill processes. Rather, it involves a shift in the basic framework for interpretation, the tectonic plates that underlie meaning-making and social action in the world.

Transformative learning thus parallels much of what Thomas Kuhn says about paradigm shifts in science. A new paradigm emerges in science when a question is posed or a problem encountered that cannot be explained within an existing scientific worldview. The sets of assumptions that undergird existing theories, research questions, and methodologies then become the focus of attention and critical examination. What emerges from such a search is a new paradigm that sets different boundaries for questions, possibilities, procedures for testing hypotheses, and phenomena to be explored. A classic example in the twentieth century was the shift from Newtonian physics to quantum physics and the new questions and research that emerged from such a shift.

Transformative learning outlines the contours by which paradigm shifts occur on a personal and communal level, particularly with respect to questions of values, social meanings, and concepts such as freedom, love, justice, and participation. It begins when learners encounter limits or constraints to their integration, growth, or understanding that cause a deeper level of questioning to occur. The transformative educational process then leads the learners into a critically reflective search for more inclusive and empowering meaning perspectives.

The Process of Transformative Learning

Research on the process of transformative learning points consistently to a dilemma or disorientation that acts as a catalyst for a person's search for more adequate explanations of what is happening. Such a disorienting dilemma can happen on an individual or a communal basis. When a marriage falls apart or a job is lost, when one's child abuses drugs or when the agony of refugees on TV newscasts sears the imagination, the question "why?" bubbles up and a significant search may begin. In the Bible we can see several shifts in understandings of God emerged when tragedies or significant disruptions to the normal order of things occurred. The Exodus challenged older concepts of

God and brought about new images and assumptions of a liberating and covenanting God. Similarly, the Judaic community was plunged into questioning its understanding of God when the Babylonian captivity wrenched it into exile. The prophetic new meanings expressed by Ezekiel consoled the people and assured them that the presence and providence of God was not limited to a particular geographic place. These broader, new "meaning perspectives" expanded once again the notion of who God is and how God acts; a larger paradigm was born. For Christians, the ultimate paradigmatic breakthrough was the resurrection of Jesus and the new meanings of life that such a reality ushered in.

These shifts represent examples of "transformative learning" that occurred within the religious community. Indeed, the notion of conversion itself is another way of naming the transformation of meaning perspectives. The shift may be sudden or gradual and it may be non-linear; it remains profound nonetheless.

Staying within old and familiar meaning perspectives can generate feelings of comfort and safety. A movement into critical reflection on unquestioned assumptions will often require a catalytic disorientation to start the process. Research still remains to be done on what contextual and personality variables contribute to the beginning of authentic critical reflection. What remains clear is that the educator needs to be aware that learners may be at various stages of readiness to engage in critical reflection and that their precipitating questions may search in differing directions. Attentiveness to what is happening in both context and person is key to fostering a growthful continuation of the exploration.

Beyond the initial catalytic event that brings new questions to the learner, transformative learning requires sustained critical reflection in order to develop either a deeper conviction of current meanings or a transformation of meaning perspectives. Mezirow and other proponents of transformative learning draw attention to the importance of a dialogical community and free-flowing discussion to support the reflective journey of those seeking new and more integrative meaning perspectives. Patricia Cranton, for example, in *Understanding and Promoting Transformative Learning,* highlights the importance of participation in a communal reflective discourse for assisting each participant to examine the coherence and validity of meanings and underlying assumptions. Distortions and biases are difficult to uncover under any circumstances. The assistance of a trusted group of companions who both challenge and are open to challenge can greatly help the process of exploration and creative transformation. Dialogic partners can also offer new perspectives and questions that the learner may not be able to see without assistance. Members of the learning community, however, must be adept at listening to one another and offering possibilities without insisting upon the acceptance of their own perspectives.

This dialogical dimension raises some values questions for the educational process itself. Stephen Brookfield, in *Understanding and Facilitating Adult Learning*, suggests that intentional learning communities need to foster a set of principles that guide members in their interactions with one another. The value of "respect" ranks high on his list. Also important is a collaborative, shared facilitation of the dialogue and a praxis rhythm of engagement in action that accompanies communal work of critical reflection.

Virtues for Transformative Learning

Paulo Freire perhaps addresses the values dimension of education most profoundly when he speaks, in *Pedagogy of the Oppressed*, of the conditions that foster true dialogue. Authentic dialogue, Freire asserts, requires the absence of domination and a stance of love, humility, and faith among all participants. Love abhors domination and seeks the integration and freedom of the other. The dialogical commitment of learning community members requires them to seek ways of becoming more aware of the moments when they seek to control others instead of allowing other members the freedom to pursue their own questions and reflections. The learning community itself grows in capacity to love as it develops a keener awareness of its communication patterns and seeks to foster a deeply respectful conversation. The quest for greater empathic listening and respectful expression is itself an invitation for members to engage in critical reflection as members challenge one another to examine their manner of interacting.

A second stance or virtue that Freire advocates is that of humility. This virtue calls community members to acknowledge the limits and conditioned nature of their own perspectives and to remain open to views that may differ widely from their own. Omniscience is not a quality that humans can claim, and the stance of humility keeps one planted firmly in the "humus" of finite existence. The stance of humility requires each person to embrace his or her own humanity and to own personal feelings, observations, and opinions.

Freire also calls members of dialogical communities to the virtue of faith–to a belief in the potential of the human heart and human energy to flow into true community on both a micro and a macro level. He calls for a stance of optimism that overcomes paralysis in the face of overwhelming social problems and empowers action for the sake of justice.

Together, all of these virtues–love, humility, and faith–lead to a ground of trust in the dialogical community. Without such trust, no true critical reflection can happen in dialogue; the risk of vulnerability is simply too great. Trust provides the emotional net of safety that enables a thorough examination of meaning perspectives in community. It also develops the comraderie needed for praxic action on behalf of social transformation.

The need for a dialogical community in transformative models of education leaves this educational paradigm ripe for religious dialogue and an examination of the virtues and values for human discourse that arise in the major wisdom traditions of the world. Recent developments in transformative education also call attention to the need for spirituality and a holistic view of the person as learner. The discourse on transformative education itself is expanding the model's horizons, resulting in more encompassing perspectives on the human person that include spiritual as well sociocultural dimensions.

THE INTERPLAY BETWEEN PRACTICAL THEOLOGY AND TRANSFORMATIVE LEARNING

Christian practical theology centers on questions such as "who are we to become and what kind of world should be labor for, because of God's presence and call in our lives?" It honors the deep and wide river of Christian experiences and interpretations that preceded us, and it explores the cultural streams of each age that helped to shape each tributary. It drinks deeply from the well of biblical metaphors, especially those centered on the reign of God, and explores the responses and responsibilities that such images call forth. Practical theology moves the Christian community toward engagement in Christ's salvific mission. With historical, hermeneutical, and sociocultural sensibilities, communities engaged in practical theology search the stories and meaning structures of Christian communities throughout the centuries in order to understand each layer of interpretation and draw new meanings for contemporary contexts. Praxic Christian communities apply these same sensibilities to the work of reading social, ecological, and cultural realities and discerning action in light of gospel values. They celebrate their common heritage in liturgy and worship and foster a stance of listening, not only to human and natural world voices but also to the Transcendent who continually communicates Self in a myriad of ways. They combine critical and appreciative awarenesses into an awakening spirituality, alive to the workings of the Spirit in multiple dimensions. Like a great live oak tree, the praxic Christian community sends down deep roots into the moist earth of tradition while opening its branches wide into the world.

The practical theology paradigm sees the Christian community as a faith-filled learning community, one engaged in a continual rhythm of action and reflection because of its deep belief in a God who enters human history with salvific power. The church is a pilgrim people, *semper reformanda*. Never arrived but always in journey, the community seeks the face of an ever-surprising, self-communicating God and does so by entering into the work of God in history. Thus, while practical theology affirms the joys of contemplation and the necessity of instrumental knowledge and technical skills, its learning mode is centered on the dimensions of *phronesis* and *praxis*.

The work of the Christian religious educator who takes the practical theology paradigm to heart is that of fostering the development of praxic learning communities. These dialogical communities learn more about their Christian roots as well as their current realities as they move through recurring cycles of Christian praxis. Religious education in a practical theology mode involves facilitating the action-reflection spiral, where reflection is fed by ever-widening explorations of the Christian faith world as well as sociocultural analyses of contemporary realities. Educational moments can certainly follow a pattern of regular times and places but need not be limited to a classroom or regular meeting time. Critical moments in pastoral care, parish planning, city or neighborhood action, or national Earth Day celebrations can each provide openings for new levels of theological reflection and religious education. For the religious educator, transformative models of education can become a valuable resource in terms of how to connect with people's pressing questions and foster further critical reflection in light of the full Christian life world. Transformative literature provides specific strategies for fostering and sustaining critical reflection and thus provides a praxis-oriented complement to the dialogical work of practical theology.

In the spirit of maintaining a mutually critical conversation the Christian tradition can also speak to the transformative learning movement. Christian life embraces rational discourse but it is not limited to the realm of rationality. Awed silence before Mystery is not uncommon in the history of Christian and Jewish spirituality. Prophetic wildness of imagination at times takes center stage in the biblical drama. Transcendent epiphanies shed surprising new light on ordinary events and transform their meanings in extrarational ways. Art and music both express and awaken ancient echoes of wisdom with us. Christian life houses many forms of knowing, living, and being on this sacred planet. Transformative learning, as a model of education that seeks more holistic human perspectives, might well draw from the kaleidoscope of human experience found in Christian and other faith traditions.

The virtues needed for the development of a truly dialogical community also resonate deeply with Christian values. Trust is a delicate net in a learning community. It cannot be instantly manufactured or evoked on cue, yet it is vital for the depth of dialogue needed to support communal critical reflection. Trust, as Freire points out, emerges from the expressions of love, humility, and faith in a group. Christian spiritual disciplines, as well as the self-awareness and adeptness in group dynamics fostered by psychosocial resources, can enhance personal and communal growth in trust and the other virtues that support it. These necessary personal virtues highlight the value-laden basis of transformative learning and connect it well with the wisdom traditions of the world.

CHRISTIAN RELIGIOUS EDUCATION IN THE TWENTY-FIRST CENTURY

The work of Christian religious educators involves many dimensions, each of which will encounter new challenges as the human community moves into the twenty-first century. Most basically, the task of the Christian religious educator continues to be that of facilitating the growth of the baptized into mature persons of living faith, persons who can act with wisdom and grace on behalf of the reign of God, even in situations that are massively complex and troublesome. Such wisdom implies the development of hermeneutical and historical sensibililties that can reappropriate and reassess Christian interpretations from the past and can also perceptively understand the contours of social issues and their cultural contexts. Fostering Christian maturity implies honoring and nurturing movement through the various stages of human development–intellectually, spiritually, emotionally, and socially. Transitions from one stage to the next will involve the expansion and transformation of meaning perspectives to broader, more inclusive and embracing horizons. This in turn will require various approaches to both critical reflection and appreciative affirmation of new understandings of the Christian faith.

A major challenge facing all Christian communities is that of maintaining credibility and relevance in the face of quantum leaps in the scientific and technological transformations of society. The Christian community cannot afford to be isolationist or ignorant of cultural trends and language. To be faithful to its mission, the Christian community must move into greater dialogue, both listening to and engaging the challenges and questions of the wider society, as well as of other faith traditions. It must also be able to "make a difference in the world" with intelligence and discernment, avoiding past mistakes of triumphalism and cultural demolition. The religious educator must become a leader in the dialogue, assisting others to learn the sociocultural and religious languages necessary to become true conversationalists and effective social activists in the world arena.

Christian religious educators must therefore be persons of keen sensitivity and listening acuity to surface the perspectives and questions raised by persons of faith as they encounter life circumstances and search the Christian tradition for guidance and vision. They also need the emotional capacity to attune to and help explore the unspoken and voiced feelings of others, without distorting them through the clouded lenses of suppressed self-awareness. Their own appreciative understanding of the Christian faith must run deep and wide, with sensitivity to the cultural assumptions that helped to formulate questions and responses in each age's interpretative discussions. And religious educators will need more than a passing interest in psychosocial, ecological, and cultural methodologies to assist them in collaborating with others to read the "signs of the times." Educationally, they will need a

broad range of approaches in how to facilitate a deepening cycle of
critical reflection and action, a praxic approach to Christian living.

An emerging question for Christian religious educators is how to
harness the holy use of technology on behalf of gospel values. The information super highway widens every day, and technological advances emerge with dizzying speed. These innovations, however, present new challenges and opportunities for religious educators as
cyberspace communities can now form and speak to one another via
the Internet. The technology is so recent that the possibilities and
shadow sides are still emerging. What is clear is that without a Christian religious education presence on the Internet, major cultural conversations will move forward without the Christian voice as partner.
The Internet will also highlight some forms of information and leave
out others. Can effective religious education occur if it is entirely verbal and leaves out the human dimensions of body language and into-
nations? Will extended attention to computers numb our sensitivity to
earth issues and the natural world? These questions are yet to be
weighted and engaged as religious educators move their critically reflective conversations to the World Wide Web.

Whatever the future structure and locus of religious education activities, the Christian call to just and compassionate action on behalf
of the reign of God will require some form of practical theology development in Christian communities. As a body of faithful, worshiping communities, the Christian church acknowledges that its own
growth and the transformation of the wider social order is ultimately
the work of the Spirit; it also recognizes, with Paul, that the church is
the Body of Christ and continues the risen Christ's salvific mission in
history. Christian religious educators act as both catalysts and facilitators of the community's growth in Christian praxis. To engage this sacred work, they will find in the literature of practical theology and
transformative learning rich resources to enhance their efforts.

10

Creating The Undiscovered Country

Religious Education as an Agent of Forging the Third Millennium

RONNIE PREVOST

INTRODUCTION

We marvel at the incredible quality and quantity of change that took place during the twentieth century. The rate of technological changed has increased geometrically first decade by decade, then year by year, and now almost daily. Even the political/global map has changed almost totally two or three times over during the past hundred years! Many nations that did not exist in 1900 have come, gone, reestablished themselves, and gone again by 2000.

How much more change has occurred over the past millennium! The world we know today would seem to be another planet (if they could conceive of a planet!) to the people of A.D. 1000. These changes have happened—and, thus have shaped and influenced—not only on the political maps, but also the maps of religion and education.

How much has religious education changed during that same period? Though religious education has seen considerable advances over the past millennium and in the past century, the proportion of change has been significantly less than that experienced in our world at large. Even with its "professionalization" and development as a separate academic discipline and the proliferation of degree programs—and publishing houses—in support of it, religious education (like so many other fields) has been unable to keep pace with the continually accelerating rate of change in technology and other areas of global culture(s).

Are religious educators, at this point, behind in relating to and influencing change in our world? I believe the answer is yes. Hopelessly behind? No. Is there anything religious educators in the third millennium can do to either slow down the pace at which they are lagging behind or, begin to catch up? As a cautious optimist, I think so, and in this chapter I will explain why.

In moving toward my observations and suggestions for forging a better religious education for the third millennium, I will briefly offer my explanation as to why religious education (and religious communities in general) has, as a body, historically been unable to keep pace with change. What remains after this "diagnosis", is to suggest short-term and long-term prescriptions and regimens and then to offer a prognosis.

I use the foregoing medical imagery advisedly. It has been said that, as with many professions, medicine uses the term "practice" because there are forces (such as the "human factor") at work that transcend the control of technique, no matter how well-informed, well-planned, or well-performed. For this and other reasons, the practitioner must be an artist of sorts, attempting various solutions to particular problems, and firmly rooted in the tradition of the discipline, but aware of the need and willing to try the unconventional when the foregoing has apparently failed. This is as true of religious education in particular as it is of education in general. Therefore, in speaking to challenging religious education and as an exercise in religious education, the following observations, projections, and propositions make no greater claim.

DIAGNOSIS

Parameters of the Challenge to Religious Education

By anthropological definition, religion is and always has been the component of culture by which its understandings, values, and so on are developed, expressed, and transmitted. What is not always so clear is what role religion, as a distinct part of the culture, plays in the development of cultural values. This is similar to the old chicken-and-egg question, that is, does religion play a greater or lesser role in forming culture? Or, from another perspective, is religion more semi-nal in cultural development or is it more reflective, taking on more of the character of a messenger and sustainer of culture? The relationship between any culture and any part of it is probably too complex to ar-rive at one universally correct answer, though individual anthropolo-gists, theologians, and religious educators have offered responses that differ in emphasis. (The questions certainly provide grist for reflection and for academic papers, theses, and dissertations in many different disciplines!) The same can be said of the complexity of the relation-ship between any particular religion and the culture in which it rises as well as the culture in which it currently exists. The basic issues seem to be those of proactivity versus reactivity. (Some may prefer the term "accommodation" over "reactivity." I choose the latter because it seems that whether or not what may be seen as accommodation oc-curs, what is done—for or against a specific cultural standard—will usually be done by methods normative for the culture. Reactivity is less thoughtful than proactivity and, thus, less transforming.)

The Challenge to Religious Education in History
Having been reared in a devout Christian (Baptist) family and like churches, having been educated by Baptist institutions of higher learn-ing, and having ministered in various Baptist churches and universi-ties and seminaries, I have at some level read and studied the Old and New Testaments throughout my life. What has always struck me (though I have not always understood it in these terms) is how the re-ligio-cultural tension described above has always been at the heart and core of the struggles of the people of God, often with tragic results.

Abraham was called to worship the one God out of a poytheistic culture. God's call to and covenant with Abraham was to proactively re-form the world and culture around him and his descendants. The Is-raelites, heirs of Abraham, would later succumb not only to the Egypt-ian bondage itself but also to a slave mentality, complicating Moses' task to lead them out of Egypt, through the wilderness, and into Canaan. They had become as enslaved by their culture as they were by their Egyptian masters. The same pattern can explain the Israelite *cherem* concept during the period of the conquest of Canaan and dur-ing the period of the judges. Rather than come to grips with and focus on the merciful aspects of God and seek to transform their culture, the Israelites were reactive, sharing and accommodating much of its cruelty (and misunderstanding and misrepresenting a compassionate God in the process). During the (relatively) united Hebrew monarchy and the division into the northern and southern monarchies of Israel and Judah, the move away from proactivity continued. Now divided, the Israelites continued to react to their culture by falling into the idolatry of the fertility cults that surrounded them while still seeking to maintain, for the most part, many of the rituals and other, more visible facets of their covenant life with God. The prophets called them away from this lifestyle. The oracles and visions of the challenged them to proactivity to transform themselves and their world.

The message of Jesus was prophetic and transformative—proactive—at its core. Especially as exemplified and summarized in the Sermon on the Mount (Matthew 5–7), Jesus challenged people to reorder their minds and lives in reference to God and not the culture—all toward the end of reforming and redeeming the world. Even the early church lapsed into reactivity, as shown in the struggles among the apostles regarding cultural norms and expectations concerning relationships between Gentiles and Jews, despite a plea like Paul's (Romans 12:2): "Do not conform any longer to the pattern of this world, but be transformed by the renewing of your mind" (New International Version).

The young church grew despite persecution, but this growth was also toward institutionalization, culminating in its establishment as the official religion of the later Roman Empire. By accepting this role, the church bound itself to the culture. This inevitably blinded the church to its call to be a prophetic, proactive, transformational force.

This pattern continues in contemporary churches and is reflected in the stories of most religions and faiths, which begin with a direct response to the perceived shortcomings of a status quo. This response tends to be visionary and proactive and can often be described as a leap beyond the culture in question. However, as the religion or faith progresses through subsequent stages of persecution, tolerance, acceptance, and, in some situations, establishment, it tends to become increasingly institutionalized, losing its original, proactive vision. Institutionalized it becomes more concerned with its own existence—reacting within existing cultural norms instead of transforming them. Even if this religion calls for change in an aspect of the culture, which it considers such to be a giant stride, what occurs happens in small steps and within frameworks prescribed by the culture. Even those who sincerely seek to lead the religion to rediscover its visionary and proactive origins can be almost as culturally bound as the persons and/or institutionalized religion they are trying to influence and change.

This kind of reactivity has always put religions behind culture. The philosopher Heraclitus once said, regarding the everchanging nature of things, that one never steps twice into the same river. A reactive response to culture, by the time it is brought to bear, will unavoidably be outdated at least to some degree. (Anyone who has purchased a computer in the last ten years is familiar with the continually accelerating rate of technological change.)

The Nature of the Challenge to Religious Education

I propose that religious education lags behind especially the culture because it is so much a part of both institutional religion and the culture that it has been almost exclusively reactive rather than proactive. This should not be construed as pejorative, disparaging, or derisive. It is simply recognizing the human limitations with which religious education must come to grips and overcome if it is to become more effective in the third millennium.

Religious education is not alone in this dilemma. One of the most widely read books in business world of the 1990s is *Reengineering the Corporation: A Manifesto for Business Revolution* by Michael Hammer and James Champy. The authors observe that late twentieth-century American businesses modeled themselves after what was proposed and developed by Adam Smith in *An Inquiry into the Nature and Causes of the Wealth of Nations*. But Smith wrote in the midst of the Industrial Revolution, over two hundred years ago. In a world of much more rapid change (and myriad other differences) following such an outmoded model dooms any corporation or business seeking to exist (even more so to thrive) on an increasingly competitive national and world stage.

Religious education finds itself in the same world described by Hammer and Champy. Rapid technological change can frustrate and challenge those seeking to stay abreast of the latest innovations in computer and communication technology. This is certainly true of religious education in that such advances are proving to broaden the horizons of creative pedagogical methodology. However, the technologies of many other areas (the multifarious forms and subdiscipline of biomedicine, for example) are also increasingly fluid and impact religious education directly and indirectly and should be influenced by it.

Expressions of the Challenge to the Philosophy of Religious Education

What may not be so obvious is that the many varieties and degrees of technological development also demand the rethinking of the metaphysical, epistemological, and axiological dimensions of educational philosophy. Digital technology is simple at some levels. For instance, I am writing this chapter and typing these words on a computer using a popular, general-use word processing application. As I type, the computer translates digital code into a visual image and, when I direct it, saves that code to disks (hard drive and two "floppies"). I see the words, but I also know that the image is only a visual reflection of the digital reality. As you read these same words, they are probably on a printed page, also visual images (but generated by ink on paper). Whether the medium is digital (on a monitor screen) or physical (on the printed page), some aspects of technology are held in common with other modes or levels. The type of communication in which we are engaged is one in which technological differences can be simply expressed in terms of methods and forms of storage.

Complexities of change are also characteristic of the communication made possible by the Internet. As a relatively new development (having been in existence only a few years as of this writing), the Internet itself is evolving and spreading, and certainly will continue to do so. As the Internet and other forms of communications technology change and multiply, so will the complexity, quantity, and quality of the questions they will surface. So it will also be with other currently existing technologies and those yet to emerge. The rest of this section includes a brief overview and sampling of just *some* of the issues and questions that technology generates for religious education. I would encourage the reader to think of others and similarly reflect.

Issues of Metaphysics. The digital world, cyberspace, and so on, just by generating the term "virtual reality" and creating the possibility of artificial intelligence, evokes the most basic of metaphysical issues: the very nature of reality and existence of the natural, personal, and interpersonal.

Many schools, colleges, and universities are exploring the use of computers, the Internet, various forms of telecommunications, and other new technologies in delivering education of at all levels, from preschool through doctoral work and beyond. Many churches, synagogues, and other religious communities are already on-line and have the capability not only to generate their own cyberframework for various types of religious education experiences in addition to traditionally understood schooling but also to connect with geographically dispersed schools. The potential is astounding for catechetical instruction, teacher education, and collaborative research. Many more types of educational media are becoming immediately available in many more venues. This prospect alone requires the reconsideration of many traditionally understood definitions of educational concepts and components. The ability to link students from around the world in either a synchronous or an asynchronous "virtual classroom" offers the opportunity for learning from a greater variety of immediate and wide-ranging global perspectives. However, this also surfaces the question of how community in its truest sense can be developed in such a class.

Thus it is necessary to reexamine the very nature of community and its role in the educational process, especially for religious education. Most religions, at some level, call their adherents to corporate relationship among their respective adherents. The ontological expression of the matter is similar to that experienced by the early Christian church as it considered the nature of Jesus. There was a heretical group called gnostics—dualists who believed that the spirit was good and the flesh was evil; and "never the twain shall meet." Some of them, known as "docetics," reconciled this with the Christian belief that "God was in Christ" by stating that Jesus was spirit and only *appeared* to be in the flesh (a "phantom," if you will). What emerged as the orthodox Christian understanding was at great variance with the docetics. The issue continues to be understood as one of the most basic and foundational among Christians of all sorts, regardless of how their answers might differ. Expressed in terms of religious education, the question is: Can true community exist in a "virtual classroom" in which the members can be seen but not touched or experienced in person?

Issues of Epistemology. The answer to the preceding question gives rise to epistemological questions of, for example, how vital community is to learning, how community can be developed in a digital environment, and so on. Since epistemology is concerned with the nature of knowledge, its sources, and how learning takes place, it stands at the very core of pedagogy of any religious education and any other area of education. The ever expanding landscape of communication technology broadens potential exposure to various epistemologically understood sources of knowledge (i.e., reason, senses, authority, revelation, and intuition) and can enhance complementary interaction among them within the individual as well as dialogue about them within a group.

However, this broader exposure may also afford greater opportunity for questioning a source in light of what is learned from another. *Time* magazine (May 10, 1999, p. 42) reported the results of a poll regarding the effect of on-line learning on youth. One question was on levels of trust ("great deal," "somewhat," "not at all") invested in five varying sources of information by youth (parents, teachers, religious leaders, friends, TV news and newspapers, and the Internet). Ranking highest in "great deal" were parents (83%); the Internet was lowest (13%). (Religious leaders were in the middle at 55%.) Conversely, the Internet ranked highest in not being trusted at all (24%) and parents lowest (1%). (At 11% religious leaders ranked second in not being trusted at all.) Seventy-eight percent responded that it was a good idea "for teenagers to have access to the Internet." It seems safe to assume that if so many adolescents think Internet access is a good idea, they will be using it more. A follow-up poll among youth after more years of access and other exposure to the Internet (especially if there are significant shifts in the rankings) would be interesting.

Because of its very nature, a great deal of technology resonates with rationalism, especially as it uses formal logic as an epistemological source. An increasingly technologically oriented people may inexorably drift toward reason/rationalism and thus become inured to the need for balance in their sources of knowledge. The perceived need for empirical knowledge as obtained through the senses may subsequently erode, though some may see empiricism and rationalism as similar. It also can deny intuition as a valid source of knowledge, denying the creativity and the creative learning that can happen when in a burst of personal understanding one leaps beyond commonly understood answers to a question or problem.

This should be of particular concern for religious educators because of the primacy of revelation (i.e., revealed knowledge) in religion. Any person who can only think in a narrowly understood rational manner will find it difficult (if not impossible) to even conceive of "knowing by faith." How much less would such a person be apt to believe and internalize any religion holding illogical (in terms of purely human rationality) or empirically unverifiable tenets?

Epistemological questions quite naturally speak not only to sources of knowledge but also to basic issues of pedagogy. Each source of knowledge may be valid, yet individual theorists prioritize them and call them to interaction differently. Educators design teaching/learning strategies and activities according to that educational design. That may seem simple. However, educators also need to take into account the consciously or subconsciously preferred learning style of the students as well as their differing types and levels of intelligence. If it may be assumed that students of the third millennium will be required by the very force of technological advances to be adept at the use of those technologies, pedagogical complexities arise and abound. If the skills required of those students predispose them almost exclusively toward one mode or method of learning, what are educators to do? Acceding to that one means of learning will lead to the epistemological imbalance discussed above. On the other hand, is it reasonable to expect students to "learn to learn" by means and methods so different from those by which they are continuously inundated? And if so, how?

Issues of Axiology. Axiology, which comprises ethics and aesthetics, speaks to issues of worth and values, and to questions of the good. Both ethics and aesthetics ask questions regarding the existence of universal foundations and absolutes of values, ethics relating to moral thought and conduct, and aesthetics to beauty. Although most would readily accept the centrality of ethics to religion (and therefore to religious education) not so many would do so with aesthetics unless or until contemplating the importance of graphic art, music, dance, and so on to the rituals and other expressions of most religions.

Axiology, in terms of both of its components, will (like metaphysics and epistemology) also affect the core of pedagogical curriculum, content, and methodology. At this juncture the scientific and technological advances so emblematic of the late twentieth century not only precipitate cultural change but also pose marked problems for religion and religious education.

Nowhere is this more apparent and confounding than in the area of biomedicine. The tenets of some nonmainstream religions have long stood at odds with such currently standard procedures such as blood transfusions, immunizations, and so on. Persons from mainstream denominations often find it difficult to identify with these groups and may view them as either quaint or unnecessarily radical. However, even the most orthodox can better sympathize with nonmainstream religions by struggling with the basic questions of the nature of life, soul, and spirit posed by cloning and genetic engineering. In vitro fertilization and similar technologies surface similar complexities. The same can be said of medical technologies that have provided mixed blessings, extending life expectancy while (in some instances) ignoring the quality of life. Such issues have rendered the meanings of death and life much less metaphysical and more immediately, practically, and ethically important every day to millions of people, regardless of religion.

The bioethical issues extend beyond "death with dignity," "pulling the plug" (or not pulling it), infertility, ownership of frozen gametes and zygotes, the spiritual status of clones, and so on. These issues deal with technologies that either already exist or are assumed will exist. More questions need to be asked in anticipation of the ethics of opening up certain areas for research. Few ask whether or not science *should* explore certain horizons. It seems to be accepted by most that "if it *can* be done it *will* be done."

The above issues are neither isolated nor hypothetical. They are being considered by countless people across the religious spectrum, particularly in industrialized countries, every day. This concern should be reflected in the educational curricula and content of any religion that cares about the speculative and realized quality of human life. It strikes at the very heart of where people live. This is where people will try to make and/or find meaning in life; many will be looking, as they always have, to their own or another religion for help and instruction in making informed choices as their religious worldview and their reality come into juxtaposition.

The marriage of various forms of art with emerging technologies offers the promise of broadening both the availability and variety of aesthetic experiences. Various visual arts will continue to become more widely available through diverse digital media from CDs to tele-computing and beyond. Further, because of their digital nature, art-work delivered by these means will be subject to creative manipulation and application by individuals, opening up heretofore unexplored vistas of personal expression. The use of electronically produced "visual sound" (such as that used in the 1996 movie *Mr. Holland's Opus* by which the fictional band director/protagonist shared his music with his deaf son) can enable the hearing-impaired to experience music and other sounds. Other technologies make it possible for, as an example, even the most musically illiterate or inept to compose and perform music of their own expression. A similar dynamic is evidenced in technologies that enable the voiceless to "talk." Emerging electronic means are enabling the paralyzed to "walk" (or "dance") in a similar way. Advances in many areas of medicine are offering many para-lyzed persons more muscular control and movement so that expression through creative movement is a greater possibility for many.

Certainly debate will continue as to whether some of these expressive forms are truly "art," but these questions have always been addressed by aesthetics. Important for religious education is that greater opportunities for aesthetic expression will enable more people to engage in a "normal" part of religious life. Artistic expression serves religion and religious education as a pedagogical tool (e.g., teaching and reinforcing beliefs) and as an empowerment to look beyond the immediate and the rational, in order to more readily experience the transcendent.

PRESCRIPTION

As with so many other developments throughout history, technological breakthroughs are, in and of themselves, amoral. Both collectively and individually they hold tremendous potential for either good or ill, both of which have already been realized. Technology offers opportunities for freeing and empowering persons. However, as a definer of the age it, like capitalism and socialism can also enslave and oppress.

The challenge for the religious education of the third millennium is to be a means of liberation and empowerment rather than an accessory to the either latent or realized tyranny of technology. Forging a better religious education for the third millennium will require a significant paradigm shift. The archetype of today's religious education is based on a cultural perspective much more dated than that on which the business/corporate world, which gave rise to Hammer and Champy's call for "re-engineering." Simply stated, religious education for the third millennium must be reengineered to be more proactive and prophetic. By proactive, I mean engaged in anticipation and formation of the future. By prophetic, I mean involved in preparing persons more for the by calling them back to their core religious beliefs. By reintroducing spirituality into the cultural dialogue, religious education can be a primary player in enabling humankind, individually and corporately, to take control of and lead technology rather than vice versa.

In some ways, this will demand something radically new. It will also mean reclaiming parts of our past that have been neither lost nor forgotten but seem to have been overshadowed by other concerns. Creating something new will require significant innovation and new ways of thinking. Reclaiming our past will necessitate going "back to the future" or, in other words, discovering elements of our past that were ahead of our time and can enable us to form and inform our future.

A Proactive Religious Education

As a child I was mesmerized (and I still am) by the starry night skies and by the early stages of space exploration. Looking up at the moon and knowing that it was approximately 250,000 miles from earth, I calculated that a spacecraft traveling at 24,800 mile per hour (the speed required to escape the earth's gravitational pull) could reach it in approximately ten hours. It was just a matter of simple mathematics. However, I soon learned (still on a relatively simple level) that the matter was much more complex: as the spacecraft was speeding toward its objective, that objective itself was moving (and much faster). Astronauts following my "flight plan" would arrive at the mark only to find that the moon having moved on.

A better religious education for the third millennium will need to learn from this childhood anecdote. Until this century, knowledge increased and change occurred at a much more leisurely rate. The immediate future was really little different from the immediate (or, in some instances, even the distant) past. Like my naïve understanding of space travel, religious education was a simple matter of looking to the past and applying its truths to the present. Though some measure of the quantity and quality of differences and progress were expected, the present was nevertheless considered to be a rather close model of the near future.

The geometric progression of change we experience today, which will continue well into the third millennium demands that our approach be less naïve and simplistic. Rather, we will need to prepare people for their everchanging future, a future that will be increasingly different from their pasts and presents.

This situation holds two particular implications for religious education. First, since there will always be certain aspects of the future that are beyond human control, religious education must improve its ability to anticipate what the future will be. Second, some aspects of the future will be subject, at least to some greater or lesser degree, to human influence and form. Religious education must be more proactive in creating the future and in teaching others to do so. Only then will religious education prepare and empower its students for their future when it arrives (and rapidly passes) and be relevant in all their tomorrows.

Further, religious education must accomplish this by precept, methodology, and example. It will influence the curriculum, content, and pedagogy of every level and dimension of religious education, from that which is based in the congregation through theological higher education.

A Prophetic Religious Education

In his comprehensive and very influential book, *Christian Religious Education: Sharing Our Story and Vision* (1980), Thomas Groome described "shared praxis" as an approach by which religious educators could bring into community the past, present, and future. A major portion of the value of Groome's approach to our discussion lies in his call us to move beyond an Aristotelian, straight-line concept of time and understand and deal with its very fluid nature. For Groome, shared praxis is an experiential method by which past, present, and future are brought into dialogue, enabling the individual to become a participant in each.

Many, even some of Groome's enthusiasts (myself included), have seen the past both as a source (that out of or from which we have grown) and as the primary resource, owing more to what has been than to what is and what will be. The present is seen as the time for action. The future is that for which we must "have an eye" and toward which we must work.

The result of this perspective is that the fleeting present and the rapidly approaching future get short shrift. Given the continuously accelerating rate of change, this is something we can ill afford. I am convinced that, as a paradigm for religious education, shared praxis will continue to hold great promise. However, to use a wonderful metaphor offered by Mary C. Boys in *Educating in Faith: Maps and Visions* (1989), our "maps" have been too focused on where we have been and where we are, and we must pay greater attention to developing maps of the future where we will be.

What, then, are we to do with the past? Must we deny our heritage and the very foundation of our religious belief? By no means! The task for religious education is to reexamine the foundational principles of religion and its history to sort the essential from the extraneous. This, in fact, is at the heart of Groome's appeal for Christians to critically reflect on the "Christian community story and vision" as found in Scripture, tradition, and history. As we rediscover the essentials of faith, we concurrently learn how adherents of various eras and cultures have appropriated and applied those same essentials in their own times and lives. This is valuable in itself and affirms the value of being mindful of our history and heritage. Nevertheless, what is at the core and nothing else must remain at the core. Only by ridding itself of the unnecessary will any religious education be able to keep apace of the future.

This is what I call prophetic mostly because of the precedents I find in the Bible, more specifically, the Old Testament. The essence of the Old Testament prophets' collective ministry was to call Israel and Judah back to their religious origins. These nations had strayed from those origins and had accrued much spiritual deadweight:

> I hate, I despise your religious feasts; I cannot stand your assemblies. Even though you bring me burnt offerings and grain offerings, I will not accept them. Though you bring choice fellowship offerings, I will have no regard for them. Away with the noise of your songs! I will not listen to the music of your harps. But let justice roll on like a river, righteousness like a never-failing stream." (Amos 5:21–24, New International Version). Micah (6:8) said "He has showed you, O man, what is good. And what does the Lord require of you? To act justly and to love mercy and to walk humbly with your God" (NIV).

Impact on Curriculum and Content

Religious education in the third millennium will need to be better informed on, and more concerned with, an even wider range of subjects. Historically, religious education has attended to matters across the spectra of theological, philosophical, social, and educational disciplines. As those various disciplines have grown, deepened, and expanded, as a practical and applied discipline corresponding to each, so religious education has grown too. Religious education has always utilized the results of those conversations in forming the structure and subject of what it has taught both in macrocosm and microcosm. This eclectic, interdisciplinary dialogue must continue.

However, religious education must engage even more areas of life in conversation and must let them inform and influence its curricula and content as well as its pedagogy. Of particular interest should be science and existing and emerging technologies. Some points of interface between religious education and some particular technologies have been mentioned above, especially in terms of how these technologies impact elements and components of educational philosophy. The curricula and content of religious education will continue to need to take into account existing and emerging technologies for similar reasons. However, in order to become more proactive, religious education will also need to include science and technologies as part of the curriculum and content for the sake of having a voice in forming and shaping the technologies as they develop.

This does not mean that all religious educators must become experts in all areas of science and technology, although they need to become better informed and more widely read. However, more academic research needs to be done in more areas by those who can then inform the larger academic community of religious educators. Ensuing academic conversation should deal with issues of immediate impact on educational philosophy and application, and also on how religious education can, should, and will influence the directions technology takes and its destination. This informed proactive model can also be applied in the curricula and content at any (preferably all) of the levels of religious education of any faith community.

This approach reflects the liberating and empowering praxis that Paulo Freire (and Thomas Groome) championed. Although it falls short of being revolutionary, it puts a new spin on what was at the heart of the origins of liberal arts education. In classical and medieval education the liberal arts were defined as those disciplines necessary to develop the rational powers of persons. They were intended for teaching people skills for particular tasks (the Greeks felt that skills needed to be taught only to those who would be doing the work and not the thinkers and leaders) but were to enable and empower them to think more effectively and, thus, lead society. However, since many areas of technology are widely available and used—and directly impact so many lives—technology should be seen as another "liberal art." Religious education must be involved in enabling and empowering people to be effective thinkers and doers.

Impact on Pedagogy

One obvious goal of this model would be to have the student and teacher be a community of religious education learning to learn and bringing what is learned to bear on the worlds in which that community exists and will exist. Encouraging mutual, two-way informing among disciplines and religious education will be requisite to that end.

The pedagogical implications of this model for religious education are similar to those found in Groome's shared praxis approach, but perhaps with an even more eclectic and an intentionally and expressly heuristic twist. The dialogue and movements of shared praxis must explicitly and directly include not only the dimensions of time but also those elements (e.g., technology, literature, politics, etc.) that define the culture. The task of this shared praxis should be to discover how the faith community, by applying its foundational beliefs, can develop long-term answers to contemporary questions and concurrently influence the future in which that solution can exist.

This, then, will require that a teacher, as a fellow pilgrim both in the faith and culture and toward the future, develop for students experiences in class that will simulate what is experienced outside of class. Functionality and creativity are not mutually exclusive. The teacher should encourage students to creatively incorporate and apply a broad, diverse range of disciplines while neither consciously nor subconsciously relying on an "orthodox" way of doing things that has both strayed from the origins of the faith and is so mired in the past that it is incapable of speaking to the culture and issues of the present, much less lead toward, inform, and form the future. The point would not be to encourage students to fantasize, at least not in the sense that they (the students) are left in inaction. It would be to engender dreams in which they have ownership and in which they can, will, and do invest their energies, lives, and futures.

PROGNOSIS

The prescription I have written conveys one understanding of what *should* be. The more daunting task is to describe what *will* be, but such is the nature of prognosis. Perhaps my safest approach would be to say that the outlook is "guarded."

I am a cautious optimist. My optimism and hope are based on my faith and confidence in those with whom I share a commitment to the profession and discipline of religious education. It is my (admittedly biased) opinion that, as a group, professional religious educators already are committed to an interdisciplinary, heterogeneous mode of working and being informed. For most religious educators, what I propose is a natural next step and an extension of what, to varying degrees and in differing forms, religious educators have always done.

My caution rises out of an awareness that the type of changes my proposed approach will ultimately demand of the institutions involved come slowly. The institutions of those disciplines invited to the dialogue I envision may hesitate, for some will fail to see the enriching opportunities for all, blinded by discipline-related chauvinism, protectionism, or paternalism. Publishing houses, understandably concerned with their already closely met margins, may find themselves unwilling to take the risks required of being truly cutting edge and more amenable to business as usual. Also (and perhaps most important) the existence and/or power of those offices and other expressions of any institutionalized religion that may be extraneous to the very core of their respective religious roots may themselves feel (and may actually be) threatened.

By whatever means, forging a better religious education for the third millennium will inescapably involve risks for all involved. Certainly there will be instances of, at the very least, perceived failure, loss, and frustration. However, religious education that refuses to reform itself, its faith community, and its culture is doomed to the tragedy of general failure and irrelevance. The excitement, wonder, empowerment, and freedom experienced by those who form the future come to those who dare to dream dreams and labor to realize them.

11

Vision, Prophecy, and Forging the Future

JAMES MICHAEL LEE

"Ecclesia semper reformanda." (The church in all its aspects must undergo continuous reformation.)
— ancient Church motto

Oh, I suppose that we possibly have a few things that might not be completely perfect. But overall, we really don't have any problems. Everything is wonderful here in our operation."
— religious education administrator

INTRODUCTION

This chapter deals exclusively with religious instruction axis and intent. The word "instruction" does not in any way mean a separate way of doing religious education. Instruction is a term which includes all larger forms of teaching and all specific kinds of teaching procedure whether high structure or low structure, whether programmatic or nonprogrammatic, whether in formal or informal settings. Instruction means to teach with intentionality and purposefulness. I prefer the word "instruction" rather than the bald word "teaching" because instruction makes more salient the inherent intentionality and purposefulness of the teaching act.

243

Spirit of this Chapter

This book is lies squarely in the prophetic line. Thus, this chapter is unabashedly and very pointedly prophetic, as is true with everything I have ever written.

A major thrust of the prophetic role is basic transformation. The primary goal of the prophetic role in any field, including religious instruction, is accommodative learning rather than assimilative learning, to borrow Jean Piaget's terminology (1952). Assimilation is the process of placing new learnings into an already existing framework. In marked contrast, accommodation refers to the kind of learning that either radically changes an already existing framework or actually establishes a fundamentally new framework capable of accommodating the new learning. This fundamentally new framework is required when the old framework is not capable of satisfactorily dealing with the new learnings. Affectively, assimilative learning is comfortable and reassuring because it is safe; it does not upset one's basic way of interpreting or valuing reality. On the other hand, accommodative learning is typically quite upsetting because it wrenches one out of one's accustomed comfortable way of interpreting and valuing the world and places one in a far different and often unfamiliar world. One of the basic reasons why prophets in the civil, church, and religious instruction arenas have so frequently been reviled and persecuted is they cry out for accommodative learning as a prerequisite for hastening the future.

The prophet foresees what persons need to learn. Most persons, including many church members, a large number of religious educationists and educators, and notably an overwhelming percentage of ecclesiastical officials do not seem to want to learn what they need to learn. The prophet is thus a genuine threat to these individuals who, in turn, strenuously resist the prophetic message and spurn the prophet. One sign of a true prophet is the individual who stands squarely in the stream of accommodative, transformational learning. Conversely, one mark of a false prophet is the person who habitually tells people what they yearn to hear in an attempt to be popular, and in the process becomes a slave to the plaudits of the multitude.

The message of the prophets, particularly those in the religious domain, is more likely than not to be forthright. Aiming as it does to be prophetic, this chapter stands unashamedly in the strong stream of forthrightness. Additionally, this chapter is confrontational, not only because prophets tend to be confrontational but also because dissonance theory has clearly shown that confrontation is one of the most effective devices for crowbarring persons out of the tightly nailed boxes of their comfortable pattern of assimilative learning thus making it possible to open the lid for the acquisition of accommodative learning. Candor and confrontation fall squarely within the tradition of the exercise of the prophetic role, as witness, for example, Amos and Jeremiah. In the spirit of Amos and Jeremiah and all the rest, I am not using confrontation for the sake of confrontation. On the contrary, I am using confrontation as a necessary device to produce transformational growth, in this case transformational growth in religious instruction. When done in the prophetic spirit, outspoken forthrightness and confrontation are not at all negative but rather are robustly positive because these qualities are directly aimed at effectively bringing about the kind of growth that really matters. There are times, possibly many times, when confrontational critiques call for the destruction of older, outmoded, and thus mission-hindering structures and patterns so that basically new and more effective patterns and edifices can be built on solid ground rather than on the rickety structures of past ineffective ways of operation. In this chapter, as in all of my writings, I take pains to offer general proposals and also concrete, specific ways of making religious education as successful as possible. Persons standing in the prophetic tradition typically follow up their critiques with proposals for doable ways of building anew and building better.

Sharp intellectual critiques have nothing to do with love or unlove of the person being intellectually critiqued. Intellection and love are two different categories of reality. Just because one disagrees, and even disagrees sharply, with the position of another person does not mean that one lacks love for the other individual as a child of God, as a human being, and as a colleague. Critiques of the prophetic sort are typically done with love—burning love for the truth, and often love of the person with whom one disagrees (Rev 3:19).

If religious educationists and educators truly love the field of religious instruction, they will not snub or isolate or persecute those who disagree with one or another of their positions, but rather do everything they can to ensure that all positions are heard so that out of the clash of positions the truth can emerge. If religious educationists and educators love the field first and foremost, they will welcome critiques and will work energetically with the persons offering the critiques to openly and unegoistically seek the truth. If, on the other hand, religious educationists or educators love their own egos (and by extension the positions that they advocate) more than they love the field, they will become angry at critics and attempt in divers ways to silence or exclude these critics in one way or another. I never cease to be shocked when I read or hear religious educationists and educators who at one minute strenuously cry out for the necessity of critical and emancipatory reflection in religious education and at the next minute become furious when a colleague critiques some aspect of their position. And I am simultaneously amazed and disillusioned when I witness religious educationists and educators wholeheartedly advocate the necessity of diversity in all things yet grow angry and personally insulted when colleagues exercise diversity by disagreeing with a their positions. Is diversity selective? Differences should unite rather than divide religious educationists and educators as they work together to seek what is best for the field and for God. Why is it that in so many fields of activity persons who disagree, often sharply, with one another are good friends and devoted colleagues, while in the religious education arena disagreement so often brings with it isolation, exclusion, and persecution both subtle and overt? Forging the future in any field, including that of religious instruction, necessitates sharp disagreement so that the truth can thereby emerge tried and tested.

It seems to me that all religious educationists and educators in the third millennium ought to be working egolessly to seek what is best for religious instruction, and thus walk arm in arm not only with those with whom they agree but also, and maybe more importantly, with those with whom they disagree.

THE SUPREME IMPORTANCE OF RELIGIOUS INSTRUCTION

One of the most piercing and important questions ever framed about religious instruction was posed in 1974 by Charles Melchert, who asked in the title of an article: "Does the church really want religious education?" All of the information at my disposal unmistakably suggests that there is not a single Christian faith group which really and truly wants religious education to the extent to which they ought. Yet it is impossible to successfully forge a bright future for religious instruction in the third millennium unless and until the churches not only recognize the supreme importance of religious instruction, but actually mobilize their efforts in such a wholehearted way as to place religious instruction at the pinnacle of their efforts.

That religious instruction ought to stand at the pinnacle of the church's activity should be obvious. The Bible, that unshakable, infallible, inerrant foundation of Christianity, is basically a religious instruction book (Rom 15:4; 1 Cor 10:11). The Bible is a history of how God taught religion to his people; it also is a document that itself teaches religion to persons in all eras. The Bible is not essentially a theological treatise, though there it does contain some theology as part of its overall religious instruction intent.

Jesus was primarily a redeemer and a religious educator. Everything he did can be subsumed under these two co-primary functions.

Just before he arose to heaven, Jesus gave his last religious instruction lesson to his disciples, teaching them what he wanted them to do once he was no longer on earth. In The Great Commission (Mt 28: 19–20), Jesus only asked his church to do two things: confect the sacraments and teach religion.

The great apostle Paul did not even confect the sacraments preferring instead to concentrate all of his ministry on religious instruction (1 Cor 1:17), thus unmistakably indicating the supremely high regard in which Paul held the work of religious instruction.

In the Roman Catholic religion, Conciliar documents ranging from the Council of Trent (1545–1563) down to the Second Vatican Council (*Presbyterorum Ordinis*, 1965) have held that the single most important task of the priest, and thus by extension of the whole church, is religious instruction. Papal formal statements such as *Acerbo Nimis* (1905), as well as documents from various Vatican curial congregations, have stated the same thing. Protestant denominations are no different in their wholehearted emphasis on the primacy of religious instruction. Indeed, one would be hard-pressed to find a single Protestant denomination that does not place religious instruction (usually cast in the language of one instructional procedure, namely, preaching) as topmost in importance for every cleric.

Despite all of this enormous evidence and testimony about religious instruction being the most important task of the church, how many contemporary churches really want religious instruction? The record is dismal. In my own Catholic religion, very few bishops and clergy seem to regard themselves as primarily religious educators in the plenitude of that term. Despite a string of Vatican documents stating that course work in religious instruction should occupy a prominent place in seminary education, the curriculum in many Catholic seminaries does not include as much as even a single course in religious instruction. Even in those seminaries whose curriculum includes a solitary course in religious instruction, the part-time faculty member teaching that course is often a local religious educator lacking requisite academic and scientific knowledge of the field. The scandalousness of this situation can be appreciated when one compares the credentials of religious education faculty in a Catholic seminary to the professional preparation and experience of faculty members in biblics or moral theology or canon law.

A bright spot in American Catholicism as contrasted to American Protestantism is the number of full-time paid parish directors of religious education. Many of these persons are professionally prepared, but some are not. Yet the full-time parish directors of religious education are often paid less than they deserve, thus signaling the somewhat low esteem in which religious instruction is held by the pastor or bishop. And not infrequently the professional parish director of religious education clashes with the pastor, who, though not professionally prepared in religious instruction, still mistakenly thinks that by virtue of ordination and appointment he knows more about religious instruction than the DRE. This scandalous situation needs remedying.

Seminary course work in religious instruction is far more common in Protestant seminaries, especially Evangelical Protestant seminaries, than is the case with their Catholic counterparts. Yet the situation here is not nearly as good as it should be. The prestige and scholarly attainments of the seminary faculty in religious education are more often than not considerably lower than that of their counterparts in biblics and systematics. Happily, some Protestant seminaries, notably Evangelical Protestant seminaries, do offer majors in religious education. Notwithstanding, it is generally recognized that students majoring in religious education frequently are less academically gifted than those majoring in biblics or systematics. One highly intelligent religious education faculty member who was then teaching in an Evangelical Protestant seminary once told me that 75 percent of the religious education majors in that seminary were on academic probation. Once Mainline and Evangelical Protestant seminarians, regardless of their

major, are ordained and are employed in a local church, they usually
cannot move fast enough out of religious education duties, except for
a few high profile religious education events, which among other
things, put the clergymenber in the limelight.

Yet if Catholic and Protestant clergy were to conscientiously make
a log of their daily activities, they might be surprised to discover that
most of their time is spent in religious instruction ministry, especially
in informal settings. If religious instruction is to be successfully
forged in the third millennium, then the clergy must recover their
teaching office, to use the felicitous words of Richard Robert Osmer
(1990). This is not a luxury. It is a necessity.

At the national and regional levels, Catholics are quite well organized in terms of leadership. Every diocese has a person who is formally in charge of religious instruction in the diocese. These people
are usually, though not always, professionally prepared to some extent
for their post. But in Protestant denominations, the situation typically
is dismal. When we at Religious Education Press assiduously endeavored to find the name of the person or the office of the individual formally heading up the religious instruction efforts in a particular judicatory of the overwhelming number of Protestant denominations, we
found that almost always there was no office and no person for such a
position. This deplorable situation surely is tangible evidence that religious instruction work is held in low regard by the leaders of these denominations. In local churches, far fewer Protestant congregations
have directors of religious education as compared to their Catholic
counterparts. In so very many cases, even in wealthy local Protestant
churches, the director of religious education is usually paid a relative
pittance—again indicating the low regard in which so many Protestant
churches hold religious instruction ministry. As Jesus once put it:
"Where your treasure is, there is your heart also" (Mt 6:21). In modern
language, this would be redacted as: Show me your budget and I'll
show you your values and your priorities.

If we are to forge the future for the religious instruction that Jesus
deserves, then all Christian churches will have to make religious instruction ministry their foremost priority. The mind-set that the primary task of every Christian ecclesiastic is religious instruction
should totally and existentially pervade the entire seminary curriculum
and color every aspect of it. Seminaries should ensure that religious
instruction faculty and students are just as competent, just as

scholarly, and just as intelligent as their counterparts in biblics and systematics. Catholic seminaries will have to offer much more course work in religious instruction than they do now. Continuing education for the clergy in all faith groups should be stepped up and should center around religious instruction ministry. Every Catholic and Protestant church with more than three hundred parishioners should have a full-time paid and professionally prepared director of religious education. Protestant denominations should move aggressively to see to it that every judicatory has in place a professionally prepared individual (typically at the Ph.D. level), preferably a layperson, whose sole task is religious instruction. This office should be given a generous budget and endowed with considerable prestige within the denomination.

THE SCHOLARLY BASE OF
RELIGIOUS INSTRUCTION

If there is good deal of evidence to suggest that church officials do not really want religious education, the question must be asked without apology: Do religious educators and religious educationists themselves really want religious education? Put in the most favorable possible light, the answer is rather questionable. The trumpet blown by religious educators and religious educationists gives forth an uncertain sound (1 Cor. 14:8).

There is a growing tendency—or more accurately a growing fad—among religious educators, notably in Catholic circles, to want to jettison their title of religious educator (or Christian educator in Protestant circles) and instead clothe themselves in some trendy sobriquet such as pastoral associate or some other title whose supposed loftiness is matched only by its actual amorphousness and etherealness. By assuming flavor-of-the-month titles such as these, religious educators seem to be reaching out in desperation for more prestige. There is no more exalted title and no more important function in the church than that of religious educator. Jesus was a religious educator; he was not a pastoral associate. At bottom, a search for prestige is really a search for self-serving egoism. True prestige in the religious sphere comes from a job well done for the Lord and for his people. Religious educators seem to be suffering an identity crisis when they vaingloriously seek to be identified by titles other than religious educator. This identity crisis can be solved only when religious educators recognize that they are God's corps of elite, and only when they concentrate on the instructional dynamics of the glorious apostolate to which they have been called by God himself. Religious educators in the third millennium should exhibit enormous and rightful pride in their identity of religious educator.

One of the major factors contributing to the erosion of professional identity among religious educators in all likelihood must be laid at the feet of many of the seminary and university programs preparing religious educators for ministry. Some years ago I discovered to my great dismay that there was no appreciable difference between religious educators trained at the master's level and those who had no graduate preparation in terms of buying serious professional books in the field in which they worked, namely religious instruction. In the late 1990s, I visited the libraries of two important graduate programs in religious education, one in the Midwest and one in the South. Neither library was well stocked with professional books in religious education. Worse still, judging by the checkout slips in these books, only a very few of these books were ever checked out by students. If the faculty members of many graduate university and seminary programs do not value the scholarly base of the field—and thus disvalue the field itself—how can their students be legitimately expected to themselves prize the field and find their own professional/personal identity in it?

Richard McBrien, an au-courant theological popularizer friendly to religious education, once pointed out that the level of scholarship in religious instruction is regarded by the theological community as being on the weak side (1976). (This indictment is even more damning when one remembers that theological scholarship is regarded by the rest of the academic community as being notoriously on the weak side.) I think the evidence amply supports McBrien's contention. Religious instruction research and publication prosecuted by university and seminary faculty members is often less scholarly than the research conducted by faculty in other fields. Even a cursory glance at what relatively slim high-level scholarship does exist in religious instruction reveals that these books and articles frequently do not draw upon or reference many works of other religious instruction writers but rather rely primarily on writings by persons outside the field of religious education. Such a sorry state of affairs would be inconceivable in other fields. Can one imagine a scholarly book in psychology or in biblics, for example, that scarcely utilizes and cites writings in psychology or in biblics, preferring instead to draw on works in other areas? When one reads articles in serious professional journals such as *Religious Education* written by religious education faculty members in higher education, or when one listens to speeches delivered by religious education professors at annual professional conventions such as the Association of Professors and Researchers in Religious Education, one is almost immediately stuck by how arcane some of these articles and speeches are in terms of a field which concentrates nominatim on teaching religion. Such articles and speeches have little or nothing to do with the central task of religious instruction, namely, the improvement of religion teaching. It is hard to escape the impression that these articles and books are intended more to impress seminary and university colleagues in other fields and disciplines (and thus gain advancement in faculty rank and in-house recognition) than they are to push the field of religious instruction forward. (It must be noted that the Evangelical Protestants in their professional publication *Journal of Christian Education* and in the annual conventions of their professional association, the North American Professors of Christian Education, tend to direct their efforts in a far more focused manner on the major issues involved in the improvement of the teaching of religion.)

Since the 1970s, scholarship in the field of religious instruction seems to have improved considerably. But there is still a long way to go if it is to attain the level which the divinely exalted field of religious instruction deserves.

To forge a better future for religious instruction, religious educators and religious educationists alike must recognize and then prize the fact that the exercise of religious instruction has a scholarly base. The success of any field of endeavor, including religious instruction, necessarily rests on the base of scholarship relevant to that field. The success and vibrancy of any field depends on the scholarship which undergirds it. Religious instruction is an art which is grounded in science, the science of teaching and learning. Without a scientific base, the art of religious instruction will become hit or miss at best (Gage 1978). This means that religious education faculty members in seminaries and universities should engage in a much higher level of scholarship than at present, and should give their students a constant appreciation of the centrality of research as the necessary and pervasive underpinning of their future ministry. If graduate students in religious instruction do not see their faculty consistently producing a goodly amount of scholarly research, how can these students ever learn to respect the great importance of a scholarly base to their activities when they go into the local church as pastor or DRE/DCE? Additionally, the scholarship of religious education faculty members in seminaries and universities should be directed primarily at that which makes religious instruction distinctive, namely, the religious instruction act. These faculty members should base their scholarship on validated empirical research into the teaching/learning act because teaching is an empirical activity. There is a necessary and very important place for the theological, philosophical, and historical foundations of religious instruction; however, it is patently erroneous to equate the foundations of religious instruction with the religious instruction act itself. If we are to forge a bright future for religious instruction in the third millennium, then religious educationists and educators alike must focus a large portion of their scholarly activities on analyzing, synthesizing, and improving the religious instruction act itself. Armed with this scholarly base, religious educators in the local church can thus be enabled to significantly improve the success of their efforts in the third millennium.

THE PROPHETIC IMPERATIVE OF RELIGIOUS INSTRUCTION

By virtue of Baptism, by virtue of participation in the divine life in which all Christians share thanks to God's overflowing grace, each Christian is called upon to be a prophet, along with being a priest and a ruler. Because religious educators are called by God himself to be his special corps of elite, the prophetic office is especially incumbent upon each and every religious educator in the third millennium.

All religious educators must necessarily be prophets not only because God has given them a divine vocation to be religious educators but also because they are teachers. To be a teacher is to automatically be a prophet. In a famous passage in one of his books in which he discusses the great dignity of the vocation of a teacher, John Dewey (1897) wrote that ". . . the teacher always is the prophet of the true God and the usherer in of the true kingdom of God."

Prophets are persons who hasten the future—persons who make the future come into the present more quickly than it would if they were not on the scene. A prophet does not so much fore-tell the future as to fore-do the future. Fore-doing and fore-telling are in a dynamic dialectical relationship, each enriching the other. It is the fore-doing which often enables the prophet to accurately foretell the future. The prophet is one who makes the road by walking it, by blazing the trail. Most modern English translations of Ephesians 4:15 translate a pertinent part of this verse as "to speak the truth in love". For prophetic and existential reasons I have always preferred the Vulgate: *"veritatem autem facientes in caritate,"* which is, "to do the truth in love." True prophets do more than just speak the truth; they do the truth in their lives and actions. But they always do it with love and for love, even when the truth seems to burn the positions held by others.

True prophecy always incorporates vision, broadly seeing possibilities and their fulfillment. Vision differs from daydreaming in that vision is grounded in proven knowledge and unconditional love. Proven knowledge comes from being intimately conversant with the best facts, laws, and theories about a reality. For the religious educator as prophet, knowledge is gained from being acquainted with top scholarship in the field and from solid practical knowledge gained from experience and tested by theory and research.

The prophetic role of the religious educator is one of reconstruction. The religious educator as prophet seeks tirelessly not only to reconstruct the field of religious instruction but also reconstruct the whole church. Religious educators are in a uniquely favored position to bring about basic reconstruction in both religious instruction and the whole church because their way of looking at things, and most importantly their way of doing things, is quite different from theological and ecclesiastical ways of looking at things and from theological and ecclesiastical ways of doing things.

As prophets, religious educators are gadflies and troublemakers. They take on the false idols of pseudo-theories and nonempirically grounded practices. They strive against princes and principalities, against those so-called religious instruction experts whose views are more fanciful than reality based, and against those ecclesiastical officials who try to muzzle the dynamism of authentic religious instruction activity by transmogrifying it into nothing more than an arid search for rules of safety.

In the exercise of their prophetic role, religious educators must of necessity be unsparingly critical of themselves, of their own job performance, and of the field at large. Disagreement, often sharp disagreement, with conventional idols and so-called experts is thus part and parcel of the religious educator's prophetic role. Disagreement, the rough-and-tumble exchange of ideas and practice, is crucial to the genuine growth of the field. In exercising the prophetic task of disagreement, the religious educator will often make enemies, especially among those whose self-serving egos might be (and should be) bruised in the process or who do not want to be introduced to accommodative learning. It is impossible to be a genuine change agent without making enemies.

The exercise of the prophetic office in the field of religious instruction carries with it a very heavy burden. The religious educator as prophet is a troublemaker and so is always in trouble. The religious educator gives himself to the field and to others unconditionally and without reserve, and frequently receives abuse and rejection in return. As prophet, the religious educator often clashes with ecclesiastical officials. This requires considerable courage because these officials are the ones who pay the prophet's salary and on whose whims the religious educator's job depends, contract or no contract. In the end, the religious educator as prophet is typically all alone. As powerfully demonstrated in the classic motion picture *High Noon*, so-called friends and colleagues all desert the prophet when the going gets very tough because only the prophet is willing to pay the heavy price of reconstructing the field and reconstructing the church.

The aloneness of the prophet is difficult for the religious educator and educationist to endure. Religious educators and educationists rightfully expect their colleagues in the apostolate to be in solidarity with their prophetic activities. But all too often these very colleagues, who also are supposed to be prophetic, cravenly distance themselves from the genuine religious instruction prophet because they fear that being in any way identified with the prophet or worse still being seen in the company of the prophet, will get them in trouble with their institutions, with other colleagues, and with "those who count." In this climate of fear, the prophetic religious educator needs to remain steadfast in his resolve and not in any way diminish his prophetic activity on behalf of significantly improving religious instruction. But there is a bright side to the aloneness of the religious education prophet. By enduring aloneness, an aloneness that often hurts deeply, the prophet is showing in a most powerful way that she is working for the Lord and the church and not for the praise of colleagues or the approval of the ecclesiasticum in its various forms. It is their tremendous love of religious instruction and unquenchable passion for its improvement that bestow on religious educators and educationists the sometimes superhuman strength to press forward in the unremitting exercise of their prophetic office, even though this love is more often than not un-requited by fearful colleagues, and even though the blood of this pas-sion is so frequently spilled on the ground in wanton fashion by an un-grateful ecclesiasticum.

History has also shown that it is the prophets in any given era who, at great sacrifice to themselves, forge the future of the next age. So too it is with religious instruction. It is from that group of religious educa-tors and religious educationists who are not frightened of assuming their rightful prophetic office that the future of religious instruction in the third millennium will be forged.

THE FOUNTAINHEAD OF ALL RELIGIOUS INSTRUCTION ACTIVITY

The fountainhead from which all the streams of religious instruction activity flow is, of course, religious instruction. A viable and bright fu-ture for religious instruction throughout the third millennium can be forged only when the field concentrates on the two major elements that make up the field, namely, religion and instruction.

Religion

Religion is the way persons live their life unto God. It is essentially a holistic lifestyle in which cognition and affect play a contributory role. Full-blooded religion is the substantive content and goal of all authen-tic religious instruction.

Theology, in marked contrast, is a cognitive science that cogni-tively reflects on God and his activities in himself and in the world. It is essentially an intellectual activity. I know of no major theologian of any Christian faith group who has equated religion and theology.

Empirical research from Pleasant Hightower (1930) down to the present day has persuasively shown that the neither the process of the-ological reflection nor the substantive content of theological knowledge is inherently capable of directly generating religion. These empirical research findings are an instance of the broader group of re-search data which indicate that cognition does not directly produce noncognitive results such as affect or lifestyle. Activities from one domain of human functioning are unable of themselves to generate outcomes from a wholly different domain.

Consequently, both the substantive content and the objective/goal of religious instruction is always religion and not theology. There is a vast difference between religious instruction and theological instruction. The subtantive content and goal of the former is religion, whereas the substantive content and goal of the latter is theology.

Religion in its finest form is what I like to term "red-hot religion," that kind of religion in which the person having religion burns unquenchably for Christ, is consumed with the fire of love for God (Jn 2:17), and strives totally to enact every aspect of life for and in and with God (Gal 2:20). This is the kind of religion which, if taught, will forge a bright future for religious instruction in the third millennium. Religion always has primacy in the eyes of God over theology (Jas 1:27), and must always have primacy in any religious instruction that is true.

So very often the source of red hot religion is religious experience. Persons in our era yearn so very desperately for religious experience. Those churches that deliberately give congregants religious experience are thriving, while those that substitute rationalism in its stead are either dying or moribund. I never cease to be amazed that so very many Protestant religious educationists, especially those of the Evangelical persuasion, place theology as the process and goal of religious instruction when, in fact, the Reformers emphasized that it is a person's religious experience, the personal burning encounter with Jesus, that forms the basis of faith and indeed the foundation of Christianity.

What, then, should the role of theology be in third-millennium religious instruction? Theology has two proper major functions vis-à-vis religious instruction. First, theology forms one internal part of the substantive content of religious instruction because it composes one (and only one) dimension of religion. Thus theology becomes part of the religious instruction event to the extent to which it furthers the overall religious process and goal of that event. Second, theology forms one, and only one, of the external foundations of the religious instruction act, alongside of the historical foundations of religious instruction, the philosophical foundations, the sociological foundations, and so forth. It is important to remember that the foundations of the religious instruction act are separate and distinct from the act itself. The foundations cannot validly substitute for the religious instruction act.

Successful religious instruction in the third millennium will be forged when religious educators center their efforts on teaching red-hot religion and when do not substitute any correlative substantive content such as sociology or theology for religion, for the real thing.

Instruction

In the term "religious instruction", the word religious is the adjective–it specifies the substantive content that is being taught. Instruction is the noun in which the word religious inheres. Instruction specifies how religion in a cohesive set of instances becomes operative; it indicates the conditions in which religion is actualized. By way of contrast, in the term "religious worship", the word "worship" is the noun and specifies how religion becomes operative in that case. No one disputes that instruction is a form of education or that education is a form of social science. Therefore it follows logically that religious instruction is a form of social science. Consequently the basic macrotheory that explains, predicts, and verifies religious instruction is social science. No other conclusion is logical. No other conclusion is existential. This fact has crucial consequences to the success of the religious instruction endeavor and to successfully forging the future of religious instruction in the third millennium.

All teaching, including the teaching of religion, is an art/science. The scientific facts, laws, as well as the concepts and principles of teaching and learning form the foundation of all teaching activity and thus ought to thoroughly infuse all intentional teaching. These scientific facts and laws and theories enable religious educators to eschew fads and gimmicks, concentrating their attention on scientifically demonstrated or scientifically probable instructional acts. Because teaching is social science on the hoof, all religious educators are obliged to be researchers in action, reflectively researching, as they teach, about what are productive and unproductive teaching behaviors during the instructional event in order to improve the quality of teaching during the next teaching episode. And because teaching is grounded in and thoroughly suffused with the science of teaching and learning, all printed religious instruction curricula, which form one context for much of religious instruction activity, must be subject to the rigors of scientific evaluation to ascertain whether these curricula validly bring about the results they claim to bring about. Religious educators in the third millennium should beware of religion curricula that are rushed into print before having been scientifically evaluated as to their effectiveness in a great many varied teaching-learning activities and settings. Scientifically validated results of a religion curriculum, and not hardball marketing skills or effusive hype by publishers, should be the sole criterion by which religious educators choose a published religion curriculum in the twenty-first century.

Teaching is also an art. All performing arts are empirical activities, and teaching is no exception. (The word "art" comes from the Latin *ars,* which means any kind of making or doing.) For some inexplicable reason, some religious educationists seem to have a bias against teaching as an empirical activity, as a technical affair, as a procedural matter. These persons seem to think that procedure somehow devalues the important and supernatural work of the religious educator (Tye 1988). Others have dipped back into the Hellenistic philosophical word *techne,* which is loosely translated as technical skill, suggesting that procedure is a rather low-level activity upon which religious educators should not center their attention. Yet the antitechnical proponents seem to forget that by its very nature all art is procedure, is method, is technique. Art consists in the deployment of technical skill all along the line. Michelangelo was a magnificent sculptor because he had a mastery of technique which enabled him to carve his vision into prophetic and insightful images. Michelangelo possessed not only the technical skill to sculpt but also the high-level technical skill on how to cut stone, on how to bring it from Carrara to Rome and Florence, how to polish marble, and so forth. When the world's foremost musicians and outstanding poets describe their work, they typically discuss technical skills more than anything else. In other words all great artists place enormous store in *techne*. Indeed, many research studies have found that religious educators, especially beginning religious educators, are far more concerned with their instructional procedures than with the substantive content. Ironically, the religious educationists who argue against the great importance of technical skill and *techne* in religion teaching are often the very persons who pay considerable attention to their own speaking skills, their own computer technology skills *(techne* plus *logos),* and their own communication skills in general—all technical activities. In the religious instruction act, procedure is not everything, but everything is procedure.

University and seminary programs preparing preservice religious educators in the third millennium should concentrate on systematically helping prospective religious educators develop and hone their instructional competencies. In short, the preservice program should be competency based and competency driven. Faculty and students, ransacking the research and empirically surveying religious educators in the field, should develop and then implement a list of major competencies that prospective religious educators need to acquire to become first-rate teachers in the third millennium.

The acquisition of many of these instructional competencies should take place in the university's or seminary's Teacher Performance Center, a laboratory in which the prospective religious educator can analyze and then practice a wide-ranging repertoire of cognitive, affective, and especially lifestyle instructional procedures. In the Teacher Performance Center, preservice religious educators use a variety of observational tools such as interaction analysis devices to assist them in objectively analyzing concrete instructional performance. In the Center, preservice religious educators engage in microteaching and other performance procedures to help them concretely improve their instructional skills in a scientifically based manner. Complementing their work in the Center, preservice religious educators in the third millennium will observe, help out, and teach religion in designated professional development sites. They will serve in an appropriate fashion as interns in competently run parish and central offices of religious education. Preservice opportunities outside the university setting will not be restricted to school or classroom milieux but will also include informal environments such as the home. The inservice program for beginning religious educators will feature ongoing mentoring by a recognized religious educator who possesses superior instructional skills and solid understanding of substantive content (English 1998).

The art/science of religious instruction is deeply embedded in theory. A theory of religious instruction and, more to the point of this chapter, a macrotheory of religious instruction is a sine qua non for bringing about effective teaching. A theory is a set of interrelated concepts, facts, and laws that offer a comprehensive and systematic reality by specifying relations among variables. Theory is often misconstrued as speculation. Speculation is the process of reflecting about a reality in an armchair fashion; it lacks the scientific nature of theory because theory is the scientific fashioning of meaning from the

interplay of the facts and laws of a reality. While speculation sometimes has practical consequences, theory is always extremely practical
with respect to its formal object. In fact, one basic purpose of theory is
to make practice more effective. Derived as it is from practice, theory
has three major functions, all of which are directed toward the improvement of practice: explanation, prediction, and verification. Theory has deductive power. From theory practitioners can deduce the
most effective practices in the field in which they are working.

If religious instruction is to be effective in third millennium, it is essential that it be inextricably linked to an appropriate macrotheory. (A
macrotheory is grand theory that encompasses lesser theories of a similar reality). In the history of religious instruction, two macrotheories
of religious instruction have been proposed, namely, the theological
approach and the social science approach. The evidence conclusively
shows that the theological approach is inherently incapable of explaining, predicting, and verifying the religious instruction act. Thus the
forging of a better future for religious instruction in the third millennium necessitates an adoption of the social science macrotheory to religious instruction.

Ultimately, the theological macrotheory is directed toward a theological understanding of the religious instruction act. Theological understanding is external to the act and thus is incapable of directly improving the deployment of the act. Theology can explain what the act
means theologically; it cannot explain what the act means instructionally. The social science approach, on the other hand, is directed toward
an instructional understanding of the teaching/learning act. This so-
cial-scientific understanding is internal to the act and thus is eminently
capable of directly improving the deployment of the act. Social science explains what the act means instructionally.

A theological understanding of the religious instruction act is incapable of producing better teaching. It cannot explain why a particular
teaching method was successful or failed. It cannot predict which
teaching method would be effective in a particular situation and which
would be unsuccessful. It cannot verify the degree of learning that actually took place in a religious instruction event. Social science can do
all of these.

In 1994 I asked Randolph Crump Miller, then the most distinguished American advocate of the theological approach to religious
instruction, to edit a book in which leading representatives from

thirteen different theologies would detail, among other things, how their theology directly brought forth an instructional practice unique to that theology. Published in 1995 under the title *Theologies of Religious Education*, the book reveals that not a single contributor could accomplish this task. Every single instructional procedure mentioned by these distinguished authors was drawn in one way or another from social science. Not a single one was directly generated by theology.

This fact should not be surprising. Theology and social science have fundamentally different methods of operation and nature, both of which make it impossible for theology to generate instructional practice.

Theological method inherently precludes theology from directly generating instructional explanations, instructional predictions, or instructional verifications. Regardless of whether a theologian uses the transcendental theological method of Karl Rahner (1978) or Bernard Lonergan (1972), the existential theological method of Paul Tillich (1951–1963), the experiential theological method of David Tracy (1975), Bernard Meland (1976), or Edward Schillebeeckx (1979), the process theological method of Schubert Ogden (1966) or John Cobb (1979), the ecumenical theological method of Gillian Evans (1996) or Yves Congar in some of his work (1937), the mediational theological method of Emil Brunner (1943), the constructivist theological method of George Kaufman (1995), or a variety of other theological methods such as those of Walter Kasper (1969), Dorothee Sölle (1990), Hans Schwarz (1991), Charles Wood (1985), and William Lloyd Newell (1990), the essential method remains the same. All these theologies, and indeed all legitimate theology, explain reality theologically through the lens of scripture and the faith of the church, predict the theological implications of reality, and theologically verify reality through the theology that theologians have constructed through their methodology. Consequently, there is no way theological method can directly generate instructional outcomes. Social science, in marked contrast seeks as a major goal the direct generation of instructional outcomes because it offers valid instructional explanations of the religion teaching act, gives solid predictions on the effect of various instructional procedures, and verifies whether and to what extent an instructional outcome has been attained.

In the twentieth century, and especially in the last quarter of the twentieth century, a discipline within the science of theology has gained some attention. Its advocates call it practical theology. Its purpose is to deal directly with concrete church practice in a way that is intended to fecundate this practice. Many Catholic and Mainline Protestant religious educationists from the 1980s onward have jumped eagerly, and I would say mindlessly, on the practical theological bandwagon in claiming that religious instruction is practical theology. But this claim is no more valid than the assertion that religious instruction is systematic theology or moral theology in action.

Of the many fatal flaws in the position that religious instruction is practical theology in action, two are especially salient. First of all, practical theology is still theology, and as we have seen. theological goals and methods are inherently incapable of adequately explaining, predicting, and verifying the religious instruction act. Second, practical theology is cognitive reflection, whereas religious instruction is concrete action. Practical theology, like all theology, reflects theologically upon the religious instruction act but is inherently incapable of validly intervening in an instructional manner in the religious instruction act. The basic principle here is that theological reflection on instructional practice is in no way tantamount to that practice itself. Reflection and practice are two separate ontic orders of reality. Virtually all practical theologians with whom I am familiar characterize their work by the words theological reflection. These practical theologians, or other kinds of theologians who sympathetic to practical theology, include but are not restricted to James Poling and Donald Miller (1985), Don Browning (1991), Denise Ackerman and Riet Bons-Storm (1998 introductory statement), Stephen Parker (1996), Dennis McCann and Charles Strain (1985), and some other authors like David Tracy and Edward Farley (in Browning 1983), and Lewis Mudge (in Mudge and Poling 1987).

Don Browning, one of the leading proponents of practical theology, claims that religious instruction is a form of practical theology (in Mudge and Poling 1987). Careful examination of the Browning essay reveals that he regards practical theology as revolving around the axial reflective cognitive methods of hermeneutics and ethics. But, as already noted, reflection on practice can in no way be equated with practice itself. And, most especially, theological reflection on instructional practice is by no means the same as instructional practice. Browning asserts that practical theology does have a predisposition toward producing action. For religious instruction, he proposes the action-reflection method as the way religious instruction-as-practical-theology can be realized. But there are at least two major insuperable problems confronting Browning's position. First of all, practical theology reflection (and theology must be essentially reflection if it is to be theology) is not the same as the action toward which it might be predisposed. Second, what Browning has done in proposing the action-reflection teaching method for religious instruction is to appropriate a teaching procedure from the domain of social science (education in this case) and then gratuitously claim that this teaching method is practical theology. One byproduct of this second insuperable difficulty is that if practical theology is predisposed to only one instructional method, then practical theology is inherently a rather sterile vessel with respect to religious instruction. There are a great many instructional methods and techniques available to achieve differential cognitive, affective, and lifestyle outcomes. Of itself, practical theology is incapable of directly devising any of these instructional procedures; indeed it can know about them only from an external theological perspective and not from an internal instructional perspective. (I should note that the instructional method that Browning claims is congenial to practical theology is not action-reflection as Browning states, but rather a reflection-reflection model.)

Because practical theology, like all of theology, is a process of (cognitive) theological reflection seeking to interpret and otherwise discern the theological import of reality, it is not surprising that those religious educationists who identify themselves as practical theologians have not only failed to devise genuinely new instructional procedures but also have either neglected teaching methods or have even looked down on those who concentrate on the pedagogical dynamics of the religious instruction act.

The proper and legitimate role of practical theology in the religious instruction enterprise is to reflect theologically on various aspects of life, personal development, culture, and the like, and then in concert with other foundational areas such as philosophy, cultural anthropology, and sociology place these important conclusions at the disposal of instructional science to use according to the mode of instructional science in preparing, deploying, and evaluating the religious instruction act. Practical theology can also legitimately form one but only one contributory dimension to the substantive content of religious instruction.

There seems to be strong valence among some proponents of practical theology toward theological imperialism, sometimes of the most naked and all-consuming sort. This imperialism goes far beyond the old position of theology as the queen of the sciences. Practical theology, it is claimed, includes not only religious instruction but also church music, pastoral counseling, church finances, church administration, and the like (Browning 1991; Nichols in Ferm 1945). If this claim were true, then all one has to do is to study practical theology to compose church music skillfully, to enact well-developed counseling skills, to be an excellent church administrator and finance specialist, and the like. Some advocates of practical theology have even gone so far as to claim that empirical methods developed by and unique to the social and statistical sciences such as survey research, multiple regression analysis, experimental research, and the like are aspects of practical theology (van der Ven 1993). The equation of practical theology with all these particular areas of practice is as patently absurd as it is imperialistic because the method, formal object, and goal of practical theology is substantially different from the method and goal of church music, pastoral counseling, church finances, church administration, statistics, and so forth. The theological imperialism of some proponents of practical theology is so voracious that it does not even exempt other areas of theology. Indeed, some practical theologians claim that all theology—systematic theology, historical theology, biblical theology, moral theology—are forms of fundamental practical theology (Browning 1991). Given the seemingly total omnivorousness of practical theology, one can legitimately ask where it will all end? For example, does a surgical operation performed by a Christian physician in a Christian hospital fall under the rubric of fundamental practical theology? Is this physician a practical theologian?

In the final years of the Vietnam War, when it became evident that the United States was losing and the nation's leaders could not agree on whether to escalate the bombing or what do next, one clever politician declared that what America should do is to declare that it had won the war and then unilaterally withdraw from Southeast Asia. There seems to be an apt analogy here between religious instruction and practical theology. What practical theologians and those religious educationists who claim they are practical theologians have done is to declare stipulatively that religious instruction activity is practical theology, period. No evidence is needed. The stipulative declaration becomes the reality. Victory is achieved. But surely we deserve better than this.

In a sense this whole subsection on practical theology and religious instruction is really moot because in actual practice all religious educators in the field and all curriculum builders base and enact their religious instruction activity on the social science macrotheory. Some of them might sprinkle a few theological phrases like holy water on their activities, but in essence what they are doing when they teach and build curricula is to fashion their activities completely around the principles and procedures of the social science approach and not the theological approach.

GOOD MORNING, THIRD MILLENNIUM

Authentic optimism flows not from any giddy, unrealistic, oversanguine mentality but rather from encountering and listening truly to the withinness of a particular reality where God's grace acts pervasively and dynamically through the integrity of the special essence and distinctive operations of that reality. It is in this spirit that I am highly optimistic about the future of religious instruction in the third millennium if, and only if, religious educationists and educators concentrate their attention on the religious instruction act itself. Everything in our field flows from this act, works through it, and returns to enrich it. It will be the concentration on the act that will give birth to the prophetic vision and the prophetic action that are going to light up a bright future for religious instruction in the third millennium.

To concentrate on the religious instruction act is to listen attentively to its inner dynamisms with profound respect and humility, much as we listen to the rushing flow of a river or to the mighty sweep of the heaving ocean in order to authentically understand each and to harvest their power. The act can teach us how to understand religious instruction and what to do with it—*if* we listen carefully, scientifically, and heartfully to it, *if* we embrace it in all its empirical reality and sweep of grandeur. We must listen to the act on its own terms, to its inner empirical dynamics, and not be clouded over by any a priori preconceptions or ideological orientations. If we do this, religious instruction in the third millennium will attain heights never before dreamed of.

It will be up to religious educators, God's special corps of elite who are equipped by their divine calling, by God's ongoing grace, and by professional preparation to prophetically hasten the future of the whole church, especially its instructional efforts, in the third millennium. And it is the sublime task of religious educationists to humbly and competently serve preservice and inservice religious educators to enhance their understanding and improvement of religious instruction practice all along the line.

As this book is published, we are at the dawn of the third millennium. The sun is rising. It will be up to us to genuinely understand and effectively deploy the religious instruction act so that we can thereby release the enormous power of this act in order to help all learners, young and old, to become saints. This is our task. This is our mission. This is the source of our glory.

Profiles of Contributors

(in alphabetical order)

NORMA COOK EVERIST is Professor of Educational Ministries and Church Administration at Wartburg Theological Seminary. She was born in Des Moines and is an ordained minister in the Evangelical Lutheran Church in America. She received her doctorate from the joint program at The Iliff School of Theology and the University of Denver. Reverend Everist's books include *Education Ministry in the Congregation* (Augsburg/Fortress, 222 pp.), *Where in the World Are You?* (Alban Institute, 140 pp.), coauthored with Nelson Vos, and *Connections: Faith and Life* (Evangelical Lutheran Church of America, 340 pp.), also coauthored with Nelson Vos. Her articles have appeared in such journals as *Currents in Theology and Mission*, *Clergy Journal*, *Parish Teacher*, and *Lutheran Partners*. She has taught at Yale Divinity School, Princeton Theological Seminary, and the Lutheran School of Theology in Chicago. Dr. Everist was the recipient of the Outstanding Alumni Award from The Iliff School of Theology.

BARBARA J. FLEISCHER is Associate Professor of Pastoral Studies, and also Director of the Loyola Institute for Ministry at Loyola University New Orleans. She was born in New York City and is a Catholic laywoman. She received her doctorate from St. Louis University. Dr. Fleischer has written the book *Facilitating for Growth* (Liturgical Press, 160 pp). Her articles have appeared in *Religious Education*, *Irish Theological Quarterly*, *International Journal of Addictions*, and *Church Personnel Issues*. Dr. Fleischer has taught at the University of Southern Mississippi. She is the recipient of the Loyola University City College Distinguished Teaching Award. Dr. Fleischer is listed in *Who's Who of American Women*.

CHARLES R. FOSTER is Professor of Religion and Education in the Candler School of Theology at Emory University. He was born in

Reardan (Washington) and is an ordained minister in the United Methodist Church. He received his doctorate from Teachers College, Columbia University. Books authored or edited by the Reverend Foster include *Educating Congregations* (Abingdon, 160 pp.), *Embracing Diversity: Leadership in Multicultural Congregations* (Alban Institute, 136 pp.), *We Are the Church Together* (Abingdon, 187 pp.) in which he was the senior author, and *Working with Black Youth* (Abingdon, 124 pp), which he coedited with Grant Shockley. Professor Foster's articles have appeared in *Religious Education*, *Living Light*, and *Teaching Theology and Religion*. He has taught at the Methodist Theological School in Ohio and at the Scarritt Graduate School affiliated with Vanderbilt University. He was the recipient of the Emory Williams Distinguished Teacher Award from Emory University.

KENNETH O. GANGEL is Distinguished Professor Emeritus of Christian Education at Dallas Theological Seminary and currently serves as visiting professor at a variety of institutions of higher learning. He was born in Patterson (N.J.) and is an ordained minister in the Christian and Missionary Alliance Church. He received his doctorate from the University of Missouri. Books written by the Reverend Gangel include *Feeding and Leading* (Baker, 329 pp.), *Team Leadership in Christian Ministry* (Moody Press, 480 pp.), *Ministering to Today's Adults* (Word, 307 pp.), and *Building Leaders for Church Education* (Moody Press, 432 pp.). Some of Dr. Gangel's many articles have appeared in *Bibliotheca Sacra, Christian Education Journal, Religious Education*, and *Theological Education*. Dr. Gangel has taught at Calvary Bible College, Trinity Evangelical Divinity School, Miami Christian College, and Toccoa Falls College. The Reverend Gangel is the recipient of an honorary doctorate from Taylor University, the Gold Medallion Book Award, and the Alumni Achievement Award from the University of Missouri at Kansas City. He is listed in *Outstanding Educators of America*, *Who's Who in America*, and *Contemporary Authors*.

JAMES MICHAEL LEE is Professor of Educational Foundations at the University of Alabama at Birmingham. He was born in Brooklyn and is a Catholic layman. He received his doctorate from Teachers College, Columbia University. Books written by Professor Lee include *The Sacrament of Teaching*, vol. 1 (Religious Education Press, 312 pp.), and his foundational trilogy *The Shape of Religious Instruction* (Religious Education Press, 330 pp.), *The Flow of Religious Instruction* (Religious Education Press, 379 pp.), and *The Content of Religious Instruction* (Religious Education Press, 803 pp.). Some of his many articles have appeared in *Religious Education*, *Living Light*, *Theological Education*, and *Catholic Educational Review*. He has taught at the University of Notre Dame, St. Joseph's College, Spring Hill College, Seton Hall University, and Hunter College of the City University of New York. Dr. Lee was the recipient of a Senior Fulbright Research Fellowship at the University of Munich and a Lilly Research Fellowship of the Religious Education Association. He is listed in *Who's Who in America*, *Who's Who in the World*, *Who's Who in Religion, Dictionary of International Biography*, and *Contemporary Authors*.

MARY ELIZABETH MULLINO MOORE is Professor of Religion and Education, and Director of the Program for Women in Theology and Ministry, in the Candler School of Theology at Emory University. She was born in Baton Rouge and is an ordained deacon in the United Methodist Church. She received her doctorate from the Claremont School of Theology. Books written by Professor Moore include *Education for Continuity and Change* (Abingdon, 222 pp.), *Teaching from the Heart* (Fortress, 232 pp.), *Ministering with the Earth* (Chalice, 226 pp.), and *Called to Serve: Diaconate in the United Methodist Church* (General Board of Higher Education and Ministry of the United Methodist Church, 80 pp.) in which she was the third named author. The Reverend Deacon Moore's articles have appeared in *Religious Education*, *British Journal of Religious Education*, *International Journal of Practical Theology*, and *Cahiers de l'Institut Romande de Pastorale*. She has taught at Southern Methodist University and at the School of Theology at Claremont. She was the recipient of an honorary doctorate from the University of Judaism, 1998 Alumna/us of the Year of School of Theology at Claremont, the Social Justice Award of the Methodist Federation for Social Action in the UMC's California / Pacific Conference, and the Christian Education Award of the California / Pacific Coast Conference of the United Methodist Church, an honor she shared with her husband and former teacher, Allen Moore.

GABRIEL MORAN is Professor of Religious Education at New York University. He was born in Manchester (New Hampshire) and is a Catholic layman. He received his doctorate from The Catholic University of America. Among Professor Moran's many books are *Uniqueness* (Orbis, 160 pp.), *Religious Education as a Second Language* (Religious Education Press, 254 pp.), *Showing How* (Trinity Press International, 250 pp.), and *Reshaping Religious Education* (Westminister / John Knox, 202 pp.) which he coauthored with his wife, Maria Harris. His articles have appeared in such journals as *Religious Education*, *Living Light*, and *Education Week*. He has taught at Manhattan College.

RICHARD ROBERT OSMER is Thomas W. Synnott Professor at Princeton Theological Seminary. He was born in Larchmont (New York) and is an ordained minister in the Presbyterian Church (USA). He received his doctorate from Emory University. Books authored by the Reverend Osmer include *A Teachable Spirit* (Westminister / John Knox, 298 pp.), *Teaching for Faith* (Westminster / John Knox, 240 pp.), and *Confirmation: Presbyterian Practices in Ecumenical Perspective* (Westminister / John Knox, 260 pp.). Professor Osmer's articles have appeared in *Religious Education* and *International Journal of Practical Theology*. He has taught at Emory University and at Union Theological Seminary in Richmond.

ROBERT W. PAZMIÑO is Valeria Stone Professor of Christian Education at Andover Newton Theological School. He was born in Brooklyn and is an ordained minister in the American Baptist Churches. He received his doctorate from Teachers College, Columbia University. Reverend Pazmiño has written *Basics of Teaching for Christians* (Baker, 124 pp.), *Foundational Issues in Christian Education* (Baker, 267 pp. in the second edition), *By What Authority Do We Teach?* (Baker, 160 pp.), and *Latin American Journey* (United Church Press, 170 pp.). Dr. Pazmiño's articles have appeared in *Religious Education*, *Christian Education Journal*, and *Apuntes*.

RONNIE PREVOST is Professor of Church Ministry and Coordinator of Special Academic Programs in the Logsdon School of Theology at Hardin-Simmons University. He was born in Athens (Georgia) and is an ordained Southern Baptist minister. He received his doctorate from New Orleans Baptist Theological Seminary. Reverend Prevost coauthored *A History of Christian Education* (Broadman and Holman, 386 pp.). His articles have appeared in *Religious Education, Theological Education, Review and Expositor*, and *Baptist History and Heritage*. Dr. Prevost is listed in *Outstanding Teachers of America*.

ANNE E. STREATY WIMBERLY is Professor of Christian Education and Church Music at the Interdenominational Theological Center in Atlanta. She was born in Anderson (Indiana) and is a laywoman. She received her doctorate from Georgia State University. Books authored or edited by Dr. Wimberly include *Soul Stories* (Abingdon, 155 pp.), *Honoring African American Elders* (Abingdon, 209 pp.), *The Church Family Sings* (Abingdon, 96 pp.), and *Liberation and Human Wholeness* (Abingdon, 143 pp.) which she coauthored with her husband Edward Wimberly. Her articles have appeared *Religious Education, Journal of Pastoral Theology, Journal of the Interdenominational Theological Center*, and *International Review of Mission*. She has taught at Worcester State College, Oral Roberts School of Theology, Atlanta Metropolitan College, and Africa University Faculty of Theology in Zimbabwe. She is the recipient of the 1987 Martin Luther King Jr. Service Award from Garrett-Evangelical Theological Seminary, and the 1994 Woman of the Year in Religion Award from the Delta chapter of the Iota Phi Lambda Sorority in Atlanta. Dr. Wimberly is listed in *The International Who's Who of Music, Men and Women of Distinction, Who's Who of American Women, Who's Who Among Black Americans*, and *Who's Who Among America's Teachers*.

Index of Names

Index of Subjects